RECLAIMING

Challenging every

Miriam E. David

P

To all my children and grandchildren
and future generations in the hope that
they will continue to strive for a more
socially and sexually just world

First published in Great Britain in 2016 by

Policy Press
University of Bristol
1-9 Old Park Hill
Bristol BS2 8BB
UK
+44 (0)117 954 5940
pp-info@bristol.ac.uk
www.policypress.co.uk

North America office:
Policy Press
c/o The University of Chicago Press
1427 East 60th Street
Chicago, IL 60637, USA
t: +1 773 702 7700
f: +1 773 702 9756
sales@press.uchicago.edu
www.press.uchicago.edu

British Library Cataloguing in Publication Data
A catalogue record for this book is available from the British Library.

Library of Congress Cataloging-in-Publication Data
A catalog record for this book has been requested.

ISBN 978 1 44732 817 9 paperback
ISBN 978 1 44732 819 3 ePub
ISBN 978 1 44732 820 9 Mobi

Cover design by Soapbox Design
Front cover: image kindly supplied by Shutterstock
Printed and bound in Great Britain by Clays Ltd, St Ives plc
Policy Press uses environmentally responsible print partners

Contents

About the author

Miriam David, known to family and close, older friends as Miki, has been a feminist and activist throughout her adult life. As an academic, she has worked in several universities and institutions of higher education in the UK, and on occasion, in North America. She is now professor emerita of sociology of education at University College London Institute of Education. She has a worldwide reputation for her research and scholarship on education, family, feminism, gender and social policy. She has published numerous papers and books, including most recently *Feminism, gender and universities: Politics, passion and pedagogies* (Ashgate, 2014). Together with colleagues in the USA, she is editing the *Sage International Encyclopaedia of Higher Education* to be published in 2018. She remains involved in campaigning for social and sexual justice, nowadays through the Feminist Forum - Seventies Sisters and as chair of the trustees of the Women's Therapy Centre in London.

Acknowledgements

Many friends and family have helped me with the preparation of this manuscript. I am immensely grateful for all your friendship and support. I hope that I have portrayed your insights, views and values appropriately. I am also very grateful to Alison Shaw of Policy Press for believing in me and bringing this book to fruition.

In particular, there are colleagues and friends with whom I have collaborated on various research and book projects. Many contributed to my recent studies of feminism and women's studies in academe, and to the European Union-funded project on challenging gender-related violence for children and young people.

I should particularly like to thank those women who talked to, or wrote to, me for these studies.

They include all my dear friends from the Bristol Women's Studies Group (BWSG) and others in and around Bristol at the time, namely Sandra Acker, Alison Assiter, Liz Bird, Avtar Brah, Sarah Braun, Claire Callender, Davina Cooper, Sara Delamont, Carol Dyhouse, Mary Fuller, Naomi Fulop, Jane Gaskell, Helen Haste, Maggie Humm, Tessa Joseph, Hilary Land, Ruth Levitas, Ellen Malos, Caroline New, Marilyn Porter, Teresa Rees, Sheila Riddell, Susie Skevington, Helen Taylor, Linda Ward, Jackie West, Fiona Williams, Lyn Yates.

I should also like to thank friends and colleagues in London and abroad from my numerous feminist international networks including Pam Alldred, Madeleine Arnot, Barbara Biglia, Jill Blackmore, Mimi Bloch, Penny-Jane Burke, Pam Calder, Kelly Coate, Fiona Cullen, Vaneeta D'Andrea, Rosemary Deem,

Rosalind Edwards, Debbie Epstein, Sharon Gewirtz, Dulcie Groves, Gigi Guizzo, Val Hey, Carolyn Jackson, Ileana Jimenez, Heather Joshi, Jane Kenway, Terri Kim, Annette Lawson, Gail Lewis, Ruth Lister, Wendy Luttrell, Frinde Maher, Jane Martin, Sue Middleton, Heidi Mirza, Louise Morley, Gemma Moss, Diane Reay, Emma Renold, Jessica Ringrose, Sasha Roseneil, Maxine Seller, Bev Skeggs, Corinne Squires, Mary Stiasny, Kathleen Weiler, Gaby Weiner, Lois Weis, Elizabeth Wilson, Nira Yuval-Davis.

More recently my U3A group on 'Women and Wisdom', my Knit and Natter 'sisters', and the London Seventies Sisters and Feminist Forum, including Gail Chester, Irena Fink, and Amanda Sebestyen, have been important sources of on-going support. Other more recent important feminist friendly colleagues include Melissa Benn, Leslie Gardner, Chloe Stallibrass and Gill Yudkin.

As I was putting the finishing touches to the manuscript I learnt of the appointment of another dear feminist friend – Becky Francis – as my 'boss' or Director of UCL IOE. This makes the future prospects for feminism in higher education much less gloomy.

Finally, I would like to thank my family for all the support and practical help you give me as well as the fun times we have: Jeff [Duckett] for thinking with me about our ageing, Charlotte [Reiner] and David [Hershman] for allowing me to share in the care of your delightful Jacob, and Toby [Reiner], Meg [Winchester] and Matt [Duckett] for supplying me with political critiques and nous from the US.

The author and publisher gratefully acknowledge permission to reproduce excerpts from the following publications: *What should we tell our daughters?* by Melissa Benn (© Melissa Benn, 2013; published by John Murray Press); and 'A Women's Liberation Movement woman' by Judith Viorst (© Judith Viorst, 1970; published by A.M. Heath & Co Ltd).

A note about the waves of feminism

It is important to note that the waves of feminism are not separate and necessarily different but may be distinctive in responding to the wider sociopolitical and economic contexts.

- First wave (19th/early 20th centuries): struggles for women's suffrage
- Second wave (1960s–80s): civil rights, women's rights and the era of social democracy
- Third wave (1980s–90s): the era of diversity and globalising feminisms
- Fourth/fifth wave (21st century): feminisms in a digital era with 'millennials', the 'selfie generation' and the rise of everyday sexism

ONE

Feminist reflections on a lifetime in academe

This book is a feminist memoir about political activism and scholarship over the last 50 years to enable us to reclaim feminism, given its resurgence in endangered neoliberal public spaces. Quite clearly, we women now have a place in politics, public life, in education, higher education, employment, and in personal 'family' life, including in sexual and social relationships.

Just five decades ago, feminism was barely on the public agenda. Today, by contrast, we see feminism in countless media, public and political places, although as women, we are still treated as 'other' and different from men, especially those in power. There has been an increase in patriarchy, sexism and misogyny in various media, particularly with the rise in social media – the 'selfie' generation – within a sharply competitive global economy. So what have been the obstacles to and opportunities for change, which have led to the resurgence of feminism in the 21st century? In this book, I argue about the importance of feminism to women's lives, even if equality, respect, fairness and social justice for women remain a distant prospect. Despite the everyday misogyny experienced by women, we feel empowered by feminism.

I started writing this reflection some time ago, returning to it after my 70th birthday. Given continuing ageism and sexism in society today, I find this both scary and daring to admit, but necessary. My children gave me badges to wear: Toby's an 'outrageous older woman' (along with a Seneca Falls Women's

1

Rights scarf), while Charlotte's was a massive '70 years young', with both children thinking of me as a 'champagne socialist-feminist'. So what can I say to them, to their children, and to future generations?

At this juncture, the long march of history has led us to changed personal and political lives, from where feminism was occluded in public places to a time when feminism seems to be everywhere and yet nowhere. This is a good time for me to 'take stock', as Penny Tinkler and Alexandra Allan (2015) did in a special issue of the journal *Gender & Education*, considering what has happened to gender equality in education across the globe over the last 25 years. I wrote a commissioned piece for this special issue where I focused on academic developments (David, 2015), while also looking at the part played by political activism in creating the Gender & Education Association (GEA).

In this memoir I go beyond what I consider to be the narrow confines of academia to reflect on how I feel changes in the cultural, economic, educational and sociopolitical contexts have had an impact on women's social and sexual lives. To what extent have women been empowered, or constrained, by the very changes that they themselves have set in train, influenced and been influenced by? How has the zeitgeist, culture or ideology had an impact on our possibilities to challenge everyday misogyny?

Since the surprise election of Jeremy Corbyn as leader of the UK Labour Party on 12 September 2015, there has been much feminist debate about the appropriate place of women in public life and gender, or women's, equality in law and politics. The question of the place of feminism within party politics has received fresh energy, not only within Labour, but also with the creation of a new political party – the Women's Equality (WE) party. In the run-up to the Labour leadership election, in which there were two women contenders (Yvette Cooper and Liz Kendall), and an interim woman leader (Harriet Harman), there was little debate about the efficacy of feminism in party politics. While Harriet had been a strong and resilient woman since her entry into party politics over 30 years ago (in 1982), on occasion espousing feminist policies, she was frequently sidelined and not supported to become the official leader: a form of everyday misogyny. She had developed a very strong manifesto for women (together with Yvette Cooper and Gloria de Piero) within the Labour Party manifesto for the general election in May 2015. This was launched with much quibbling about the pink bus to take the manifesto around the country and little emphasis in the main party political debates. It was the Labour Party's loss at this election that prompted the resignation of Ed Miliband and the search for a new leader.

The election of Jeremy Corbyn has ignited new contentions among feminists about women's representation in party politics and leadership, and the place of feminism within socialism. The old debates about the 'unhappy marriage' of socialism and feminism are being re-asserted without reference to this history, perhaps inevitably as new generations have no knowledge of it, and older generations tire of its marginalisation. Media and feminists instantly focused on Corbyn's 'same-old' sexism in not appointing women to the ostensibly three senior positions in Labour's shadow cabinet, as Chancellor of the Exchequer, Foreign and Home Secretaries, arguably the critical political positions in the 19th-century origins of British parliamentary democracy. Social welfare policies in the second half of the 20th century led to the growing importance of education, health, housing, social security and local policies to democratic governance. When Corbyn's shadow cabinet was completed, he had ensured that over half (17 out of the 33) appointments comprised women. In these days of instant media it was contended that Corbyn had already shown his political ineptness and sexism in how he went about his business, being a rather senior old-fashioned socialist, despite his appeal to the vast majority of those who elected to join the Labour Party. He ignited more popular appeal, especially in the young, and possibly older, generations by the growth of Labour membership to well over half a million, with 60% voting for him.

These are heavily contested questions about participation in politics, dividing both feminists and socialists. Many feminists eschew participating in parliamentary politics, given the difficulties of the policy context for achieving our feminist aims, with frequent, feisty debate within the Older Feminist Network (OFN) and the London 70s Sisters email list, and

3

about the efficacy of the WE party, a feminist organisation, founded at the Women of the World (WOW) festival in March 2015. Others feel that it is important to participate and be chided for collaboration at the expense of being more activist and involved in campaigning groups. These questions also affect men in thinking about democratic and social justice issues, including the ethics of war. Tony Judt, from a similar academic and Jewish refugee background as myself, provides a guide through the debates in his posthumously book published with Timothy Snyder (2013), despite the lack of attention to gender or women's issues.

Whatever involvement or activism is chosen, in parliamentary or extra-parliamentary activities, in education, academe or forms of (professional) employment, opposing forms of sexism or misogyny remains treacherous. A recent example supports this: Charlotte Proudman, a young feminist barrister, who had worked with victims of sexual abuse and violence, was subject to what she experienced as misogyny through her professional page on LinkedIn. A senior male barrister, prefacing his comments as politically incorrect, praised her good looks rather than her professional acumen. Her objection to this objectification left her subject to torrents of abuse, being termed 'feminazi' and targeted by trolls on the internet: evidence of everyday misogyny.

Feminist knowledge and feminist practice

My argument for how relations between men and women could be equal and fair is based on what we know about relations between women and men in contemporary society – in education and employment, politics, public and family life – and how these relations could be different: how they could be equal and fair. This memoir is a plea for dignity and respect for women and girls – where they should be less subject to abuse, harassment, intimidation and violence – and how both girls and boys, women and men can learn how to develop more respectful relationships. How can we develop a conscious education and social policies that provide for this set of relationships in public and in private, making life better for both men and women?

I have been struggling with these questions throughout my adult life – as a woman, as a feminist, and as an academic/ professor. I have spent my entire professional life in higher education, what is now known in the UK colloquially as 'HE'. I became a feminist early on, now seeing myself as a 'second-wave' feminist. Given the various rising 'waves' of feminism, there are major contestations on campus not only around sexuality, sexual harassment, rape and gender segregation, but also about academic freedom or freedom of expression. How inimical is the patriarchal neoliberal academy to feminism, and how does it produce and regulate misogyny, 'laddism' and sexual harassment? These questions particularly concern younger generations or the fourth and fifth waves of feminists in their academic practices, questions including strengthening relations between generations of feminists.

I had hoped that I would no longer feel marginal and 'out-of-step', that my feminist work in teaching and researching education and social policy would by now be finished, or at least passed on to another generation, and feel safe in the knowledge that our impact had been positive. Sadly, it feels as if our influence has been either incorporated into forms of neoliberalism, such that it is claimed that gender equality, especially in education, has been achieved, or it remains sidelined and ridiculed as old-fashioned and out-of-date. Personal and family change – such as for my own children – has been important, but it really is not enough. We still need a collective endeavour to transform social and sexual relations in society today.

Feminism has been vitally important to our understandings and knowledge about what it means to be a woman in contemporary society, linked with other changes in education and the economy, as we have provided new practices and new models of ways of living and working. In my view, feminism has quietly revolutionised education, not to speak of public life, in ways that people may often be too blinkered or even prejudiced to see. So this is a plea for more careful attention to education in particular, because the processes of knowledge-making influence and are influenced by gender and sexual relations. Although there is now a feminist resurgence, it is often engulfed by misogyny.

5

Feminism as a set of ideas and values has been a collaborative and cooperative venture, providing positive evidence of complex gender, sexual and social relations. It has come to prominence in public discourse, and in HE especially, because of its powerful ideas. Many feminists, especially those in academe, are now public intellectuals. Nowadays the term 'feminism' has far more currency and caché than when I was starting out. Far more women subscribe to these ideas, articulating them in public arenas – as students, as academics, as activists or campaigners, as writers and journalists. Changing technologies, with the advent of the worldwide web and social media and networks, have facilitated these processes, Facebook and Twitter especially.

Yet at the same time, old systems of male power and dominance – patriarchy – continue to hold sway, and women continue to be invisible or belittled within political and business systems. Indeed, the worldwide web actually provides new opportunities for forms of sexism, patriarchy and the marketisation of old power relations, in the form of 'trolling'. These often become ever more misogynistic, a term that has recently developed new currency. New forms of sexual or gender violence through 'sexualisation' or 'pornification' are made possible with these new technologies of power, including for the 'selfie' generation. The transforming media and education remain full of contradictions.

HE and me

While I have never actually left education since my early childhood – I moved from school to HE from pupil to student, to researcher and then professor – not all of my time has been spent in universities but in a range of colleges or HE institutions, including in the US and Canada. During my working life, HE has been expanding as part of global socioeconomic transformations. As a feminist social scientist, I have always been passionately interested in the relations between sociopolitical changes, family, work and education. I have written extensively about these in an academic activist vein, including an intellectual biography (David, 2003) and a study of feminists in universities (David,

2014). I have played a part in leading change in academe from a feminist perspective.[1]

I use the term 'leading' advisedly, but it is in the new language in education as well as politics. Indeed, *Leaders in gender and education* (Weaver-Hightower and Skelton, 2013) arrived on my desk as I was originally penning this introduction. It is a book to which I had been invited to contribute, as part of a series, Leaders in Educational Studies. I was both flattered and daunted by the invitation from the two international editors. What we, the contributors, had been asked to do was to review our academic work and to talk about which of our publications we felt most pleased with and why.

The reason I mention this is that, funnily enough, all of the contributors struggled to find a mode of writing that did not feel self-indulgent. They also felt uncomfortable with the term 'leader', given the collaborative nature of our endeavour. It is fascinating to note how uncomfortable the new leader of the Labour Party also feels with this title, and how he, too, wants to pursue a more collaborative style. In our different ways, as authors, we all felt that we had little to say about our lives that would be of interest to others. But collectively what has been produced is a most interesting story of how we have all contributed to educational change from a gender and feminist or pro-feminist perspective. It illustrates the power of telling stories about our lives that builds a picture of a changing social and sexual world.

With some temerity this is the picture that I want to paint, also drawing on others' stories. Quite clearly this is a huge canvass and there is a vast literature, but I want to paint an alternative picture to that which is contended and contested. Given how knowledge has become part of the processes of change, and

---

[1] My own working life is illustrative of the complexity of the changes in HE institutions and the reforming of elites. I have not always worked in universities as I also had a period in what was then known (almost 30 years ago) as a 'polytechnic' in the UK, which became known as a 'new university' while I was there. I also moved between colleges of the University of London and the University of Bristol, as well as a year at Harvard University in the US (now elite institutions, and in the UK, known as the Russell Group).

something of an industry, are women's lives now completely different from their mothers' and grandmothers' lives in terms of education and employment?

My teaching and scholarship has fortuitously but fortunately gradually centred on families, gender, education and social policy, drawing on critiques of the situation to frame challenges to the status quo. Feminists have gathered knowledge and garnered wisdom about gender and social structures using a variety of methods, drawing on ideas and values from an array of sources – civil or human rights, social and political movements – within and outside of universities. Feminist social scientists have increasingly developed an approach that draws on the complexity of people's lives and includes social class and ethnicity, 'race' and/or religion. In academic circles this is often nowadays called 'intersectionality' or 'diversity', but at the same time, it is still about our lives, whether personal or political.

My own circumstances have nudged me to be concerned about how I am not just a woman, but how my identity has been formed and reformed by being part of various social groups and relationships, changing as I have grown and developed a more nuanced understanding of what it is to be a woman. My Jewish background was particularly important, committed as my parents were to education, seeing it as an avenue to achievement and successful employment. And yet there were unwritten rules about how far I could and should go in defying convention and women's roles. Education, yes, but full-time employment while a mother of young children, no....

HE as part of my parents' backgrounds, and influences on me

My mother and father inevitably had rather different influences on my journey. Both were highly educated and from refugee backgrounds, although experienced differently. This is particularly pertinent in the current crisis of refugees and migration across continents. My mother went to the University of Manchester, unusually for a woman of her generation. Although her mother (my grandmother) was a child refugee from what was then called Russia and had had her family as a very young woman, she strove for her children to be highly educated, with all three starting at university. My mother's father died aged 50, when my mother was not yet a teenager, and so she grew up in a lone-parent family, and this had a lasting influence on her. She became a schoolteacher after graduating with a degree in geography and history. First, she taught at secondary schools, and then, daunted by the problems of disciplining teenagers, she became a teacher in a Jewish primary school in north Manchester. My mother encouraged all three of us, her daughters, into education, although she did not particularly want us to be teachers, which we all three ended up becoming, in our different ways. My mother was a married woman returner while I was growing up, and this was not an easy path, balancing family and education in a changing world of expectations for women, as I noted in my intellectual biography (see David, 2003). I return later to how these changing expectations have played out across my life, experiences and education, including HE and in family life.

My father was a Jewish 'refugee' from Nazi Germany. I use the term advisedly as my mother always objected to its use, because my father came to the UK to a professional job – another current referent! My father had been attending the Technische Hochschule in Berlin, beginning his doctorate in mechanical engineering, at the time of Hitler's rise to power. Now named the Technical University, it was the first in Germany, founded in 1886 in a palace in Charlottenburg (*Hochschule* translates as 'higher education'). Having lived a relatively prosperous middle-class life of *Kinde, Kuche and Kirche* ('children, kitchen, church'), growing up in the heart of Frankfurt-am-Main, my father went first to study in Darmstadt, and then Berlin. On Hitler's accession, my father was forced to leave his post at the university, and went to work for a time in Prussia (now Poland). My father realised there that war was brewing, and decided to leave for a post in Manchester, arriving on his 28th birthday.

Persuading the rest of his family – parents, grandmother, great-aunt and brother – to leave was a more difficult task. Getting permission for them to leave was even more difficult, and was only successful after Krystallnacht, the night that the Nazis burned and looted Jewish shops and synagogues (see Levitt, 2015). My uncle was deported to Dachau the following day, 10 November 1938. It was a Herculean task for him to be released and for the family to get the visas and permits to leave, including financial guarantees from English people. It was my mother's family who had to do this, with my uncle, married to my mother's elder sister and 20 years my mother's senior, acting on behalf of my father's brother. My widowed grandmother supplied the guarantees for the other four family members, and was able to do so as a householder; my mother, despite her professional status as a teacher, was not considered capable of acting as a guarantor. Indeed, later in wartime and on marriage to my father, she lost her British citizenship, and was only able to regain it on payment of a substantial sum of money![2] Vestiges of this system for refugees remain today.

My parents, and my father especially, therefore had strong feelings about education, family life and politics, which has also influenced how much I am able and should say....

Family political discussions were the mainstay of my upbringing, including standing up for political change, but precisely what that should entail is entirely another matter. Engaging in debate and questioning became fundamental to my emerging identity. However, I am not, and never have been, interested in armchair theorising, but rather in questioning the way things are, to mount campaigns to change policies and practices at the institutional, local, national and even the international level. The specifics of family and gender relationships have changed as the context and concepts, or the ways we think and talk about these, have changed. At heart I am an activist and campaigner, but what have we actually achieved? What have we managed to change, if anything? And what has changed around us? What might we now change for the better? Or is society now changing for the worse? Can changes be undone and refashioned in a fairer and more equal way?

Feminism as political and educational

For me, feminism is and has been not only a social movement or political project, but also an educational project. And I want to

---

[2]   It was 5s, or five shillings, for a certificate of re-naturalisation; see David (2009, p 5).

demonstrate how this is the case, to show how we have developed knowledge and understanding to question everyday life and how it is lived. During my lifetime this process has become an explicit one of researching and writing about women's lives in ways that were not done hitherto. Nowadays there is a massive literature in popular and more scholarly publications, codified and classified as feminist, women's and gender studies, and taught variously in an array of universities and colleges. So why, you may ask, is it necessary to have yet another book on this topic?

What I want to show in this memoir is how rich and richly important all this work is, building in particular a corpus of knowledge and understanding about women's lives, lived under the current and increasingly competitive economic systems of capitalism. And while women are clearly more visible in education and employment, at the same time they also remain invisible or belittled by the ruling powers in education, HE and political systems. While there is a rich seam of knowledge, it remains hidden, especially from public view, and indeed is specifically ignored by the political classes, so this is my way of trying to contribute to a new approach to women, gender and equality and fairness.

In the past this kind of approach was marginal to education and was done by lone writers or scholars outside of the mainstream. There were clear examples of what could be done, but they remained beacons in a more obscure world. Mary Wollstonecraft's *A vindication of the rights of woman* (1792) is one such light by an avowed feminist of 18th-century Britain. This book is now recommended to and read by multitudes of students of 20th and 21st-century Britain and worldwide. Virginia Woolf is another such beacon, as she railed against the limitations of university education for middle-class women at the turn of the 20th century, particularly in her *A room of one's own* (1929). She, too, is now recommended to and read by countless students, especially those of feminist literature.

The term 'feminism', while commonplace nowadays, remains scary as it hints at unconventional change, at attacking the roots of women's oppression. But it is not necessarily as scary as it sounds, and it certainly does not overturn all our cherished social relations. Personal and family life remains intensely political in the sense of power relations, and yet they are still kept relatively separate and obscured from public and political interventions. For some of us this is regrettable, but at very least we can learn and begin to understand why these processes of cultural, political and social change in how women are regarded are so difficult to achieve and sustain.

Becoming a feminist, and enjoying it!

I became both a feminist and a professor quite by chance and certainly not by design, but increasingly by desire. This desire to learn and to understand more about these ticklish and difficult questions on relations between men and women grew through my personal and political friendships and working relationships in academia. I now want to share what I have learned, using the insights of the scholarly and reflective approaches of feminist sociology. These draw on the amazing scholarship and insights not only of colleagues, but also of students and others; indeed, we can begin to think of colleagues as remaining as students, eager still to learn and change.

Complementing this book, I have written *A feminist manifesto for education* (David, 2016: in press) about how education itself could be different and fairer for both boys and girls and for future generations. And similar issues have also been taken up by Melissa Benn (2013), in *What should we tell our daughters?* There is also countless other feminist writing, too, to which I will refer, and much that, regrettably, I will have to miss, given word and knowledge constraints.

In this memoir I review the lessons that I have learned from these myriad activities and consider the future, drawing on my ageing wisdom, and that of others. I now have the chance to sit back and reflect on these questions in ways that were not possible in a busy working life and one subject to the rigours of academia. And these rigours seem to have been getting ever more tightly constrained as business approaches are increasingly applied to academe, and knowledge becomes ever more commodified and marketed rather than seen as a free and public good.

My objectives are intertwined. I want to make sure that the theories, ideas and campaigns of women of my generation, formed through the social movements of the 1960s, my so-called 'sisters', are not lost to history. Many of the really important and significant women who created the knowledge and wisdom from this period are becoming old and ill, frail, and some have already passed away.[3] And as the years roll on, those passing away inevitably increase while yet others are retiring. I also want to make sure that the legacy of such ideas is available to other generations, and to see how feminism has already had an impact on subsequent waves of feminism.

Have feminist ideas, theories and practices been changed as education, and universities, have expanded? How could these ideas now be used for future generations? As Mary Evans (2004) pointed out, the women's movement was one of the major social movements of the 20th century. Given the current global economic recession and the changing political complexions of government, there are also urgent questions about the changing role of universities as part of the global economy as well as the changing contributions of women, especially university-educated women. Indeed, universities are increasingly contested places as forms of women's empowerment and liberation.

And there is another reason, an urgent reason, and that is that many of the ideas and work of my fellow feminist activists may soon be lost to history, if a collective portrayal is not provided. Assembling the evidence about what we know and what we have learned is important, or we may find ourselves forever reinventing the wheel, as the late feminist scholar and activist educator, Diana Leonard, argued (Leonard, 2002). By constantly having to retrace our steps and revisit our histories, we may not to be able to take it forward and propose appropriate initiatives for change.

---

[3]   Others have recently passed away, such as the well-known American education feminist, Jean Anyon and the equally well-known British feminist Doreen Massey.

Academic feminism: politics, passion, pedagogies

To tell the story of how feminism became not only a political project but also an educational one, and to remain true to feminist principles of collective and collaborative action, I have relied on many friends and colleagues – what we have called 'sisterhood'. 'Sisterhood and After' is the name of the British Library's most recent archival collection of oral histories of the Women's Liberation Movement (WLM), collected together by the University of Sussex in association with the Women's Library, and funded by the Leverhulme Trust. It was launched at a celebratory event on International Women's Day (8 March 2013), and is a major project to ensure a collective record of the 20th-century women's movement in the UK, so that the lives of these women would not be lost to history. Over 60 interviews are available on the 'Sisterhood and After' learning website (see www.bl.uk/sisterhood).

Some of the women involved in the oral histories were also participants in my study of feminist academics, which was published as *Feminism, gender and universities: Politics, passion and pedagogies* (2014), which I embarked on to ensure that women are not erased from the histories of the transformations of global higher education in the 20th century.

My study participants were not only British academic feminists, but also from as many countries as I could reach out to, and include women from Australia, Canada and the US, largely what is now called 'the Global North'. I decided to construct a collective portrayal, memoir or biography, using life histories and stories to reflect on these changes, and opted for an account as seen through the eyes and in the words of the participants in these changing processes.

By concentrating on how a select group of feminist academic women's lives have been transformed, I was able to demonstrate how important education has been in these changing contexts, and what further changes are necessary. A tapestry of their values and voices has been woven, to dig deeper into the echelons of education that are often seen as all too private and hidden from view. I now want to show how contested the current managerial or business approach to university and education systems is, and how odiously different in approach to that of feminism.

Quite simply, we women, as academics, teachers and others (professionals), have benefited from the array of social, economic and cultural transformations, including the technologies that sustain them. But has this been enough? While there have been myriad changes in education and universities over my lifetime, as I want to show through the stories that I tell here of women's learning and women's lives, there are some stubborn obstacles to change.

Perhaps most resistant to change are the power relations between men and women in the higher echelons of society, what have been called 'patriarchal relations' or 'hegemonic masculinity'. So, despite all the welcome developments, such that education and universities especially are now critical to the global economies, as exemplified in the widely used term 'knowledge economy', patriarchy or misogyny still rules. Interestingly, universities today remain bastions of both male power and privilege. And as austerity or economic changes bite harder, the male hold is ever tighter, perhaps illustrated by HE as its personification. I now have the chance to reflect on what opportunities I have had, and what the obstacles have been to these possibilities. Some have inevitably been of my own making: my own feelings of trust and safety to express my views openly and honestly, fearing for my safety at work or at play. Others I have learned to see as more structural barriers – social and cultural.

My work has been in collaboration with other scholars, researchers and with students, both undergraduate and postgraduate. I have learned a great deal about their lives and values as I have accumulated this knowledge through these developing and changing relationships, and have become particularly fascinated by and committed to feminist work, although I have not always had the luxury of being able to write or work in this vein.

Our feminist past and feminist presence

As I am now partially retired, I want to share my thoughts, knowledge and wisdom that I have gained from my feminist involvements and scholarship. But why, you may ask, would anyone want to read about these issues written by someone you might regard as an 'old crone'? What do I have to offer that is fresh, new and inspiring? I have found over many years that learning and sharing ideas is exciting, and many women feel passionately about this. Knowledge and wisdom is a basis for both understanding and possibly changing the way we live our lives.

This kind of biographic approach is now quite commonplace as it is a way of illustrating how our knowledge and understanding are not separate from the way we live – there is no one objective truth about the world around us. A key issue in *Leaders in gender and education* (Weaver-Hightower and Skelton, 2013) is that it is written from a personal and subjective perspective, but all the authors in this volume talked about their struggles with this style of writing. In their introduction the editors highlight that we struggle with this genre of personal or subjective writing while being fundamentally a part of it. Instead of using the notion now current in the literature of biography or auto/biography or memoirs, the editors invent the term 'intellectual self-portraits', which neatly encapsulates the notion that there can be more than one portrayal and more than one scholarly approach.

And this is what has become important internationally, in a loose network of scholars in gender and education, with contributors from Australia, the UK and the US. The contributors to this volume edited by Weaver-Hightower and Skelton also illustrate some of the changing nuances in approach to gender and education today, with a majority of now feminist scholars, but a large minority of (male) pro-feminists. Definitions of both 'gender' and 'sexuality' are carefully interrogated with instances of homosexuality, lesbianism and transgender or sexuality and diversity (LGBTQi).

The women with whom I have spoken are similar, drawn from various informal social networks. A key network for me has, of course, been the feminist network of women working on gender and education, such as the GEA, including scholars who are self-professed 'education feminists' and loosely linked through the professional association of the American Educational Research Association (AERA). The AERA is a vast professional organisation of teachers and researchers, not only in the US, but also internationally. It holds annual meetings around the US at which a multitude of teachers gather together, including a growing number of feminists and women researchers.

Others include networks of women's studies scholars, one of which was formed in Bristol when I was starting out on my journey of becoming a feminist activist and scholar, over 40 years ago, the Bristol Women's Studies Group (BWSG). This group celebrated its 30th anniversary of the publication *Half the sky: An introduction to women's studies* belatedly, but in 2010. We discussed our assessments of the changing situations and continued our enduring conversations that we had committed to in our younger days. Yet other networks are of sociologists and social policy experts stemming from those Bristol days, before and after, linked together in networks of older British feminists, such as the Women's Budget Group, the OFN and London 70s Sisters.

Having decided to talk to feminist activists and others mainly in universities, and as public policy analysts – professors and researchers – I asked them a series of questions designed to target certain key issues that I see as the criteria to zero in on what feminism is, and how it plays out in their and in others' lives. I asked them to assess and reflect on how successful feminism has been in educational arenas, in politics and public life, and how important it remains to them today. I wanted to capture their initial feelings of excitement about being part of the women's movement and campaigning for sociopolitical changes, and I also wanted to see whether they felt that they had achieved their personal and political goals, and how far these goals had changed over time. Had the goals of the WLM, or feminism more broadly, been achieved, as some were beginning to argue at the turn of the 21st century?

I also wanted to assess what the obstacles as well as opportunities to social change had been. Just how far had we been successful in transforming academic, educational and political lives? What had not been achieved? Could the transformations that were desired yet be accomplished? Were some of the social and political changes during our lives inimical to feminist aims? Was it possible to continue to campaign to change these? It was also important to capture the range of emotions that the women had and have, the passions for being feminists and also the desires for and disappointments of being in academia, and the pernicious effects of the business and managerial systems in global education today.

Initially I focused on the generation of women formed through involvement in university education from the 1960s, like myself. Universities were expanding then, and opportunities for women, not only as students but also as researchers and academics, were opening up: women, including feminists, were quickly afforded opportunities to enter academia. In the UK, for example, the policy to expand HE was initiated through the Robbins Report, published in the autumn of 1963. This built on a secular trend in expanding education and creating new universities as a public rather than a private good.

Over the last 50 years, this pace of change has speeded up such that women now comprise over 50% of university undergraduate students across most countries, especially the developed world or Global North, although these percentages do not translate into academia, and nor do they transform gender relations (European Commission, 2012; UNESCO, 2012). The question of gender equality in universities, and the contribution of feminist or women's studies, is still a highly contentious topic, arousing very strong emotions. The claim that gender equality has been achieved usually refers to the question of the balance of male and female students, whether of undergraduate or graduate degrees and courses (Bekhradnia, 2009). It is rarely about the numbers or proportions of women as academics, teachers or researchers. *She figures* is a European Union (EU) annual publication, and illustrates how limited women's penetration into the senior ranks of university research and administration has actually been.

As I began to gather my evidence, talking to other feminists, I decided to expand the generations of women I would talk to, to ensure that I captured the range and diversity of change, although I saw how awesome the task was of trying to capture all the changes. Could I confine my work to just what was happening in universities, even though they were playing a bigger part in international and national economies now than in the 20th century, and becoming known as 'academic capitalism' (Slaughter and Leslie, 1997; Slaughter and Rhoades, 2004)? Just what part did growing inequalities, and poverty or social disadvantage, especially for women, have in this story?

My feminism had always included activism as part of the picture: campaigning as well as theorising and reflecting. Aiming to change the world in the direction of greater equalities, and transforming it for women, inevitably, in my book, means for social class, ethnicity and 'race' too. So I also spoke with other feminists and women who had benefited from the changes but who had not remained in either HE or as active feminists. They did see education as vital, and included former school and university friends and members of the University of the Third Age (U3A), an informal national network of retired people, organised into local and regional groups. They have all remained in some form of education – school, primary or secondary – advising on teaching subjects and working in what are now called the 'knowledge industries'.

The initial generation that I focused on became known as 'second-wave' feminists, by contrast with the 'first-wave' feminists of the turn of the 20th century, who had campaigned for political changes such as women's suffrage. While I think that this wave analogy is problematic, I used it to analyse my stories of women across three generations of feminist academics. Several others have also used this kind of approach, and I borrowed from Olive Banks (1986), a respected feminist sociologist of education.

I aimed for international feminist 'voices' drawing on several overlapping 'networks' of academic and educational researchers, but all in English. I did not anticipate a large number of respondents, but hoped for a spread among Anglophone metropolitan countries, and some countries of Africa and Asia where I knew of feminist academics. As I proceeded I found that some of my 'respondents' preferred to be interviewed while others were happier to write to me by email. I had an amazing and extensive array of responses, far more than I had initially anticipated, and finally ended up with well over 100 participants, who provided interview materials, conversations and transcripts or written replies to my questions.

I also obtained a spread of feminists across the arts, humanities and social sciences, as well as across the ages and generations, although, perhaps inevitably, most of my participants' replies were from women either already or partially retired, or in that age bracket of women about to retire. Sadly I rarely found natural scientists. Especially important here were the reflections on feminist work in the academy put together by a group of Canadian feminist scholars, entitled *Minds of our own: Inventing feminist scholarship and women's studies in Canada and Quebec, 1966-1976* (Robbins et al, 2008). The contributors show the importance of preserving the memories of the heydays of feminist involvement in creating new knowledge and wisdom for global education. Lorna Marsden's article was especially important in arguing that 'second-wave feminism breaks on the shores of academe.' Marsden's work encapsulated the notion of feminist knowledge being created in academia.

A partial study, partial to feminism?

While I had a fascinating array of participants, my study was inevitably *partial*. It celebrates the feminist scholarship and knowledge that has grown apace in academe, although there are debates about what exactly this now constitutes. It is also *partial* because of the limitations of my networks and my resources. Many were far too busy to participate, and I did not want to put further pressure on such pressurised academics, as this might be seen as a further instance of the intensification of academic work today, rather than the pleasurable and passionate engagement with feminist scholarship.

While there have been innumerable studies of feminism and the women's movement, changing politics and policies, there is relatively less about how feminism has become part of education and academe, developing feminist knowledge, contributing to critiques of the traditional academic subjects, and as a subject in its own right, as, for instance, women's studies. Many of the women who wrote the initial books and pamphlets of 'second-wave feminism' were, indeed, women who had been college students, as the American women in Friedan's (1963) hugely important feminist study – *The feminine mystique* – of housewives and mothers and their dissatisfaction with 'the problem that has no name' had been (Stambach and David, 2005).

Studies of HE and of women today

Alison Wolf's (2013) *The XX factor: How working women are creating a new society*, is an engagingly written and well-documented review of the societal changes that have been occurring for women, and well-educated women especially, over the last several decades. She interviewed women from across the generations – some of hers and my generation, and many younger women who are now rising up in education and professional jobs – her book is about elite university-educated professional women. But there the similarities between our arguments end and we part company. Wolf argues that the expansion of universities for elites has meant that such women are now in the ascendance in the professions and in business, and are able to live the lives of privileged and non-traditional women, dependent though they may be on other less privileged women for forms of care and support such as childcare. Wolf applauds this system of individual class-based educational and professional success as heralding a new society, and does not appear to question its downsides.

Sylvia Walby's book, *The future of feminism?* (2011), also promised a reflection on the future as seen from an educational perspective. However, her current version of feminist politics is not about the processes within universities, although she is an extremely distinguished professor of sociology, also holding the title of the UNESCO chair in gender research at the University of Lancaster. Rather, Walby is interested in exploring the impact on European politics and issues of gender equality or equity within the polity, and she does this with considerable flair.

Both books and arguments stand in marked contrast to my interests. I am interested in both a more traditional and radical notion of feminist politics as they relate to the personal, and within an institutional arena, of education: about both activism and understanding the roots of women's oppression within the family, work and the political systems or power relations. Illustrating quite how important reassessments of the contemporary state of affairs are, another exciting book is that by Janet Newman, *Working the spaces of power: Activism, neoliberalism and gendered labour* (2012). Like Walby, Newman is interested in traditional politics – through the local as well as the national state, as well as lobbying and pressure groups or social movements. Like Wolf, Newman, too, uses a similar method to mine: of interviewing women across the generations, and mainly, but not only, academics: some academics manqué. Newman is interested in talking to her feminist participants about involvements in activism – in local or national politics – and their involvement in pressure groups for social change and social welfare. So we have complementary interests: in the transformations achieved by feminists and in the blockages to change wrought by more conservative and constraining contemporary governments. Newman doesn't focus on education or changing politics specifically in academe, leaving yet another space for feminist assessments of the past, and thoughts about possible future scenarios. This is where our differences lie.

In a different vein from Walby and Newman, Kathy Davis and Mary Evans (2011), as editors of the *European Journal of Women's Studies*, were interested in the development of feminist theories among generations of scholars in the global academy. As sociologists, and both from my generation of 'second-wave' feminism, Davis and Evans invited their contributors to consider the 'feminist canon', drawing on the US by contrast with European and/or UK ideas. The contributors to *Transatlantic conversations: Feminism as travelling theory* all produced autobiographical reflective essays. While Davis and Evans focused on the transatlantic context, I have not, given my focus on obtaining international contributors. My approach addresses a slightly wider canvass, and does not engage with the dominance of American English or indeed, American feminist theories.

Most recently, a presentation at the biennial conference of the GEA, held in London in 2015 at Roehampton University, alerted me to the continuing appeal of investigating the trajectories of international feminist academics. Three Brazilian women from the University of Paraíba presented a collective biography of feminist academics in northern Brazil, mainly around Recife. They concentrated on a group of women from the age cohort born between 1930 and 1960, looking at how they had established a feminist network of gender studies and research centres. They argued that 'activism was the key to the women's academic identification', considering the role of social and university movements for change as central to the women's identities and their strategies for empowerment. They concluded that change through federal programmes in Brazil remained a distant dream.

Given this increasingly intensive nature of international academic work in universities today, and the constrained and constraining individualised academe, I was not surprised that the responses from the older and retired women also tended to be more full: those who had been fired by feminist passions for political activism and who had eventually become, as I had too, jaundiced by the constant struggles within academia to maintain an emancipatory place and space. Yet all my participants felt passionately about how important the feminist project has been to their own learning, involvement in the academy, and to their own lives.

My study was therefore made up of a diversity of women, and mainly, but not only, academics, across the generations and ages, and was also extremely varied in terms of the women's social and geographic locations, illustrative of the mobile, transnational academics who are characteristic of the overall academic profession in the 21st century, as Terri Kim and Rachel Brooks (2013) have argued so cogently. The proportion of women from overseas in the major research universities, such as the Russell Group, in the professoriate are higher – around half. These foreign nationals are not only from the EU, but also from the US and the rapidly developing economies such as Brazil, China and India. Similarly, Rajani Naidoo (2011) has also shown how diverse and transnational the global academy is.

While most of my participants are now resident in the UK, many were not born in the UK but come from former British colonies such as Australia, Canada, the Caribbean, India, Pakistan, South Africa and the US and other parts of Europe – France, Greece and Spain. Equally, my participants from

Canada, for example, were originally from other countries such as Germany, Norway, the UK and the US, all part of post-colonial trends.

Importantly, the stories of how these over 100 diverse women entered the global academy and became feminists – through university or not – and specifically by types of subject – women's studies, sociology, psychology – is immensely varied. The theories and/or books or writers who contributed to and had had an impact on their learning is, interestingly, much less varied, and their stories are much clearer about the developments of feminist practices and influences, including Eureka moments, and their work for PhDs and teaching courses. A range of accounts of feminist activism in the academy, changing positions and changing lives shed light on the obstacles, opportunities and impact of gender relations in the 21st century.

In pulling together these stories, there were inevitably ethical questions to be addressed, particularly about the travails of life in academia today. I note that Alison Wolf did not raise this question, naming all her women quite openly, although Janet Newman (2012) problematised the balancing of giving voice and recognition to the creativity of feminist activists as opposed to maintaining confidentiality and anonymity.

Despite their seniority as professors, some of my participants felt that giving detailed biographical material would provide too much exposure to personal and intimate matters at the expense of broader professional questions. But many, while being members of feminist communities, are also unique and easily identifiable. So the question of attribution is never straightforward. I want to ensure that this story is neither dispassionate nor impassive, that 'the personal is political', as this is a feminist thread since it was coined in the 1960s. This is similar to how 'personal troubles become public issues', as the famous sociologist C. Wright Mills (1959) claimed, linking biography with social structure, although his democratic optimism is no longer as simple to maintain.

I am struck by how feminist networks have become more than professional and collegial, but also based on shared values and knowledge: the desire to maintain feminist knowledge through our daily and pedagogical practices as collective actions. Increasingly, as the sociopolitical climate in a global era of austerity tightens, there is resistance to the limitations for women, particularly as feminism has increased and become more dramatic. Anti-austerity and misogyny are now locked in combat.

U3A and Women's Learning Lives

As part of the process of retiring, I also became involved in the U3A. This choice was not accidental, as I could not keep away from learning and teaching. I felt safer in the U3A than in a more formal educational setting where I might have ended up having to be assessed and examined. Ironically, I don't like that process of examination, fearing that I might be found wanting, despite having had to develop ever more finely tuned criteria of testing over the years. Perhaps this is why I find the new league table approach to schools and now universities such an anathema, and I am certainly sympathetic to those who are frightened of such judgements. I am also disparaging of those who hold dear the ranking systems of schools and universities on what I know to be such flimsy criteria. We come back to this approach to elite and selective education later, as we recognise its exclusionary tactics.

I chose a branch of U3A close to home in north London, and suggested coordinating a group called 'Women's Learning Lives'. I was told that recruitment might be slow, and so it proved, but five or more years on, and we are still going strong, now as 'Women and Wisdom', although group membership has changed. We have all relaxed as we have told our stories, sharing our hopes and fears about learning. What is most remarkable is the group's love of learning, and the fact that learning is so important, lighting up our days, and seeing it as an act of sharing. We don't all agree, and why would we? But we do share a desire to think through the questions together, discussing ideas in what feels like a safe environment (and somewhat akin to the old consciousness-raising [CR] groups of the early days of the women's movement). We feel safe in the group because we have begun to know and trust each other not to disparage or judge our ways of living.

HE in the lives of my school friends

I also discussed these questions with former university and school friends. My old school friends and I met up on the 50th anniversary of our entering secondary school – Keighley Girls' Grammar School, in what was then the West Riding of Yorkshire, where the redoubtable Sir Alec Clegg led the then local education authority (LEA). (He was knighted for services to education, some time after we had left school. Interestingly, as I recently discovered, having attended the biennial conference of the Feminist and Women's Studies Association (FWSA) at the University of Leeds, in September 2015, that a studio in the new theatre on campus was named after him.)

As we enjoyed our initial reunion, we have since met together regularly to reflect on the impact of education, with at least five of us remaining in education throughout our lives. While some of my school friends may not see themselves as feminists, they do illustrate how their changing lives have led them to be strong and powerful women. Being of a similar generation to my U3A friends and my study participants, their stories confirm the robust impacts of feminist ideas that live on in all these women's lives.

I now turn to my stories of the enduring influences of feminist ideas, not only through HE, but also across women's lives. I want to weave a story of my own biography with the stories of others, within the bigger tapestry of the postwar British settlement for education and social welfare, to show how 'she' has made some progress in the world of HE and public life, but that much remains to be done to change the world in the direction of a more fair and equal society, for both men and women.

TWO

Changing feminism

I now explore facets of the changing cultural, socioeconomic and political contexts over the last 50 years. Feminist methods of study have been created with the development of substantive knowledge, within the social sciences or social and educational history. These methods draw on those in the arts and social sciences, although there is a question about which came first. But let's not be detained by debates about the chicken and the egg; suffice it to say that ideas about using narratives as ways of gleaning wisdom about the lives of others, women especially, has become an acceptable approach of what became known as 'the biographic turn' in the late 1980s. It had been prefigured in the developing methods of the social sciences in the postwar period. While these ideas remain contested, they remain critical to feminist studies.

I also provide some statistical evidence about changing demographic trends of university education, starting with the UK, by contrast with the US and other European countries. It is clearly the case that HE, like feminism, is far more prominent in public life and employment than 50 years ago. It is also more prominent in global economies, leading to the notion of knowledge economies. As already mentioned, in 1963, the then UK Conservative government received a major report into HE, which it immediately accepted. This report, the Robbins Report, was the subject of much public and policy discussion in 2013, given the celebrations for its 50th anniversary. I revisit its details to set the scene for subsequent discussions about women's changing lives and the consciousness of feminist ideas.

Lord David Willetts, elevated to the House of Lords in the Dissolution Honours of August 2015, was the former UK coalition government's Conservative Minister for Universities and Science (2010-15). In *Robbins revisited: Bigger and better higher education*, he reviewed the report, producing a very useful summary (Willetts, 2013). To identify the changing balances between men and women as *undergraduate students*, he had the figures carefully re-analysed. In 2013 there were 54% female undergraduates as opposed to 46% male undergraduates, whereas 'in the 1960s only 25 percent of full time students at UK institutions were female' (Willetts, 2013, p 26).

Of course, given his very traditional views of men and women's roles, which he has written about separately (Willetts, 2011), Willetts provides no information about academics themselves. (Ironically, he is now a visiting professor in the Policy Institute at King's College, London.) Indeed, Willetts shares views about women's role in the family that were current (in the 1960s) and clearly articulated in the report. For many of us, his views are old-fashioned and do not accord with how we women now live our lives, which Willetts appears to abhor, writing that 'feminism trumped egalitarianism' (2011, p 208). In other words, he wants socioeconomic equality or social mobility for men alone, seeing feminists as entirely the middle-class beneficiaries of HE. What a bizarre contrast. But he does mention the changing balances between subjects and faculties in universities, which may have implications for graduate and professional employment. His concerns are about what are now called STEM subjects, namely, science, technology, engineering and maths (or medicine). And in his case, the focus is firmly on medicine, and the fact that nowadays there is a predominance of women as students, and therefore, presumably, of women doctors.

A critical political and social moment: 1963

As it so happens, I was just becoming a student in the autumn of 1963 at the moment when the Robbins Report was published, and although I have only a hazy memory of its publication, I am aware of the surrounding events, and their subsequent re-evaluation. I have been a witness, a participant and integral to movements for change, especially the women's and other social movements, including socialist and civil rights movements. My own reflection has a gloss that includes my own emergence as a feminist academic and critic. Feminist analysis of patriarchy and subsequent studies of sexism and misogyny had not emerged back then.

At the time, HE reached a very small segment of the population, and university education was an even smaller proportion. The official figures and statistics in the UK did not routinely show sex or gender. Students were a rarity in the early 1960s, being less than a quarter of a million overall – 216,000 undergraduate (and postgraduate) students (Robbins, 1963, p 15). They were not commonly on the public agenda for discussion, and as women students, we were even more rare, a tiny minority of a small minority of young people coming of age in the 1960s. But students became increasingly vocal as the decade wore on, and this led to the emergence of a strong and campaigning international women's liberation movement (WLM), of which I quickly became a part.

I have witnessed and participated in the changes as feminism has framed my adult life in HE, and I represent one of a small minority of academic women activists influenced by the changing effects of the report. My reflections are inevitably partly arising from those effects, and I cannot step outside of or escape the implications. But none of the terms now used about the relations between men and women in HE and beyond were then in either common currency or in the official lexicon. These are all part of the changing discourse of HE and its political situation – terms such as 'gender equality', 'feminism' and the 'women's movement'. And even less so notions of 'sexual harassment' or 'abuse', 'patriarchy' and 'misogyny'.

The celebrations for the anniversary of the Robbins Report took place alongside several other 50th anniversary events, which I also discuss to locate our stories in a wider cultural and sociopolitical framework. Another celebration in the spring of 2013 in the UK and the US was about US feminist Betty Friedan's book, *The feminine mystique*. This arguably launched the feminist movement in the US initially, and later in Europe and beyond. It was based on Friedan's study of suburban housewives, the majority of who lived in middle-class areas and who had been college students prior to becoming wives and mothers. They all identified what Friedan called 'the problem that has no name', namely, women's dissatisfaction with their lives as merely wives and mothers, hidden from public and professional lives for which they had studied. This was a major cry for social change, and the book quickly became a bestseller, launching the National Organization of Women (NOW) in the US. Several women I spoke to mentioned this as formative: for example, Professor Helen Taylor, the feminist literary critic, and Professor Sandra Acker, the feminist sociologist of education, both mentioned reading the book as graduate students in the US, remarking on how influential it had been in their journey of thinking about new ways of being a woman. Professor Bronwyn Davies, an Australian feminist sociologist of education, was also captivated by how the book had transformed her life.

Similarly, there were public debates about the 50th anniversary of US President John Fitzgerald Kennedy's (JFK) assassination on 22 November 1963. At one time, most people could remember where they were when they first heard of the assassination, but as the years have worn on, this event has slowly dimmed in significance, and other public events taken over. Nevertheless, I can still remember being an undergraduate student in Glasgow and telephoning home, that Friday night, with my younger sister telling me through a tear-stained voice of the assassination a few minutes before. JFK's assassination is significant as part of the process of civil or human rights and social movements aimed at transforming political life in the direction of social, sexual and racial equalities. Arguably, this event contributed to the emergence of student movements across the Global North, including the women's movement. It was also around the same time of the start of the so-called 'sexual revolution', which included moves towards campaigns around different forms of sexuality, and expressions of homosexuality and lesbianism. Opening these up for public debate was part of these widespread social and political movements for human, civil, economic and social rights.

These social movements built on earlier movements in the postwar period, and although there are many accounts of these political developments, they rarely include the question of women's role in the processes of political and social change. Indeed, some of the international developments had arguably begun during the Second World War (Plesch, 2011). For instance, the United Nations (UN) was formed as an organisation of allies to try to defeat Nazi Germany during the war. At the end of the war, the UN Commission on Human Rights was created, producing the Universal Declaration of Human Rights in the late 1940s. This included reference to women. The UN has subsequently been at the forefront of developing international human rights, including the status of women, hosting decennial conferences, although it took another 50 years to create a special division of the UN responsible for women's equality, UN Women.

Other changes included the growth of student movements as a response to changing contexts such as postwar political changes and developing antagonisms between Western liberal democracies, as represented by the US, for example, and communist or socialist democracies. Indeed, in the 15 years from the end of the Second World War to 1960, tensions between these regimes mounted to such an extent that it was described as 'the Cold War'. In 1961, in Berlin, this was solidified by the Berlin Wall, which separated the East's communist regime from the West's liberal democracy. Shortly after its construction and before his assassination, President Kennedy visited Berlin, famously declaring 'Ich bin ein Berliner'. The wall contributed to the rise of sociopolitical movements opposed to such a separation barrier. But it was to take almost another 30 years before the wall came down, and East and West Berlin and East and West Germany were reunited in 1990, with celebrations for 25 years as I write.

Student protests about the increasingly harsh forms of political and social control began to hit the air waves towards the end of the 1960s, not only in the UK, but more spectacularly in France, and in other parts of Europe, Germany especially, and the US. 'Les événéments' in France in 1968, followed by events in the US, especially at the University of California in Berkeley and Kent State University in Ohio, came to symbolise the later mood of civil disobedience and campaigning. It was the stirrings of consciousness for women, for students, and for campaigners for civil, human and social rights.

The question of divisions between types of democracy and political regimes were the source of the growth of sociopolitical movements, with the women's movement being but one. Women inevitably played their part within these various movements, and their analytic studies have met with varying amounts of acceptance. In particular, it should be noted here that another contribution to this debate about the characteristics of totalitarianism and particular regimes was that developed by the German Jewish refugee from Nazism, Hannah Arendt, who, postwar, became professor of political philosophy at the New School for Social Research in New York in the US. In particular, her political and philosophical analysis of the Adolf Eichmann trial held in 1961 was a key contribution to these debates, although it was then seen as highly controversial. It is only much later, and well into the 21st century, that her political philosophy has been taken up in feminist debate and circles. Arendt herself might never have defined herself as a feminist, however, being of an older and more sceptical generation.

Origins of second-wave feminism in the 1960s

The origins of the feminist project lie with these sociopolitical movements for change in the postwar period: movements for civil and human rights across the now so-called 'Global North', in North America, Europe and parts of Australasia, but subsequently spreading to the Global South – Africa, Latin America and Asia. Many of the early participants in the WLM, or what has become known as 'second-wave feminism', were students in these expanding systems. During the 1960s, there was a resurgence of the feminist ideas that had been in currency during the pre-war period. Indeed, feminist ideas originated in the 18th and 19th centuries, mainly outside the academy, where women were not excluded. While Hannah Arendt might not have seen herself as a feminist, many originators of second-wave feminist ideas were of her generation – women as students within the inter-war years from across countries of the Global North. Arendt had been a student in Berlin in the early 1930s when Hitler came to power.

Simone de Beauvoir, the French intellectual and existentialist, who was also of the generation born in the first two decades of the 20th century, began to address these ideas in her own life and writings, especially through *The second sex* (de Beauvoir, 1949), but her works were not taken up as feminist ideas until the 1960s, first in France, and later in the UK and elsewhere. Both Professor Elizabeth Wilson and Dr Ellen Malos mentioned their excitement as young students on reading this book. De Beauvoir had been a particularly able and highly achieving woman at France's premier university, the Sorbonne, in the 1920s. In her story, *Memoirs of a dutiful daughter*, published in the 1960s, and providing one of the first biographical narratives of a feminist, she mentions that she gained a higher qualification than Sartre in the examinations, although this was not recognised.

Similarly, Betty Friedan, the American Jewish feminist writer and socialist campaigner, was of this early generation of feminists, formed during the inter-war period. She had been a student at the elite women's college, Smith, in the 1940s, and was followed there by Gloria Steinem, feminist founder of *Ms* magazine and the National Women's Political Caucus in 1971, and Sylvia Plath, the feminist poet and icon. Others include Alva Myrdal, sociologist and wife of the Swedish-American politician and demographer Gunnar Myrdal, who launched her studies of *Women's two roles* (with Viola Klein) in the early postwar period. The British feminist sociologist Olive Banks was also of this generation, studying at the London School of Economics and Political Science (LSE) in wartime. Banks went on to become one of the first women professors in sociology.

Some writers who inaugurated 'second-wave feminism' to distinguish it from the 'first-wave feminism' of the late 19th and early 20th centuries were of a later generation – women born in the late 1930s, during the Second World War and its immediate aftermath. Feminist ideas and writings were part of a wider cultural, social and political context, including universities and HE. Several of the books that 'inaugurated' the women's movement, between 50 and 60 years ago, were written by women who had been students in the postwar period, formed and framed by this turbulent context. Many of these publications were produced during the later 1960s, with 1970 becoming a key moment. They include Eva Figes, the German Jewish refugee to England in the late 1930s, who wrote *Patriarchal attitudes* (Figes, 1970), later becoming a novelist, and Shulamith Firestone, the Canadian orthodox Jewess born in 1945 who sought refuge in New York after her student days, and whose *The dialectic of sex* (Firestone, 1970) was critically important for the launch of the radical feminist arm of the women's movement. Kate Millett, the American artist who wrote *Sexual politics* (Millett, 1970) as part of her doctorate in New York, and Adrienne Rich, the American lesbian feminist poet and essayist, who wrote *Of woman born: Motherhood as experience and institution* (Rich, 1977), were also influential in framing our ideas.

Germaine Greer, the Australian émigrée academic to England, was also critically influential initially in the UK, with her polemical study *The female eunuch* (Greer, 1970). So, too, was Juliet Mitchell, the New Zealand–born socialist-feminist academic, who later became a psychoanalyst and writer, returning to academia in her later years. Her 'Women: The longest revolution' (Mitchell, 1966, 1984) was influential in the forming of a socialist-feminist movement in the UK, along with Sheila Rowbotham, the English feminist historian, educated at Oxford in the early 1960s, whose *Hidden from history* (Rowbotham, 1973a) and *Women, resistance and revolution* (Rowbotham, 1972) provided useful, previously uncovered, materials to aid the growth of women's studies and feminist history.

These writers were all passionate about changing women's lives: in the family as daughters, sisters, wives and mothers, as sexual beings, and in education, paid and unpaid work or employment. How could women's lives be transformed and made more equal with men's lives, in both public and private? How could patriarchy and sexual oppression be overcome?

While there have been innumerable studies of feminism and the women's movement, changing politics and policies, there is relatively less about how feminism has become part of academe, developing feminist knowledge, contributing to critiques of the traditional academic subjects, and as a subject in its own right, as, for instance, women's studies. Just how did feminism continue to have an impact on HE itself? Before we address this question, there is the prior question of how feminist knowledge emerged, and how it become a vital part of the transformations of HE.

Feminist ideas in changing historical contexts

During the late 19th century and into the first decades of the 20th century, feminist political campaigns became serious debates about strategies, which were very turbulent among suffragists and suffragettes.[1] These campaigning ideas, together with those about women's education, came to dominate some agendas. The women's educational movement in the UK in the 19th century had been a very strong, controversial, and lively component of feminist campaigns, too. While these movements for social and political changes for women – for education, including university education, and for the vote, and for family changes such as birth control and abortion and for women's employment – were only of limited success, other campaigns took precedence.

What is important is that by the early 1960s, women remained subordinate to men in all walks of life, whether in politics or in education or in the family. While women had achieved the vote in most countries of the Global North during the first half of the 20th century (the exception being in Switzerland, affording women the vote only in 1971), and there were educational provisions up to and including HE, this was not extensive, and women felt relatively excluded from political, public and social life. From an educational perspective, women were still not entitled to participate on a par with men. For example, while there were schools, colleges and university places also available for women, most of the elite and middle-class places remained single-sex, separate and different from men's opportunities. The argument of 'separate but equal' was used frequently to justify these differences.

---

[1] 'Suffragette', a film about the British suffrage movement starring Meryl Streep and Carey Mulligan, opened in October 2015.

Perhaps the postwar period – from the 1940s to the 1960s – can be seen as one of quiescence for feminist ideas, given the need to recreate a stable and secure society. Nevertheless, this postwar period was, as we argued in *Closing the gender gap: Postwar education and social change* (Arnot et al, 1999), a time when there was a growth of educational opportunities for women and girls. The seeds had been sown for major social changes, including feminist campaigns for more equal educational provision, in the UK and in other countries, initially of the Global North.

HE institutions in 1963: single-sex or co-educational?

Given that going to university was not crucially important for professional employment, such as the law, many men did not go. And some of the women who went on to gain qualifications in what were then seen as key female occupations – teachers, nurses and social workers – did not have to go to university but to specialist schools and colleges. Willetts makes the point that of the 216,000 students in the UK in 1962-63, only 118,000 went to universities, while the other 98,000 went to other institutions, such as colleges of technology and teacher training colleges (2013, pp 22-4). So very few of the age cohort of 18- to 20-year-olds went to university, and of that tiny proportion, less than a quarter were women. (This was also the case in Canada, Australia and the US.)

Even in universities, the more elite institutions were, like many of the secondary and public (private) schools that contributed the lion's share of their students, single-sex. In the UK in 1963, all the constituent colleges of Cambridge, Oxford and several of the colleges of the University of London were single-sex. In Cambridge, there were just three colleges – Girton, Newnham and New Hall – for women from among 30, and similarly in Oxford, there was Lady Margaret Hall, Saint Hilda's and Somerville for women from among a similar number. In London, Bedford College, Royal Holloway and Westfield were women's colleges, although other colleges of the university, such as the LSE, King's College and University College, had been co-educational from their beginnings. This pattern of co-educational institutions was a feature of the creation of the major civic universities, such as Birmingham, Bristol, Edinburgh, Leeds, Liverpool, Manchester, Newcastle and Nottingham, although all their halls of residence were, at that time, single-sex (Grant, 2016). The origins of this differentiation link with changing social class and occupational patterns as much as with the politics of individual institutions. Professor Carol Dyhouse has provided an intriguing analysis of these complex patterns in her book entitled *No distinction of sex?* (1995), and her studies of women as students.

This pattern was similar in the US, where the Ivy League colleges were all-male, with the Seven Sisters, a loose association of seven liberal arts colleges in the Northeastern US, historically women's colleges. They are Barnard College, Bryn Mawr College, Mount Holyoke College, Radcliffe College, Smith College, Vassar College and Wellesley College, and all were founded in the mid to late 19th century. These colleges were for the sisters of the men in the Ivy League colleges (Horowitz, 1993). The major public universities, however, were again, largely co-educational, although again, like in the UK, their residences were single-sex.

During the 19th century there had been arguments about women's difference from men that prevented women having the same education. These arguments and evidence of them have also been uncovered and highlighted by feminist educational historians and researchers. For example, Henry Maudsley, who founded one of the major psychiatric hospitals in the UK at the turn of the 20th century, was known to argue that women's menstruation meant that they were not as capable of study as men. His arguments also led to the prevention, therefore, of women gaining admission to undergraduate degree qualifications.

So it was only after considerable struggle during the late 19th century that women gained admission to university, and in some of the more elite colleges, they were still denied qualifications on a par with men, until well into the 20th century. For example, women were able to study at women's colleges in Oxford and Cambridge, but were not entitled to gain degrees. In Oxford, women were able to obtain degree qualifications from the 1920s, but Cambridge remained a male bastion until after the Second World War. Women were finally admitted to a degree qualification in 1948 in Cambridge.[2] Rosalind Franklin, for example, did not actually gain a degree from the University of Cambridge, only from her college, Newnham.

The term 'blue stocking' is used for an educated, intellectual woman, based on a specific group of 18th-century intellectual women. Until the late 18th century, it had referred to learned people of both sexes or rather, gender. However, it was subsequently applied primarily to intellectual women, and the French equivalent *bas bleu* had a similar connotation. It has since developed negative and sexist implications. The feminist social policy expert Professor Fiona Williams mentioned that to acknowledge her evident intellectual abilities and yet malign her womanly being, one of her male schoolteachers at her co-educational secondary school called her 'a frightening blue stocking' in the classroom. This sexist insult has remained with her and framed her desire to campaign for political and social changes for women. No small wonder, then, that with the rise of the WLM, a magazine and socialist group in the US would call itself 'Red Stockings' to parody the notion!

In the UK as in North America, teacher education was distinctive, and there were colleges specifically for women to train to become teachers at this time that did not even require them to study for an undergraduate degree. Teacher training, especially for women, had commenced in the mid-19th century in the UK with Whitelands College opening in London in 1841, followed by Borough Road in the later 1840s for elementary schools.[3] Becoming a teacher for older children and young people could also take place in universities, as a graduate professional qualification. Inevitably, this was initially the case more often for male than female teachers, who would subsequently be employed in academic and secondary schools.

It was in the period from the 1960s that these distinctions of both sex or gender and professional qualifications began to erode in both the US and UK. And it was only in the last

---

[2] This was the subject of the play *Blue Stockings* performed at The Globe in 2013, drawing on Jane Robinson's *Bluestockings* (2009); see also Grant (2016).

[3] It later became Borough Polytechnic, renamed South Bank, becoming a new university in 1992.

quarter of the 20th century that the single-sex colleges in Cambridge, Oxford and London became co-educational. Several of my contemporaries from my single-sex girls' school went to single-sex colleges, one to read mathematics at St Hilda's at Oxford, and others to single-sex teacher training for primary schools such as Avery Hill, subsequently to become part of Greenwich University. Interestingly, this was also part of an international process, with similar changes taking place in the US as elsewhere. These changes in university education were also part of HE becoming a more fundamental component of economies, whereby women's involvement in employment, graduate and professional employment was gradually becoming more acceptable, because it was economically necessary.

Quite how do we now portray what is happening to the relations between men and women in education, universities especially, and into forms of employment and public life? How have political or power relations been changing across changing times and landscapes, including the growth of knowledge economies? As feminists, we argued for political changes on the basis of our emerging views of how our personal lives were not unique. Relations between men and women, in the privacy of the family and in the wider public, were political, in the sense of being about power and inequalities of power in the minutiae of everyday relations.

Feminist testimony or reflections on 'the personal is political'?

If we look at the changes in terms of class and gender, some forms of social equality have been achieved by changes in HE. Quite clearly, however, this has not been enough, as it has not given rise to forms of social equality among women as graduate students, researchers and academics. It has also not equalised employment opportunities and family responsibilities, despite the massive expansion of universities, creating what we called 'massive universities', although not for the masses (Langa Rosado and David, 2006).

'The personal is political' became a major slogan of the WLM in the 1960s and 1970s, framing our approaches to the sexual division of labour, women's rights and women's work, and, more importantly, the rise of intellectual curiosity about how these structured gender relations had come about (David, 2003). Through the WLM, based, as it tended to be at that time, around young women as students or new graduates, feminists began to develop new 'knowledge' and methods, including feminist pedagogies grounded in personal experience. At the same time, HE was expanding, and opportunities for women not only as students but also as researchers and academics were opening up: women, including feminists, were quickly afforded opportunities to enter academia.

Looking back on my own life as an emerging feminist activist, I remember, for example, that ideas about sex and sexuality were not on public agendas and rarely talked about. We had no notion of how abusive and damaging some such forms of behaviour could be, as they were indeed, as the feminist writer and researcher Sheila Rowbotham put it in her 1970s study, *Hidden from history*. Given the public debates about child sexual abuse and violence against women and children, for example, in the wake of revelations about Jimmy Savile, the BBC celebrity, after his death five years ago, I recall that he was launching his career as a DJ on the public stage when I was returning to Yorkshire to become an undergraduate student of sociology at the University of Leeds. Among my friends and acquaintances in Leeds were young women who had encountered him, and around the same time other women friends were beginning groups as part of the early stirrings of the WLM that was later to become known as 'feminism'.

Even more intriguingly, at the FWSA conference in Leeds on 'Everyday encounters with violence: Critical feminist perspectives' in August 2015, no mention was made of Savile, the 'Yorkshire ripper' or Doctor Harold Shipman.[4] All these men originated their 'everyday violence or misogyny' in and around Leeds in the 1960s. The 'Yorkshire ripper', Peter Sutcliffe, was almost the same age as me (born in June 1946), and grew up in Bingley, close to where I lived. Having left Bingley Secondary Modern aged 15 in 1961, he had worked as a grave digger in

---

[4] I am grateful to Fiona Cullen for alerting me to this at the conference.

Bingley cemetery until the late 1960s and his marriage to Sonia, who had trained as a teacher. In 1981 Sutcliffe was convicted of murdering 13 women and attempting to murder seven others in Leeds and its environs over a five-year period in the 1970s. It was a very high-profile case, and many of the women were accused of being prostitutes, meaning that they were not regarded with the same respect as other victims of violence.

Harold Shipman was also the same age, born to a working-class family in Nottingham (in January 1946). He trained to be a general practitioner (GP) at the University of Leeds Medical School in the 1960s, after his mother's death, when he was 17. He began working as a GP in Yorkshire, later moving to his own practice in Lancashire. He became an even more prolific serial killer, mainly of elderly women patients, by lethal drug doses. At his trial in January 2000 he was found guilty of 15 murders. The Shipman Inquiry was subsequently launched and took over two years to complete. It is suspected that he actually killed over 250 people, with over 80% being women. Shipman is the only British doctor who has been found guilty of murdering his patients. He committed suicide in a Yorkshire jail in 2004. Although his treatment as a serial killer was different from Sutcliffe's, all three men have nevertheless been treated as unusual, but with more respect than the women who had been the victims of their violence. It is indeed curious that there were three high-profile cases of men who were committing everyday acts of violence in Leeds around the time that I was a student. These men were unknown at the time, but their kind of sexual behaviour was unremarkable and not on public agendas. Today, this kind of behaviour is still not recognised as remarkable or reprehensible. And even new generations of feminists forget quite how common and usual it may be. So what does this say about everyday encounters with violence?

It was in CR groups that women began to talk personally about intimate sexual relations, but in the relative safety of the privacy of groups of like-minded women, reaching out towards some understanding of sexual power relations, and how they were not only individual but also political. Yet they were certainly hidden from the public gaze. Now they are in the social media, but not necessarily dealt with appropriately there, or in criminal law.

Misogyny has replaced sexism as the analytic term for this, but little else has changed in sexual relations, albeit that women now have a public place, including in education. Issues are now in the public eye and on educational agendas but are still not dealt with satisfactorily for women despite the changes.

Socioeconomic and political context for the Robbins Report

The Robbins Report was commissioned in 1961 by a British Conservative government. There was anxiety at the time about how to sustain and develop economic growth in the postwar period, and education was gradually seen as a key strategic component, given other international developments. Thus the government's aim was to use HE for the purposes of economic growth, and it therefore appointed an eminent economist to chair the proceedings, namely, Lord Lionel Robbins, a professor at LSE. He was commissioned to report on the state and future of HE contributing to economic growth. This was one of the measures embarked on by the then Conservatives, given that the Robbins Report was published less than 20 years after the end of the Second World War.

The policy to expand HE was not initiated through Robbins, but rather, the government wanted the Robbins committee to legitimate and enhance a policy already set in train. By the beginning of the 1960s, the government, through its autonomous University Grants Committee (UGC), had already sanctioned the expansion and creation of new universities on green field sites, universities such as Essex and Sussex. It was a time of commitment to socioeconomic change, to human and civic rights, in the shadows of the war. Governments were committed to bringing about social change through peaceful solutions.

When I became a lecturer in what was then called 'social administration' at the University of Bristol in 1973, we offered undergraduate courses on the role of the state in social policies. Consideration of the Robbins Report, published only 10 years earlier, was on my syllabus. It was conventional wisdom to argue that there was a bipartisan social consensus on the role of the state in socioeconomic policies, especially around the expansion of educational opportunities. The desire to expand education beyond the compulsory stage, which in the UK had only just been raised to the age of 16, was seen as central to achieving economic growth, using public funds. Institutions had grown up in response to different and specific economic needs such as teaching and technologies. Hence there were separate and often locally funded and supported colleges of technology and teacher training.

The period was also one of the rise of the social sciences within universities, linked to social reforms and social welfare. I was one of the beneficiaries of this expansion of the social sciences, and was enabled to continue to use my newfound knowledge in developing courses about this, together with other women colleagues. We did not have the materials to teach, and had to garner ephemera for the purposes.

Willetts' tables constructed for his commentary on Robbins show these developments and changes in university subjects quite dramatically. In his table 3.2, entitled 'Full-time university students by sex and faculty, 1961–62 and 2011–12', he shows that in 1961–62 there were only five groups of faculties or subjects, namely, humanities, social studies, science, applied science and medical subjects. The balances for all students were that a third were in humanities, a quarter in science, and almost 20% in applied science, with just over one in ten in social studies and almost a sixth in medical subjects. Across all faculties in 1961–62, there were 75% men and 25% women. The proportion of women was highest in the humanities, where there were 42%, which represented over half of all women students (53%).

By 2011–12, these faculty groupings had increased to include other subjects and, far more importantly for my story, the balances between both the faculties and men and women had completely reversed! So, in 2011–12, social studies accounted for almost a third of all students, and humanities had dropped to one in ten, while science and applied science had also reversed in balance, too, so that a quarter of all students are now in applied sciences and only 12% in science, with now only 4% being in medical subjects! It is clear, then, that there has been a major growth in the social sciences, and accompanying this phenomenal growth has been the rise of women as students – women now represent 54% of such students and men only 46%, with women being the majority (almost two-thirds in humanities and other subjects [65%], and well over half in medicine [59%] and social studies [57%]). It is clear where the rise in interest in social change has developed, and how feminism has taken hold.

Feminism was one of the social movements linked most clearly to social reform and political change. Indeed, some of the early and most important studies conducted by feminists in academia, which inevitably led them into changing women's roles in families and social welfare, were those by the British feminist family policy experts, for example, Professors Elizabeth Wilson and Hilary Land.

When I started out as a student in 1963, all these ideas were unknown to me and to students of my generation. Our lives were lived in the dying shadows of the Second World War, where educational opportunities were growing and being seized. While it did not seem so at the time, the war was only just behind us, and creating a new society was a major endeavour. This was a political context of hope, but where there were few actual opportunities for young women starting out as either the women or the daughters of those who had suffered throughout the war years. Indeed, there were social expectations that we should marry and raise families, rather than continue in paid employment after marriage or motherhood. Hilary Land's 'The myth of the male breadwinner' in the 1970s was a captivating account of these familial assumptions and how they were not played out in practice.

Women and the family, and the Robbins Report

The Robbins Report recommended that 'university places should be available for all ... qualified by ability and attainment', defining eligibility as two passes at GCE Advanced level. This became known as the *Robbins principle*. The Robbins committee advised a commitment of public funds to create a *system* of HE that meant transforming some colleges of advanced technology (CATs) into universities (such as Aston, Bath and Strathclyde) alongside the already newly created universities (Essex, Sussex and Warwick). The intention was for there to be more universities as autonomous institutions funded through the UGC. The report also recommended four liberal principles or,

> ... objectives essential to any properly balanced system: instruction in skills; the promotion of the general powers of the mind so as to produce not mere specialists but rather cultivated men and women; to maintain research in balance with teaching, since teaching should not be separated from the advancement of learning and the search for truth; and to transmit a common culture and common standards of citizenship.

Robbins considered the culture of society, recognising how few women students were attending university: there were more than twice as many men as women students in the early 1960s. Only 2.5% of 17- to 30-year-old women went to university, in contrast to almost 6% of men. The report also noted that parents were expected to support their daughters on marriage, and so Robbins argued against the implementation of student loans, especially as to the potential impact that they would have on parental decision-making about their daughters:

> In particular, where women are concerned, the effect might well be either that British parents would be strengthened in their age-long disinclination to consider their daughters to be as deserving of higher education as their sons, or that the eligibility for marriage of the more educated would be diminished by the addition to their charms of what would be in effect *a negative dowry*.... (Robbins, 1963, para 646; emphasis added)

> On balance we do not recommend immediate recourse to a system of financing students by loans. At a time when many parents are only just beginning to acquire the habit of contemplating higher education for such of their children, *especially girls*, as are capable of benefiting by it, we think it probable that it would have *undesirable disincentive effects*. But if, as time goes on, the habit is more firmly established, the arguments of justice in distribution and of the advantage of increasing individual responsibility may

come to weigh more heavily and lead to some experiment in this
direction. (Robbins, 1963, chapter 14; emphasis added)

The then Conservative government accepted all the
recommendations, including encouraging the provision of
more places for women.

In Willetts' review of the Robbins Report (2013), he starts
by setting out the context in an ostensibly dispassionate but
knowledgeable way:

> The Robbins report appeared fifty years ago, in October 1963.
> It was a remarkable year: the country was ... staggered by the
> assassination of JFK in November. Aldous Huxley died but the
> title of his most famous book, *Brave New World*, was an apt
> description of the age. It was a big political year too. On 1
> October 1963, Harold Wilson promised the "white heat" of a
> new technological revolution at the Labour Party Conference. A
> few days later, during the Conservative Party Conference, Harold
> Macmillan resigned as Prime Minister, citing some health problems
> ... the new Conservative ... Prime Minister... Alec Douglas-Home
> ... took charge. Less than a week later, on 23 October, his new
> Government formally received the Robbins report.... A day later,
> the new administration accepted Lord Robbins's conclusions in
> full.... (2013, p 8)

Willetts mentions the creation of new institutions, 'Because
existing universities were not keen to deliver all the extra places
[needed as seen by the UGC], there was an unprecedented
opportunity to bring some embryonic ideas to life. New
universities were established in Sussex (1961), East Anglia (1963),
York (1963), Lancaster (1964), Essex (1964), Kent (1965) and
Warwick (1965). Keele University was founded in 1962...' (2013,
p 12). He also comments that:

> ... the report makes two key assumptions about this growth
> which proved hard to reconcile in practice. First, it assumed a
> substantial proportion of these extra places would be in science
> and technology.... Secondly, as women were particularly under-
> represented at university and their forecasts for growth rested

on forecasts of better school attainments, this would mean a particularly dramatic surge in the number of female students from 68k in 1962 to 253k in 1980. Together these assumptions required a massive shift of girls towards science and technology. This may have been right and desirable but it required a shift in cultural attitudes and patterns of school teaching which could not be delivered in the time available. Robbins correctly forecast a big increase in female students but many more of them went into arts and humanities, which is where overcrowding and resource pressures proved most intense.... (Willetts, 2013, pp 25-7)

The gloss that Willetts puts on the issue of student loans is different from my point of view:

... to pay for all of this Robbins toyed with the idea of loans repayable as a percentage of future earnings. He decided not to go down this route as he was afraid that positive attitudes to higher education were not sufficiently widespread, especially among young women. Looking back he increasingly came to regret his caution. Eventually, after over 40 years, we have ended up with a financing model very close to the one Robbins really preferred. One might conclude that on this issue all three main political parties whilst in government have followed the logic of the remark attributed to Churchill about Americans, that they "eventually do the right thing, but only after exhausting every other possibility". (Willetts, 2013, p 70)

1963, Robbins and me

Robbins' recommendations were accepted in the autumn that I went to university. Having been a somewhat rebellious teenager, active in social and political movements, I did not do well in my GCE A-levels, although I had more than reached the Robbins minimum requirement, and found myself without a place at university. So I initially went back to school, to retake my examinations in a third year in the sixth form, becoming the head girl prefect. However, there was a surfeit of places in the expanding HE sector, and I applied and was accepted for a place to study for a Bachelor's degree in social sciences at what was then the Glasgow College of Advanced Technology.

In early October 1963, I left school and embarked on my student life in Glasgow. The college was one of the CATs that Robbins had earmarked for transformation into becoming a university, and so it proved to be. In the spring of 1964, Quintin Hogg, later Lord Hailsham, was appointed Secretary of State for Education in the Conservative government and was charged with officially opening the new universities. In May he came to open what had become Strathclyde University, and I had the privilege of meeting him. One of my fellow students was Sandy Macmillan, grandson of the former Conservative Prime Minister Harold Macmillan, and he invited a group of social studies first year students to meet Quintin Hogg at the official opening.

Our school was relatively working class and had a small sixth form, but we all went on to either college or university – the expansion of universities meant more places for women, and for women from an array of social class backgrounds, and the expansion of HE produced social mobility and opportunities for women from a range of backgrounds. It also altered the ways in which women began to live their lives as wives and mothers, and in terms of sexuality. My family was middle class, with my university-educated mother, although it was relatively impoverished because of wartime strictures. Nevertheless, my mother gave up paid employment as a teacher when she got married. When I went to secondary school my mother became a 'married woman returner' to teaching. This meant that for the next 30 years she resumed her professional status as a teacher, although she continued to feel committed to her role as a housewife.

The Robbins Report was a social scientifically informed document, arguing that societal norms were such that parents, by implication fathers and from the middle classes, were expected to provide financial support for their daughters on marriage, with a traditional dowry. As feminists such as Christine Delphy and Diana Leonard (1992) subsequently argued in *Familial exploitation*, systems of marital property and inheritance were key to understanding patterns of women's subordination, especially for the upper and middle classes. They rendered women subordinate and exploited in families by their patterns of work, inheritance and familial support on marriage. While the formal dowry system was no longer legally sanctioned, it remained a cultural and religious phenomenon in many sections of British society, largely among the aristocracy and upper to middle classes and those who remained linked, however informally, to certain religious groupings. It was of sufficient importance as a cultural tradition for Robbins to mention it with reference to parents' abilities and/or willingness to finance their daughters' HE, given the continuing expectations that women would marry in their early twenties, to bear and raise families.

While the British welfare state, which had come into being 20 years previously, was providing financial support from the public purse through mechanisms such as family allowances, and the funding of universities and colleges for tuition, student support for participation in HE through maintenance grants was controversial. There was a competitive system of scholarships for some universities, which was regularised by 1960. Maintenance grants had been introduced on a means-tested basis for full-time students, alongside the provision of student halls of residence and the notion of 'relocation' or study away from home, on a formal basis in 1960, through the Anderson Committee (Dyhouse, 2006).

My father had the remnants of a dowry system in his head – his own mother and grandmothers had had dowries. One of the few things that they managed to bring out of Germany were some of the embroidered linens with CR (Clementine Rothschild) woven together with AD (Adolf David), my grandparents' initials. Given that my parents married during the Second World War (and my grandmother was a widow), my own mother's dowry was much more limited, although she had gone to university, as had my father in the late 1920s, but given the circumstances of the Second World War, they did not make as much as they might have. My mother's elder brother went to Cambridge, but left when his father died, to become a journalist on the then *Manchester Guardian*, and her elder sister studied pharmacy, marrying a pharmacist 10 years her senior. My father worried about his ability to support his three daughters financially at university and beyond, although he never wavered from his belief that all three of us should go to university. In part it was so that we might meet suitable men to marry, akin to Vikram Seth's novel *A suitable boy*, and with whom to have children, the bearers of the next generation ... but precisely what was that to entail, and how far have we come?

This, and the Robbins Report, illustrates the changing times dramatically. Fifty years ago most women were not expected to pursue a career throughout their adult lives: marriage and motherhood remained a more important official focus. Robbins' reflections on funding and how students should be helped illustrates neatly how different it was then. While I did not know the Robbins Report's arguments at the time, they confirm the expectations that many women, myself included, were brought up with then. How things have changed for us all as a society, and in terms of the balances between employment and education in an expanding global knowledge economy.

Second-wave feminism, HE and the wider society

Having mapped the changing cultural, educational and social values about students and women's place, I now consider second-wave feminism, HE and the wider society. It is clear that the changes have, indeed, been enormous. In the UK alone we now have more than 2 million students in HE, making for a massive increase in participation such that females are in the ascendance. The worldwide increases have also been fivefold, making HE a major component of global economies, or what is called 'academic capitalism'. Women now account for a majority of students in most countries, (and this is part of) an increase of around 500% in enrolments over less than 40 years (1970-2009). UNESCO commented that 'the capacity of the world's education systems more than doubled – from 647 million students in 1970 to 1,397 million in 2009 ... [and] from 33 to 164 million in higher education' (UNESCO, 2012, p 9). They go on to say that 'female enrolment at the tertiary level has grown almost twice as fast as that of men over the last four decades. The colleges, schools and universities to which students now go vary greatly, as do the students themselves.'

In Willetts' review, he commented that:

> ... the situation we face in today's society is one that might have seemed unlikely in 1960s Britain, with more women entering university than there are men even submitting a UCAS form. This is a remarkable achievement for women, who were outnumbered in universities by men as recently as the 1990s. *It is also the culmination of a longstanding educational trend, with boys and men finding it harder to overcome obstacles in the way of learning. It is a real challenge for different policy-makers.* (2013, pp 27-8; emphasis added)

Willetts laments the demise of male power through the shifting gender balance, arguing for policies to rectify this, exemplifying everyday sexism or misogyny today.

We still know very little about who the teachers and academics are, whether they are women, where they have come from and what the future holds. Willetts adopted a pessimistic, conservative view, concluding that 'The demographic background now is the opposite of that facing Robbins. We are currently in the middle of a 10 year period of decline...' (2013, p 28). While expansion may not be the issue, given the size of HE globally, the values about our culture, economy and society still need to be challenged. Indeed, global expansion has led to increasing inequalities, including, but not only, for women. While women have secured a foothold in universities, they remain belittled and subject to forms of sexual harassment, rather than being treated as equals.

THREE

Feminist pioneers

Women, and feminism, and the zeitgeist

'It was the zeitgeist' is how women of my generation – born in the shadows of the Second World War across cultures, countries and continents and 'baby-boomers' – described how they became feminists. What changes have there been to the zeitgeist or 'spirit of the times'? Even this term is one that has only recently come to have meaning in public quarters and is used in various media. I originally assumed that it was either a Yiddish word, hence its more recent common currency, as these have become more acceptable as part of popular rather than strictly Jewish culture, or drawn from sociology and such analysis. I discovered that the term is indeed German, but that it draws from Hegel (a forerunner to Marx), a German 19th-century philosopher, and from other political philosophers, psychologists and psychoanalysts rather than sociologists. No matter its origins, it is certainly a useful term to review changing ideas.

It is extraordinary how extensive change has been, especially in the 21st century, with an explosion of media interest in feminism. Mostly this is not about politics at the grassroots level, but about gender or sexual politics, sociocultural relations between men and women in everyday life. This is in the context of massive change in markets and neoliberalism, with the internet representing new forms of competitive capitalism. For instance, Hadley Freeman, a *Guardian* (feminist) columnist and film critic, turned the notion of zeitgeist on itself, writing that:

... *zeitgeist enthusiasts* will delight in how weirdly plausible the film feels. When Jonze started writing *Her*, Siri hadn't been invented; now expecting one's smart phone to talk back is near commonplace.... Internet addicts like me will see the film as a bang-on indictment of how so many of us use technology as a form of escape from our lives, while trying to convince ourselves it enhances it... (Freeman, 2014; emphasis added)

Interestingly, despite her feminism, she did not comment on the continuing sexism or misogyny in the film she was celebrating. Entitled 'Her', the film is about how a smart phone, variously called 'Samantha' or 'mother', talks back to the film's protagonist played by Joaquin Phoenix. Surely it is no accident that the robot is a woman while the star of the film is a man? In what sense is this film feminist rather than an extension into new spaces and places of traditional relations between men and women: another case of everyday misogyny?

It is in online media that many new debates are now taking place, as Freeman argues. *The Huffington Post* is one such important political medium, akin to our more conventional online and print newspapers such as *The Guardian* and *The Independent*. It has garnered enormous coverage for sparky political comment. Intriguingly, it was set up by a woman who vocalised strong arguments about women and social change in the 1970s – Arianna Stasinopoulos, who became Arianna Huffington in the 1980s on her marriage in the US to a Republican member for California of the House of Representatives (discussed later).

The very idea of zeitgeist seems tied together with its form of expression in new media, but just how different are the times, and their expressions? Is feminism so very different from 50 years ago when the term was being re-invoked from an earlier time another 50 years back? First-wave to second-wave to third-wave and now a new online media zeitgeist about fourth-wave feminism: so are the changes to do with the ways we communicate? Is it more to do with new wine in old bottles? Have vintage 'second-wave' feminists been superseded, or have sexual politics been allowed to resurface, given the changing times and economic imperatives of increasingly competitive capitalism? Lets go back to think about feminist agendas and its zeitgeist 50 years ago.

Reflections on the zeitgeist of the 1960s and 1970s

The new media debates about feminism, sexual abuse and harassment, rape, and violence against women and girls (VAWG), have ignited many reflections, especially from 'vintage feminists'. As already mentioned, there have been anniversary celebrations reflecting on what feminism was like. Another was early in 2014, to celebrate when Germaine Greer turned 75, looking back on her *The female eunuch* published in 1970. Comments from younger feminists imply that the book had little personal impact on them – 'It felt more like an academic experiment than an awakening', was the headline for Anna Holmes' comment (an American writer and editor), although Bidisha (a British broadcaster and journalist) claimed that she is 'a defining voice in Western feminism … and Greer's devastating insight and wisdom are coming full circle.' Helen Lewis, deputy editor of the *New Statesman*, argued that 'her value is as a destructive force: tearing down stereotypes.' Rosie Boycott, a contemporary, vintage feminist from the 1970s, belonging to the British collective that founded *Spare Rib*, a feminist magazine, argued that the book:

> … makes sense only in the context of the time. In 1970, women couldn't get a mortgage, or even buy a car, unless their husband or father countersigned the documents. Horizons were low. Germaine burst into this limiting life like a whirlwind. Get a life, she said. She challenged the concepts of marriage, the nuclear family and the obligation to breed, exhorting us instead to be doctors and businesswomen … some feminists dismissed Germaine for not being political enough but, for me, her vibrancy and sheer zest for life played a key part in changing mine. (2014)

It is certainly true that there are many forms of feminism, and Greer represented a particular zestful public voice, despite coming from academia. The world is now a different place, allowing more space for media and other reflections about feminism. Private reflections also include those from the 70th birthday party of Professor Clare Ungerson, held in February 2014. Clare eloquently remarked that for her, feminism had been influential in highlighting the reversal of family and friends as friendships and family. Clare retired 10 years ago from her post as professor of social policy at the University of Southampton. Her role as an academic, she claimed, had been as a *knowledge synthesiser* around the changing role of women, caring, family and friends.

On a bigger canvass, the Feminist Library in London organised a gathering of 1960s-1970s Sisters over the last weekend of January 2014. The aim was to reminisce and to work together as we have grown older, to consider our mortality. Given the rise of feminisms, there was space for reflecting on what had changed and what had remained the same. This desire for collective reflection was more popular than anticipated, overflowing with older feminists all eager for the resuscitation of the old CR groups. Feminists gathering in safe places and spaces, with like-minded knowable and knowledgeable women: this, and the subsequent email list illustrate the new zeitgeist. It allows for these conversations to take place, albeit still in dark places.

The Feminist Library is housed in an incredibly shabby building on Westminster Bridge Road near London South Bank University, reminiscent of what South Bank was like when I was there, back in the 1980s. It is in the same building as when originally established about 30 years ago, when I went to South Bank as head of the social sciences department. I was one of three newly appointed women heads of department as part of the liberal to left mood in London of providing opportunities for women to become middle managers or leaders in HE. Opportunities were certainly opening up for women in educational arenas, and at the time, the Inner London Education Authority (ILEA) represented the vanguard of providing such for women in various levels of education, as shown by Jane Martin (2013) in 'Gender, education and social change'.

The Feminist Library is also a stone's throw away from LSE, and now the home of the Women's Library, which was, in 2013, 'sold' by London Metropolitan University (LMU). Since LMU argued that it could no longer afford to house the Women's Library, which has a 90-year pedigree dating from its days created by the Fawcett Society, it put it out for tender. LSE was successful in its bid to take over the library. It had been housed in a feminist architect-designed building, converting an old women's wash-house in the East End of London. The building was not part of the exchange, however, despite the investment of a huge amount of public money through the Lottery only 10 years earlier.

As a result, the two libraries exist cheek-by-jowl, fulfilling very similar purposes of archiving feminist materials, especially from the heydays of the 1960s-70s. The Feminist Library is committed to preserving the work of second-wave feminists, including ephemera. The Women's Library is also committed to that aim, but has a focus on women's history from 19th-century first-wave feminism. Both were part of the emerging zeitgeist of developing knowledge for the propagation of feminist campaigning and scholarship. They differ in their social class orientations, yet both want to retain their autonomy, resisting being seen as a national treasure by being housed in the British Library, for fear that the resources would be subsumed and no longer identifiably feminist or committed to the women's cause.

Another example of memorialising the old zeitgeist was the celebration of Pete Seeger, the American folksinger and civil rights activist, who died on 28 January 2014, aged 90. There were fulsome celebrations of how he inaugurated a new form of politics and political protest through his music. His half-sister, Peggy, was also recognised for her songs for the women's movement. In one obituary in *The Guardian*, Paul Buhle wrote: 'Seeger went to Harvard University to read journalism and sociology.... In 1939 Seeger dropped out of Harvard, persuaded by Guthrie that he could "learn more from hitting the road than from hitting the books"' (2014). The civil rights movement questioned the contradiction between university and life, subsequently influencing the women's movement. The 'university of life' became important, especially for women, in the 1970s and 1980s. As Professor Rosalind Edwards (1993), one of my research students, argued, many mature women students contributed to feminist critiques, including creating the knowledge on which such politics are based.

Zeitgeist of feminism and sisterhood in an age of social democracy

As budding second-wave feminists, we were influenced by the zeitgeist through the WLM as a political movement, with its emergent, often ephemeral, literature and readings on feminism. We were captured by the political mood to transform our own personal, sexual and familial situations. This led us all into creating feminist knowledge and pedagogies with a passion, drawing on collective action and camaraderie. Our own university education, across the narrow range of universities that existed, while opening up opportunities for women as students, was also very traditional and did not contain any specifically feminist courses. Few of my generation of women mentioned materials from university courses that had influenced their becoming feminists, although they themselves hoped to influence subsequent generations with their overtly feminist scholarship.

Many 'leading' feminist writers were cited, including some who had passed away in the recent past: Eva Figes, Shulamith Firestone, Adrienne Rich, to name but a few. Mary McIntosh, who died in 2013, was arguably 'an influential sociologist known for her work on gender and sociology' (Plummer, 2013), as *The Guardian* obituary headline announced. Ken Plummer went on to state that she was 'a prominent second-wave feminist, a founder member of the modern lesbian and gay movement in Britain, and one of the most influential feminist sociologists between the 1960s and 1990s.'

Joining CR groups, becoming 'sisters', working together for sociopolitical change, was seen as a political act. Our aim was to develop an analysis of women's oppression by men. The term 'sister' was adopted to express our warm and close friendships, mirroring the French revolutionary term 'fraternity', and illustrating its limitations for political and sexual equality: women were not the equal of their brothers. My account illustrates the enduring importance of these stories in feminist women's lives from the vantage point of today, when the contexts have a veneer of change for the better, despite the rise of increasingly competitive forms of capitalism. It was exhilarating and exciting, especially what we read and what we wrote – our collective scholarship to develop feminist knowledge for action.

Many of the women I spoke to mentioned their feelings of dissatisfaction with their lives growing up as female, recognising the limitations of their own mothers' lives as confined to family, housework and motherhood or childcare, and that they wanted to do something more than be 'just a wife and mother' – Friedan's (1963) 'the problem that has no name'. My participants, like Friedan's, were the beneficiaries of an expanding educational system as part of the growing social state. While this welfare state offered new possibilities for work and caring, it also remained constraining in terms of women's employment and personal lives. Indeed, for many of us, our schooling mirrored the constraints of likely adult life, with women attending single-sex schools and colleges as part of a state-sponsored system. The most elite colleges – at Cambridge, Oxford and London universities – were all single-sex. Even those participants who were 'first-generation' (the US term) or 'first-in-the-family' to go to university, aspired to and some actually went there.

All of my participants were involved as students in the 1960s. But becoming a feminist was not to do with their courses of study, but with their growing realisation about the sexual politics of the day, including opportunities for work or employment as adult women. 'Sexual politics' is how the zeitgeist was named, making clear that the relations between men and women, while based on sexual relations, were also power relations. They were not about gender only as a social distinction, but imbued with connotations about desire and fantasy. By the late 1970s, there was a more humorous response to questions of sexual harassment while also embedding a more serious political and legal response to expressions of sexual intimidation or harassment, and Italian-style bottom pinching. Typically, the Italian car manufacturer, Fiat, advertised one of its cars on a poster by saying: 'If this Fiat were a lady it would have its bottom pinched.' Some feminists spray-painted onto the adverts: 'If this lady were a car she would run you over.'[1]

---

[1]   Val Hey's talk in Sussex, 27 January 2014, and Jill Posener (1979), Acme cards.

Professor Ann Oakley is an innovative second-wave feminist sociologist. Over the course of her academic career, she has written breath-taking scholarly work about women as housewives, mothers, pregnant women and in childbirth, health and care, stemming from her early doctoral studies in the late 1960s. Inevitably, she has reviewed her feminist politics and scholarly approach, latterly developing mixed methods in *Experiments in knowing* (Oakley, 2000) and her superb parody *Gender on planet earth* (Oakley, 2002). Her essay, *Sex and gender*, published in 1972, launched a major debate about the concepts and practices of sex and gender, and although we might say that these terms have gone viral in the last 50 years, they remain vital despite all the scholarship. In addition to her distinguished academic career, she has also carved out a niche as a feminist novelist.

Together with Juliet Mitchell, the feminist psychoanalyst, they intervened in debates about the notion of 'sisterhood' as a form of collective action, arguing that it was unhelpful for promoting a politically powerful approach. It had serious consequences for the internal debates within the women's movement about how to proceed on a larger political stage. Given the recent resurgence of 'sisterhood' in a totally different context, it is a valuable concept to illustrate the nuanced differences between forms of male and female collective action, despite the binaries that it also invokes.

These issues were coming on to public agendas, as part of the general mood of protest, but not on the formal curriculum of universities. It was in the interstices that they were debated – in student unions, in social groups, in political groups and movements. Feminism was rarely named at the time; it was discussed in the women's movement, often linked with socialist movements, and it was rarely in mainstream media.

While I had two sisters and I was the middle daughter, my 'real' or biological sisters – Judy and Anne – took slightly different pathways through these exciting, complex and contradictory political times. Their choices about educational topics, sexual, marital and maternal relations inevitably differed across subjects – science and applied science as opposed to social science – when and how to start marriage and motherhood, and whether or not to work throughout or to work part-time. Our individual choices were wide and yet constrained by both Jewish and everyday culture and the continuing patriarchal structures of the times. As one Jewish feminist 'sister' still puts it most evocatively, '5,000 years of patriarchy to contend with!' These patriarchal structures remain despite all the changes. Indeed, in some respects, the 1960s and 1970s were better, and unique, in long-term historical contexts.

They were the heyday of social democracy, a time of opening up sociopolitical possibilities linked to economic growth. From today's vantage point, the state or government was benign, with a bipartisan political consensus on how to improve people's lives by offering opportunities for growth linked with social mobility. In the UK, policies and services were developed in the interests of a wide citizenry around education, employment or unemployment, children and old age, housing, health and welfare, implementing public, social policy solutions to the 'five giant evils' of want and squalor, ignorance, idleness and disease that Beveridge (1942) had laid out in his report to the UK government in the Second World War, through the creation of the welfare state. This had taken place during the decades of our childhood.

Women still had to shoulder the responsibility for implementing welfare policies, as we slowly began to realise, as we came of age. Becoming teachers, social workers for children or disabled people and the elderly, nurses and other para-medical professionals, rather than medical doctors ourselves or working for human and civil or civic rights, made the continuation of male domination explicit in all walks of life. These concerns slowly became part of our critiques of the burgeoning welfare state, with some feminist scholarship critical. Several feminists were involved in developing our critical knowledge about the less benign effects of what was, in principle, an important new form of governance.

Social democracy allied with social welfare now appears as a blip of history, since the passing of any semblance of a political consensus on social welfare provisions, through the development of economic liberalism from the 1980s, morphing into neoliberalism in the 21st century, with individualism and markets in all walks of life. Until the election of Jeremy Corbyn as leader of the British Labour Party, Syriza in Greece, and Podemos in Spain, the new zeitgeist and political consensus was about austerity and dealing with deficits in public finances rather than reducing social and sexual inequalities, and poverty especially.

Social democracy enabled the emergence of social movements for change including feminism, with commitments to women's liberation and gender equality. The women's movement, in the UK as elsewhere, began to organise collectively around various 'demands on the state', initiated through the first of a series of conferences in the early 1970s. The inaugural British conference was held in 1970 at Ruskin College, Oxford, a working men's college loosely associated with the University of Oxford. Several of my participants described this event and subsequent ones, including the socialist feminist conferences, during the 1970s.

The initial four demands were equal pay for equal work, equal educational opportunities, free contraception and abortion on demand and 24-hour day nurseries. They were about women's concerns not only in education and the workplace, but also about birth control and the care of young children – essentially, the concerns of young women about to embark on adult lives as potential mothers, or freeing them from the burdens of being mothers. More demands were added during the 1970s around economic independence – 'The why be a wife?' campaign or the fifth demand about financial and legal independence – and the sixth demand about sexuality. The seventh demand to end violence against women was also added in the late 1970s. But nothing specifically was said about sexual abuse or harassment, although these topics were clearly acknowledged as vital in the CR groups that sprang up in relatively safe environments for intimate and personal conversations: not in the public or media gaze....

The WLM and me

I 'joined' the WLM through a CR group in the 1960s in London when I was working as a postgraduate researcher at LSE, but I missed the inaugural Ruskin conference. Having graduated from the University of Leeds in sociology in 1966, I presumed that I would have to work throughout my adult life, although I might also marry and have children, reluctant though I was to bring children into what seemed a rather harsh world (and how much more harsh it is now!). I had been interviewed for a postgraduate position working with the professor of sociology, together with a close friend. She was about to get married, whereas I was not in an intimate relationship. Asked who was the more deserving, I answered that her needs were greater than mine to stay in Leeds with her postgraduate partner. I had no idea that I was supposed to sell myself as the better candidate for the job, not feeling very confident about myself. My friend got the post! My father, I still remember well, was shocked at how I had answered the question. There were only the faintest of glimmerings about the women's movement among my student friends.

I moved to London to a more cosmopolitan, Jewish life, to work as a statistical research assistant at the postgraduate Institute of Psychiatry on a US-UK project on the diagnosis of mental illness (David, 2003). I had toyed with the idea of going to a kibbutz in Israel, having been an ardent member of a socialist Zionist youth movement, Habonim, but fought shy of this. Before the Six Day War in Israel in 1967, I volunteered, going the day after the war ended on 7 June with my elder sister Judy. I was given leave-of-absence from my post at the Maudsley Hospital and postgraduate Institute of Psychiatry, and spent the summer working first in a moshav, then a kibbutz, and lastly for the Israel Institute for Social Research, interviewing settlers to Israel or Palestine. I considered staying and applied to do a Master's in sociology at the Hebrew University. I was accepted on the proviso that I take three years to do the course, given my inadequate knowledge of Hebrew! I panicked, and returned home to my post at the Maudsley.

It was here that I met Eleanor Jane Chandler, who had just been appointed on graduation from Leeds. Together with Ruth Schmidt, a childcare social worker, and newly arrived émigrée from South Africa, we joined a CR group in Belsize Park. We also attended meetings of the Women's Workshop in central London, listened to talks from Juliet Mitchell, whose *Women: The longest revolution* had just been published (1984), Selma James, of the Wages for Housework campaign, and many others. We went on demonstrations about 'abortion on demand' in the light of the Abortion Act 1967, and wrote of our own experiences, editing an issue of *Shrew*, the London Women's Workshop magazine. With other CR groups across north London, we made our common cause.

My sister Judy was also in a CR group with an old friend from Bradford, Viv Davies. They were concerned with childcare, having very young children themselves. Together, we went to the second national WLM conference in Skegness in 1971. We were amused to listen to Suzy Fleming, a major keynote speaker, as she was also from the Bradford Jewish community. At that time she was an undergraduate student at the University of Bristol, and fired up about the question of women's work as housework and sexual work. She was a leading light in Wages for Housework, a splinter group from the more mainstream approach about domestic labour. This subsequently developed into a serious international academic debate about women's employment, with contributions from Jean Gardiner, Wally Seccombe and Ellen Malos from the Bristol women's movement. When I went to work at the University of Bristol, I joined in.

This was all extremely exciting, and a complete counter to my job where I was now working in the converted ECT[2] labs – a recipe for depression! During the winter of 1967-68 I applied for and was appointed to another research post, in LSE's social administration department, on a funded project on gambling, work and leisure. This involved working with two very different relatively junior lecturers, Bleddyn Davies and David Downes, who had totally different approaches to the study. Both were absorbed with their own personal problems of domesticity, childcare and early education. This showed in the questionnaire that we developed for the study, although there was no concern for women's dilemmas of housework and motherhood. I was one of a team of four researchers, linked with others in the department.

---

[2]   Electro-convulsive therapy – given routinely to patients with depression until the late 20th century. See for example Barbara Taylor (2015) *The last asylum*, London: Penguin.

It was a most exciting professional and political time, a time of the LSE gates saga,[3] and the rise of trade unions and WLM within universities. It was here that I met Ann Sedley, Hilary Land, Hilary Rose, Tessa Blackstone and countless others, all of us jostling to understand the niceties and nuances of being professional academic women. I remained in this post for 18 months, while I also began to teach for the extra-mural department of London University – courses on women and the social structure of modern Britain, as well as social theory. It was through this teaching that I began reading studies of women and learning about sexual politics.

When the LSE post ended, I applied for several jobs, and was successfully interviewed for two on two consecutive days: one as a research officer in Queen Mary University of London (QMUL), and one as a lecturer in sociology at what was then Borough Polytechnic, about to become South Bank. I was on the horns of a dilemma, since I had accepted the job with Professor Maurice Peston, thinking that I would not be offered the lecturing post. At interview, Maurice had asked me what now would be considered an improper question, against all equal opportunities criteria, about whether I was about to get married and therefore would leave the post early. Having accepted the post, I felt duty-bound not to withdraw and take the lecturing position, given also my father's moral strictures as a refugee who was frightened of not behaving appropriately. But in my heart I preferred the possibility of the freedom entailed in such a post, which would have meant working with Mary McIntosh, among others. By some fluke of fate, 16 years later, I ended up by becoming head of the social sciences department at what had become South Bank Polytechnic, soon to become London South Bank University.

I spent three years working as a social researcher at QMUL, while also involved in the growing WLM, two completely separate activities. When pressed by Maurice to research women and education, I resisted, unsure of what it might entail, although

---

[3] LSE constructed gates to 'lock' out students who were demonstrating against the administration's appointment of Walter Adams as Director. See Blackstone et al (1970).

I did continue extra-mural teaching and teaching in QMUL's economics department. My life was exciting and simultaneously frustratingly difficult. We were always pondering new ways of living – with or without children, in monogamous or multiple relations, and as heterosexual or homosexual, whether or not the men in our lives agreed with our concerns. Inevitably there were always compromises to be made, negotiations to be had, and sexual harassment, which at the time was never publicly named, was ever present – a source of humiliation and shame, but also hard to name. It remained a constant topic of our CR group, but never surfaced on public agendas.

When my research was about to end, I was still not in a satisfactory reliable sexual relationship. I decided to go to the US, and applied for funding for a comparative study of educational policy-making, and to my utter amazement, I was successful. Armed with this precious grant from the then Social Sciences Research Council (SSRC), I wrote to many US universities, but only the Center for Educational Policy Research (CEPR) at Harvard Graduate School of Education responded. To my delight, David Cohen, Director of CEPR, invited me to be a visiting research associate during 1972-73.

I set out to find a new life (akin to Bernard Malamud), hoping also to find more women's activism, given our newfound knowledge of the international women's movement. Cambridge, Massachusetts, was not the hotbed of radical political action that I had anticipated, but I did find various new groups in Harvard and MIT (Massachusetts Institute of Technology). I learned about studies of educational inequalities and new policies to counter them, especially around ethnic and racial inequalities. I joined a Jewish feminist CR group based among graduate students in Somerville, where I first encountered *Our bodies, ourselves* (Boston Women's Health Collective Inc, 1971), a handbook for women's health, and Nira Yuval-Davis, who has remained an important friend and colleague. Nira is now an extremely distinguished professor and feminist theorist of intersectionality. She has spent the majority of her career in the UK, arriving in England shortly after I returned.

My research grant was for one year, but I toyed with staying in the US, to do an education doctorate at Harvard as a necessary prelude to an academic career. But I was offered an exciting post in England – as a lecturer at the University of Bristol – and arrived in Bristol in September 1973. Hilary Land, who had remained a good friend from LSE, where we had been active together in a new union for researchers (Association of Scientific, Technical and Managerial Staffs, ASTMS), had moved to Bristol to help set up a new department of social administration and had been very supportive of my appointment. She wrote to me about the exciting rise of the women's movement in Bristol. I arrived, and immediately became immersed in both the politics of the local WLM, based as it was in Ellen Malos' house, and in the politics of embedding women's studies in extra-mural and undergraduate courses in sociology and social policy.

These were entwined activities, and completely absorbed our professional and personal lives, including considering how to live our lives differently from our mothers and others. We fought for the Working Women's Charter Campaign (WWCC), with local women, set up a women's centre in the city, and taught women's studies locally. Ellen Malos organised one of the first women's refuges for domestic violence, and we also did regular pregnancy testing. Jackie West and I were also involved in setting up a university nursery, as there was no local provision for childcare, except on a commercial basis.

Hilary and I also worked closely with Jackie from the sociology department, developing an innovative undergraduate course entitled 'Family and social policy'. Numerous publications derived from this, including my *The state, the family and education* (David, [1980] 2015b). This has recently been re-issued, illustrating how important such early historical analyses remain, despite all the subsequent changes. We also developed courses for the extra-mural department of the university, reaching beyond Bristol to Gloucester and Cheltenham around a range of themes, including education and social welfare, developing a network of friends, some of whom coalesced as the BWSG and others into a thriving CR group.

We also had postgraduate research students who joined our circle, with one in particular significant for me – Linda Ward. Linda had arrived in Bristol fresh from her undergraduate studies at LSE, and wanted to undertake a doctoral study of birth control in the inter-war years, which I supervised. In the 1970s, it was the responsibility of supervisors to justify the title and topic of the thesis to the university's academic board, rather than the student's responsibility. Linda boldly decided to entitle her thesis, 'A feminist study of birth control', and I had to defend this at a meeting. I had not, until that point, called myself a feminist, but rather as involved in 'women's liberation.' My experience of this board meeting, where I was roundly attacked for such an inappropriate and political title and topic, forced my arm: I instantly became a feminist, and have not looked back! Linda's thesis title survived this and other onslaughts; she became a doctor and subsequently a successful academic, finishing as a professor.

Becoming a feminist was not an easy ride: it was a challenging struggle, personally, politically and also professionally.

New wine in old bottles?

Many of my interviewees differed from me: they felt that they had always been feminists because of their upbringing and their mothers' commitment to equality. Others felt more like me: reacting against their mothers being housewives. While all mentioned the personal – their cultural and social class backgrounds, relationships with parents and sexuality above all – key texts were influences on their budding consciousness, and desires to change women's situation socially and politically. Mainly, being social scientists, we aimed at social change rather than party political changes, although the debates between feminism and socialism were contentious. It was at this time that Hartman (1981) wrote about the 'unhappy marriage', also likening the debates to our collective feelings about family and marriage. We all sought more knowledge to counter strategic obstacles.

Nira Yuval-Davis told me that it was through her sociological fieldwork on new Jewish movements that she first became a feminist. Her story is like mine in reactions to the existing Jewish family culture, although her early experiences were in Israel-Palestine. She said that:

I was born in Tel Aviv in Yishuv, Palestine.... My mother was a housewife and full-time mother, and was one of reasons I did not want to live life just via and through family. My initial studies at the Hebrew University in Jerusalem were in sociology and psychology. My parents were proud of my school achievements. All this was pre my becoming feminist, although my gut feeling was as a feminist, and my mother said Golda Meir should be my role model. *I only became a feminist (and socialist) in the US.* I married in 1965 and Uri went to the US to do a PhD at Brandeis ... it was at a time when wives followed husbands.... I started to do a distance PhD at the Hebrew University on 'Different ways of being a radical Jew in the diaspora', and attended classes at Harvard, and so I was exposed more to feminist activism and ideology. I became a mother and interviewed Jewish feminists ... one told me a joke that a non-Jewish woman was a sex object but *a Jewish woman is a good sex object with a brain*.... Uri decided to settle in Britain because his father was born here, so we moved in 1973 and I finished my PhD at Sussex. I was conflicted about Harvard ... but sociology extended my world – I loved it so much.... Britain also extended my world and sociology, and another key moment was the 1974 BSA [British Sociological Association] conference on feminist sociology – with Diana Leonard and Sheila Allen ... and outside sociology the European Socialist-Feminist Forum and other feminist and socialist organisations. When I came to Britain I realised fully how sociology extended visions.... Feminism has been very influential in my learning, and from PhD work, shortly after finished my PhD, I started to study feminist aspects of the Zionist project, and the role of women in Israeli military and in national reproduction.... (emphasis added)

Intriguingly, another sociologist was also in Cambridge where she, too, became a feminist. Her story is different from Nira's and mine, as she is from an upper middle-class British background, although her parents migrated to Canada when she was a small child. Professor Jane Gaskell is now a very distinguished Canadian academic who has written about the impact of feminism on education, and has been dean of the Ontario Institute for Studies in Education (OISE), University of Toronto. She went to college in the US, including graduate work, before returning to Canada, telling me that:

In 1968 I graduated with a major in sociology from Swarthmore College, a Quaker, liberal arts college outside Philadelphia. I received an excellent academic education, and a strong introduction to activist politics, but never had a female professor and never discussed feminism. The next year I moved to Harvard to study in the Graduate School of Education. In the student paper, I saw an advert ... for a women's liberation group. Looking for political action and extra-curricular activities, I went to the address mentioned in the ad. There must have been 60 women gathered in someone's apartment. We were formed into CR groups of about 15, and I stayed with my CR group, attending meetings once a week, until I left Cambridge three years later. *This is the group that taught me feminism* ... most of us were white.... We read feminist texts, often photocopied, ephemeral material.... We shared tales of orgasms, rapes, housework and men and we discussed what it all meant for a theory of feminism and political action. This reading was by far the most exciting reading I was doing as a grad student, although I took some classes that discussed women's issues, eg, Talcott Parsons and a ... seminar with Matina Horner.... She was a model of feminist intellectual challenge and became president of Radcliffe. She was also pregnant, and talked about it in class. (emphasis added)

Professor Sandra Acker, also a distinguished feminist sociologist of education, was born and brought up in the US. Her university education experiences are similar to those of Jane Gaskell who was a colleague of hers at OISE, Toronto. I first met Sandra when I arrived in Bristol, as she had been a lecturer in the School of Education for a year there, on her arrival from graduate studies at the University of Chicago, USA, with her then husband. It was in Bristol that we formed a close friendship. She spent her early career at the University of Bristol, only returning to Canada to become a full professor. She melded together her personal reasons for becoming a feminist – her views of her mother's life – with the early stirrings of feminism in the US in the late 1960s:

In one sense I was always a feminist. I did not see why my mother, who was so intelligent, was a housewife and devoted to her children (us) without directly using her education.... My parents encouraged all of us to do well in school and go on to higher education and into careers (though we were also to get married). I think my first exposure to feminism per se was reading Betty Friedan's *The feminine mystique,* which I loved. However, I can't remember when I read it. I think it must have been when I was at graduate school, not undergraduate. The late 60s were such a time of upheaval and feminism came along with student protest and civil rights and anti-Vietnam protests. Students formed CR groups and I belonged to one of them. It was exhilarating.... I think I have approached most of my scholarly pursuits through the lens of feminism – both research and teaching. I also have a feminist way of looking at relationships, family, media, and everyday life. I have never been an activist in the usual sense but have tried to change people's thinking through my teaching and writing. Earlier in my career I did quite a lot of organising of seminars and workshops and so forth on various aspects of gender and education....

Professor Avtar Brah, a renowned feminist scholar of ethnic and 'race' relations who retired from her post at Birkbeck College, London University, a few years ago, similarly exemplifies how my participants melded together their personal and educational journeys, especially through feminist or women's literature, to create new lives for themselves. Like Nira and Sandra, she is a cosmopolitan, educational migrant, with university education crossing continents, cultures and subjects. She had an initial desire to be an agricultural economist in a developing country, given that she had spent much of her childhood as an Asian living in East Africa. She also studied in the US, before coming to the UK for further studies. She told me that her becoming a feminist predated her university education, although she did not apply her feminist ideas to her work until she embarked on postgraduate studies in Bristol in the 1970s, which is where we met.

My relationship with Avtar still feels very special, as her doctoral thesis was the first that I was invited to examine as an internal examiner of the University of Bristol. The examination actually took place in London, within an LSE building, as this was more convenient for the external examiner, for Avtar, and by chance, for me, visiting my parents, who had also come to London for my father's birthday. At the time, I had a newborn baby girl – Charlotte – and was somewhat anxious not to have to leave her for a very long period of time (balancing family, childcare and work was inevitably a key dilemma). Avtar told me:

> I went to university in California (University of California, Davis). I studied agriculture for my BSc and adult ed for MSc in Madison, Wisconsin. I took these subjects because I wanted to return to Uganda to work in the agricultural sector. But during my studies, I found that I enjoyed social and humanities courses much more than my major subjects.... I became a feminist when I was about 12 when I read novels by a Punjabi writer called Nanak Singh. I was also influenced by Amrita Pritam, a Punjabi poet and novelist and Waris Shah, another renowned Punjabi writer. They all critiqued women's position in Punjabi society. I have been deeply influenced by feminism, and have contributed to it both through activism as well as theory.... I did a PhD at Bristol University on intergenerational continuity and change among Asian and white respondents, and questions of marriage, family and gender were part of it.

Vintage feminism, Bristol-style?

Two other women whom I met in Bristol through BWSG (Bristol Women's Studies Group) spent time in the US where they became feminists. Their US studies were critically important, although they may have had earlier presentiments about feminism around their mothers' views. The renowned professor of literature, whose feminist critique of *Gone with the wind* is now a classic, Helen Taylor, told me that:

> I went to the States after a rather conventional English degree out of a sense of excitement about American literary and popular culture and discovered there a radicalism I'd not shared in Britain (despite '68 and all that). Feeling personally freer in the States allowed me to discover my feminism and participate in the early WLM. I became a feminist when I undertook an MA at Louisiana

State University from 1969 to 1971. I ... immediately joined the National Organization of Women (NOW) and CR and campaign groups.

Similarly, Dr Liz Bird told how important her time in the US was for her, as she went to:

... Oxford in the mid-1960s to do PPE (politics, philosophy and economics) but the why is interesting: I did Oxbridge entrance in English but got called for interview for PPE as the admissions tutor decided that I would make a good social scientist from reading my entrance exam essay – she was probably right, but I have always been somewhere between arts and social science. From Oxford I went to the University of Sussex to do a doctorate in the sociology of art and literature but spent a year at Cornell University while doing my studies. I was there from 1969-70 and joined the first ever women's group – we marched, sat in, and campaigned for abortion rights. I returned to the UK and went to Scotland in 1971, but did not really get involved in feminist politics there – made some good friends in the "Women in Action" group and did march in favour of abortion rights – SPUC off. This was more of a big step for my partner with whom I started living in 1972 as he was raised a Catholic but still joined in the march.... By listening to Ellen I've been reminded that I, too, was a "tomboy" and preferred playing with my brother to my sister as I regarded her as unbelievably wet, but am now much closer to her than to my brother – this could be partly the influence of feminism and indeed "sisterhood"?

Ellen Malos, another member of BWSG, well-known for her work on domestic violence, has been honoured by the University of Bristol for this exceptional contribution. She came to the UK with her husband, and studied at the University of Bristol for a postgraduate degree. Originating from a working-class family in Ballarat, Australia, in the 1950s, she was 'first-in-the-family' to go to the elite University of Melbourne:

I wanted to go to University because I had decided when I was about 10 that I wanted to stay on at school and did not want to leave school at 14, get married and have children (which at that time and place meant to be a full-time housewife and mother). I was always a voracious reader of just about anything I could get my hands on. This involved first convincing my father to let me go to the high school (six years possibly leading to matriculation) rather than the girls' school (five years, culminating in the School Leaving Certificate, working in an office or nursing etc), then getting bursaries in the last two years of school and a studentship with the state Department of Education to go to university before training as a secondary school teacher, the only way it would have been affordable. It also involved a very emotional tussle with my mother, who didn't want me to leave home, or to go to university because of her attitudes to class.... I would have done a pure English course except that it was a requirement of the Education Department to have two teaching subjects.... I was already a proto-feminist at primary school. I identified as a tomboy, climbing trees – where I would sometimes sit doing embroidery after the example of the heroine of one of my mother's books.... At university itself, being on the left wing and doing arts subjects, we didn't rub up against overt personalised sexism all that much. That came after graduation. And of course that was before we had the reinforcement of New Wave feminism, so had to fall back on our own personal resources – although Engels' *The origins of the family* helped. The first important new text was a translation of Simone de Beauvoir's *The second sex*, which appeared in the early 60s. We did, though, have communist women's groups.... Having called myself a Christian communist – à la Dean Hewlett Johnson while still at school, I had joined the Communist Party at 18, shortly after Khrushev's denunciation of Stalin.... There was a period in which I went back into school teaching, which was made exciting by the advent of the WLM. In trying to get to grips with what all this meant, I read across many disciplines, including anthropology as well as literature and history, and the burgeoning writings of the WLM itself....

Professor Marilyn Porter, also of BWSG, and now based in Newfoundland, Canada, has yet another contrasting story of how she came to feminism in the 1970s in Bristol. She was, like Ellen, 'first-in-the-family' to go to university, but from an upper middle-class family. She said her feminist consciousness was slowly awakened:

> I went to Trinity College, Dublin in the early 1960s, doing modern history and political theory. My choices were limited because of my inadequate schooling, and Dublin seemed nicer than the large red bricks. Indeed, it was. I was well taught and I enjoyed myself, though I didn't work in any driven kind of way, and came out with a respectable degree and a husband. There was no feminism around, either in the literature or on the campus, and little radical activity. The Aldermaston marches were happening, but they were a long way away, and I was still too far under my conservative parents' thumb to make the trek. I remember picketing in support of Travellers' camps but not much else. I left university with a wedding weeks away and no idea of what I wanted to do, and with the words of the dean of women students ringing in my ears: that as I was about to marry I should do something easy – like a DipEd. So I did. I did history and then education – which was all pre-political awakening. What happened then was feminism, and subsequently a transitional diploma in sociology and a PhD in sociology, which was one of the early explicitly feminist PhDs in the UK.... I first became aware of an overt feminist consciousness with an article in *The Guardian* weekly while I was teaching in Botswana by Jill Tweedie or Mary Stott – I forget which – but it alerted me to the fact that women were meeting and discussing their problems with the way women were treated and located in the world as it was. As soon as I got back to the UK I tracked down a feminist group in Bristol. I think my early graduate teaching in feminism came in that group and at the feminist conferences and demonstrations of the early 1970s. I was moving rapidly towards a more radical view of the world – both socialist and feminist – and I wanted to root this new awareness in something more systematically intellectual....

Professor Helen Haste, a retired psychologist from the University of Bath, presents a picture of coming from a relatively committed middle-class university-educated family background, saying that she:

> ... recall[ed] at age of eight asserting girls' equality and often subsequently. We were brought up to believe in gender equality (mother always worked).... Family was strong on gender equality and achievement, however, parents took traditional roles in the household.... I eventually joined WLM in 1971 when I realised the need for action on a collective scale.... Key influences on me were Margaret Mead as a teenager. Simone de Beauvoir later....

Similarly, Susie Skevington, from a comfortable middle-class family, also a professor of psychology in Bath, until she moved to Manchester in 2013, became a feminist in Bristol, after her marriage had ended, and

> ... [well] after university where I had started reading for a science degree and transferred to psychology because I was interested in "people, not dry bones". The marriage lasted five years – it ended six weeks after graduating with a PhD. In the years that followed, the analysis of this experience was core to my development as a feminist with the help of women friends. I became a feminist for two reasons: because of working on social identity theory and research work in Bristol, and teaching extra-mural studies about women's health in Bristol. Feminism developed as a result of or as a key to the divorce ... a trigger.... My women friends who were exceptionally important to me at that time and helped me develop my consciousness. It was painful and also exciting – it freed me up to become a university teacher ... important in consolidating an academic career. I went to Bath in 1976....

Linda Ward, now retired from a research professorship, thought that becoming a feminist was:

> ... probably afterwards, though tellingly my undergraduate dissertation at LSE was on "Female roles and female magazines", so I think it was already influencing me then. It has been a big influence on my life. I've probably tried to influence disability politics around women's issues more than I've tried to influence feminism. I went to Bristol University in 1974 when I was 26 and started to do a PhD on birth control in the 1920s.... I was particularly interested in Eva Hubback and wrote a chapter on the

new feminists.... Practical feminism was parallel to thesis research. I was involved in the women's centre rota ... and reading Sheila Rowbotham. Before Bristol I remember going to some kind of women's meeting or event in South London where Patricia Hewitt, then of National Council for Civil Liberties on Women's Rights, and Anna Coote showing us how to do a vaginal self exam ... and my feminism has mainly been just the women's movement rather than academic and teaching in adult ed ... not really done much teaching in uni ... mainly research ... but I've continued to be a feminist ... it has come and gone, a kind of windy path and patterns are around social justice or human rights or equal opportunities and a feeling of camaraderie....

Finally, from the BWSG, Dr Jackie West, from a solidly middle-class educated family, said that her feminism developed immediately after her graduation in sociology from Exeter:

When I moved to Bristol for a lectureship, from 1971. At Exeter I was vaguely interested in student politics but, if anything, hostile to specifically women's issues. I even resisted options on women and children in history, but since Margaret Hewitt taught so many other core and optional units (including religion, social history), I received an excellent education in it on which I drew from the outset when given the chance to teach gender at Bristol. But by the time I had completed my MA (in criminology), I was (despite a dissertation on homicide) sufficiently interested in female deviance to consider that a possible doctoral topic. This came to nothing ... but prostitution/sex work has been a strong feature of my recent work, although I have been critical of most feminist writing/activism on this. My own feminism in the 1970s developed organically with "left staff" activities, Marxist reading groups, the Working Women's Charter and CR. Having an abortion in 1974 brought me actively into WACC [Women's Abortion and Contraception Campaign], pregnancy testing and the defence of the 1967 Act, but it also created new links with my mother ... [and] inspired renewed interest in interwar history about birth control. I also became involved in education work in schools on abortion, and this led me to an invitation to join the management committee of the Brook Advisory Centre in Bristol which led, some years later, to being vice chair.... Feminism is crucial but I've always been a bit of a devil's advocate for critiques. It has framed my intellectual career, even when arguing against it. I was raised as an undergraduate on theory for theory's sake and the philosophy of social science, though alongside a heavy dose of empirical research, but have increasingly found both feminist "theory" and other theoretical paradigms (Marxist, post-structural or whatever) problematic. I was introduced to the Chicago School early on in my university education, and its grounded approach to social analysis remains a key influence for me. So in my teaching of "sexual divisions" (as early as 1972), gender relations, the family and work, or, most recently, sexuality.... I have always emphasised critical thinking, including how much gender matters or even whether it does, and activism has also played a much less significant role. In my recent research I have come to know many sex work activists, but my publications are theoretical!

While Jackie's reasons for becoming a feminist are a mixture of the personal and political, Professor Hilary Land proffered entirely intellectual reasons. She wrote a beautifully crafted piece about the readings that eventually led her to becoming a feminist, before taking political action. She, like several others, found a feminist sociology conference organised for the BSA, by the late Professors Sheila Allen from the University of Bradford and Diana Leonard, latterly the University of London, then a new young researcher attached to the University of Essex, a key moment:

I read Margaret Mead and Simone de Beauvoir when I was an undergraduate [studying maths in Bristol]. While preparing for pilot study of large families in 1965 [while at LSE] I read Eleanor Rathbone *The disinherited family* (1924). She raised questions about how and why responsibilities for children are shared between parents and the state as well as how the state defined the marriage relationship. She introduced me to feminism in theory and in practice, in particular as it can relate to social and economic policies, and I've been working with her questions ever since. Working with Roy Parker when I left the Poverty Survey in 1968 enabled me to write about the history of family allowances

– published in *Change, choice and conflict in social policy*. This introduced me to various strands of "first-wave" feminism. In the late 1960s very few either in academe or policy circles were much interested in gender equality issues in the social security system, "the twiddly bits of equity", as a deputy secretary at the then DHSS [Department of Health and Social Security] called them at the time. In 1970 I joined Roy Parker in Bristol as a lecturer.... The first WLM conference I attended was in 1973 in Bristol; 1974 was a critical year in my career. The BSA conference on "Sexual divisions in society" was an intellectual watershed for me, and at that conference, for example, I met ... Mary McIntosh as well as Diana and Sheila.... Mary Mac invited me to join a new group campaigning for financial and legal independence for women, which later that year became the WLM's Fifth Demand group. The 1974 conference established the BSA women's network, which was very supportive. The Southwest group was very active. Sharing research and publications was crucial for those of us introducing feminist issues, analyses, evidence of inequalities etc into our teaching, both inside and outside the university. (Ten years later there were still some senior members of the faculty who could not believe there was "a respectable literature" in gender studies!) Many of us were involved in WEA (Workers' Educational Association) and extra-mural teaching, as well as developing courses in the new social admin degrees in the social sciences faculty. Feminism was present in my teaching from the outset. It was an exciting time, and working collectively with other feminists across the faculty was very supportive. It could not have been done on an individualistic basis. At the same time I was involved in producing the Fifth Demand group's discussion kit, which was very popular. The group (about 14 of us) was also involved in giving evidence to various government policy committees as they affected women's legal and financial rights in the mid-70s with the creation of the EOC (Equal Opportunities Commission). Barbara Castle and Shirley Williams, senior members of the Labour government, were beginning to take these more seriously. My travel to meetings of the Fifth Demand group in London were subsidised in part by the Ministry of Defence (MOD) for during 1974-76 I was a member of the MOD's committee of inquiry on army welfare, and had to attend meetings in London.

(This experience also showed me patriarchy in the raw, but it also gave me a chance to get data on the lives of army wives in the public domain. A source of much amusement to the MOD's chief statistician – how could wives give *reliable* evidence?)....

Vintage feminism and social policy

Professors Hilary Land, Clare Ungerson and Elizabeth Wilson, who all wrote useful critical feminist studies of the British welfare state, have now retired as distinguished professors. Hilary and Clare remained deeply involved with the nuances of social policy and the changing welfare state, while Elizabeth displayed abilities over an amazing array of topics to do with women, from fashion to dress to art and style. Elizabeth and Hilary went to university in the 1950s, from relatively upper middle-class families. They were both feminist pioneers, with Hilary being the 'first-in-the-family' to go to university, whereas Elizabeth came from a long line of highly educated family members. Elizabeth said:

I went to Oxford University in the late 1950s, when there was (as I only later discovered) a debate about why women were being sent to university. In the words of the principal of my college we were being educated to be "diplomats' wives" (she actually meant civil servants' wives, but "diplomat" sounded more glamorous, I suppose). There were women dons of course, but they were largely treated as bizarre eccentrics, even Iris Murdoch – and I feel many of the faults in her novels are partly due to the Oxford atmosphere in which she lived.... I read Simone de Beauvoir at university, so in that sense I was a feminist, but it was very out of fashion then.... As I became an academic at the height of the women's movement in the 70s, feminism has been very influential in my teaching and I was also involved in various campaigning groups.... I still think that de Beauvoir probably influenced me more than any other writer, because I was so young when I read *The second sex*. I was actually more interested in general Marxist theories in the 70s. Having worked in a very conservative psychoanalytical set-up, I was much less impressed by all the Freudian stuff, although I do still think some of Freud's concepts are important. I taught women's studies, among other things, for a time, but was actually more interested in developing cultural studies during the latter part of my teaching career and actually was most interested in women artists, painters eg the Surrealists, most of whom weren't really very feminist....

Vintage feminism, university education and the zeitgeist

Professor Carol Dyhouse, the renowned feminist historian, explained the zeitgeist very clearly, arguing:

> There have been seismic changes in the scale and structure of higher education over the last century, and student experience has changed dramatically. "Going to university", an experience confined to less than 2% of 18-year olds before the Second World War, is now almost a rite of passage for something like a third of young people in the UK.... Some of the most dramatic social changes in higher education are to do with gender. A "typical" university student at the beginning of the last century was a full-time undergraduate male, whereas the part-time female student is arguably more representative of higher education today. In 1939 women constituted less than a quarter of the university student population, a proportion which remained fairly stable until the late 1960s, when it began slowly to rise. The real turning point came in the 1970s, after which the growth in female participation seemed inexorable, although it has steadied in recent years. Women overtook men as a proportion of UK undergraduates in 1996/7.... (Dyhouse, 2005, p 20)

She also recognised that:

> The "class divide" between Oxford, Cambridge and "the red bricks" continued to make a marked impression on observers. Ferdynand Zweig, whose portrait of *The student in the age of anxiety*, a comparative study of a group of (mainly male) students in Oxford and Manchester, was published in 1963, noted that none of the students in his Manchester sample had fathers who were "landed gentry, generals, admirals, ambassadors or top-rank scientists", as was often the case at Oxford. Zweig found his students a troubled lot, lacking in exuberance and anxious about a great many things:

among them, money, work, sex, religion and the atom bomb....
(p 22)

As women moved into academia, they were pioneers of an explicit consciousness of feminism and women's issues, and they tried to make changes in their own family lives: choosing not to marry, choosing to marry and later divorce, choosing not to have children or to limit their family size, choosing their sexuality. Carol told me that she is from an upwardly socially mobile family:

> I grew up in a very masculine household, having three younger brothers. I had a feeling of uneasiness about masculinity.... I read history for many reasons, some rather quirky. For example, at school I found most subjects fairly easy to get high marks in, but in the first year I got a lousy mark for history. This meant it became a challenge. I put some effort in and then got hooked. I liked the history teacher at school. She seemed sophisticated and reasonable. However, all through first degree studies I wondered whether I should have gone to art school instead. I gradually got more committed to history but the real turning point came after graduating, when I started to investigate women's history. From then on it became a passion. I think I was always a feminist but didn't use the word until the late 1960s. Feminism has probably been THE single most profound influence and driving force on my academic work....

She shows how feminism influenced educational change:

> The new universities of the 1960s, offering new kinds of curricula in the arts, particularly, proved especially attractive to women. Meanwhile the rise of "second-wave" feminism fostered equality legislation and forced an end to some of the more discriminatory practices in higher education and the labour market. The politically fraught process whereby formerly single-sex colleges in Oxford and Cambridge "went co-educational" was also crucial in opening up more opportunities, even in these institutions for girls. Meanwhile, the advent of the contraceptive pill began to reverse the trend to early marriages: girls began to take more control over their lives

and their educational successes and career aspirations changed accordingly.

Second-wave feminism was influential, especially among university students in the 1970s, as some of them moved into academia from being students. I conclude by looking at the widespread influences of the zeitgeist on women in elite colleges.

Female fortunes: highly educated women from the 1970s

These snapshots of remarkable women show that they were pioneers of new ways of living and being, and developing the knowledge base for future generations, especially through academia. Of those women who went to the most elite colleges in Oxbridge, they may have encountered other women who were pursuing similar new paths. A variety of opportunities were opening up. Becoming president of either the Cambridge or Oxford Students' Union was seen as a guarantee of a pathway to party political office. Historically it had been how many male leaders of the Conservative, Labour and Liberal Parties developed their careers.

It is notable that the first three women to become presidents of the Cambridge Union were in this zeitgeist, the heyday of the WLM. The trend in the Oxford Union is slightly later in the 1970s, with two notable women. Ann Mallalieu was a striking first, as president in Cambridge in 1967, followed by Helene Middleweek in 1969. Both were law students at Newnham College, with Helene coming from a German Jewish refugee background, like mine. Arianna Stasinopoulos became the third female and first 'foreign' president in 1971. Similarly, Susan Kramer, now a Liberal Democrat peer, became president of the Oxford Union in 1971 while studying PPE at St Hilda's, followed by the late Benazir Bhutto, President of Pakistan, who studied PPE at Lady Margaret Hall, Oxford, having previously studied at Radcliffe College, Harvard University, becoming president of the Oxford Union in 1976.

All three women presidents of the Cambridge Union represent an aspect of the public face of women's newfound higher educational opportunities – the zeitgeist – but none would claim to be feminists. They have been celebrated for their accomplishments as women of this era with illustrious political careers befitting such exceptionally able, highly educated women. Both Ann Mallalieu and Helene Middleweek (now Hayman) have had careers in the UK, while Arianna Stasinopoulos' has been in the US. Ann and Helene have had political careers in the Labour Party, both becoming Labour politicians, mainly as members of the House of Lords, with Ann becoming Baroness Mallalieu in 1991, while Helene became Baroness Hayman in 1996. Given that women's membership as life peers of the House of Lords had only begun in 1958, this was a considerable achievement.

On graduation, they diverged professionally, with Ann training to be a barrister and becoming a QC in the 1980s. Ann never contested a parliamentary seat, but on becoming Baroness, she became the Labour opposition 'spokesman' on home affairs and on legal affairs (1992-97).[4] Helene became first a campaigning officer for the housing charity Shelter, then a local government officer for social services, becoming deputy director of the National Council for One Parent Families. On her marriage to Martin Hayman in 1974, she contested the Wolverhampton South West constituency in February 1974 unsuccessfully, but was elected as the MP for Welwyn and Hatfield in the October 1974 general election.

Helene was the youngest member of the House of Commons, remaining the 'Baby of the House' for three years. She became infamous in 1975 as the first woman MP to breastfeed her baby in the House of Commons, a proto-feminist action that created much public consternation. She lost her seat, a marginal, to the Conservatives at the 1979 general election. Almost 20 years later, after the Labour Party won the 1997 general election, Baroness Hayman served as a junior minister in the Department for Environment, Transport and the Regions and the Department of Health, before being appointed Minister of State at the Ministry of Agriculture, Fisheries and Food in July 1999.

In May 2006, Helene won the inaugural election for the newly created position of Lord Speaker, after the position of

---

4   *Who's Who* (2010), 1623 edition, p 1515; and for Hayman, p 1031.

Speaker in the House of Lords was separated from the Office of Lord Chancellor as part of reforms under the Constitutional Reform Act 2005. Becoming a female first Lord Speaker was outstanding, and she was appointed Dame Grand Cross of the Order of the British Empire (GBE) in the 2012 New Year Honours for services to the House of Lords. She has had an exceptionally distinguished career.

Arianna Stasinopoulos was born in 1950 in Greece and moved to the UK aged 16, studying at Girton College. On graduation, she became a journalist and worked for the BBC, but her career trajectory diverged from that of her slightly elder Cambridge presidential sisters. Critiquing the zeitgeist, in 1973 she wrote *The female woman*, attacking the WLM in general and Greer's *The female eunuch* in particular. She became increasingly conservative on moving to the US and marrying Republican Michael Huffington in 1986. After her divorce in 1997, Huffington described herself as side-stepping the traditional party divide, saying 'For me, the primary division is between people who are aware of what I call "the two nations" (rich and poor), and those who are not.' Prior to *The Huffington Post*, Huffington hosted a website called Ariannaonline.com. Her first foray into the internet was a website called Resignation.com, which called for the resignation of President Bill Clinton, and was a rallying place for conservatives opposing Clinton. She then became associated with the Democrats, including supporting John Kerry for President. In 2011 she sold the *Huffington Post* to AOL, but still commands a major media presence in the US.

It is quite clear that the women who became students at universities in the 1960s and 1970s were distinctive in many respects, but they were also incredibly diverse: personally, politically, and in what they became professionally. Nevertheless, these pioneering women made incredibly strong waves, not only in academia, but also in education, in family (changing traditional relations such as childcare), and in politics.

FOUR

Gender and generations

Today's zeitgeist could hardly be more different from the 1970s, given explicit reference to misogyny, then normally called 'patriarchy'. To link misogyny with racism, 'misogynoir' has been coined by black feminist commentator Feminista Anyangwe (2015). Complex sociocultural and political changes in women's involvement in public life, located within a vastly changed global knowledge economy, are now characterised by rampant individualism of the 'selfie' generation, a fitting double-entendre. The 1970s zeitgeist focused on collective discussions about women's economic, education and employment opportunities, also linked to changes in family and personal lives – questions of birth control, child, family and elder care and sexuality. These were hotly debated between liberal, Marxist, radical and socialist-feminists, and whether to pursue state means to achieve these broad goals. How much public money could and should be invested in opening up opportunities for women, especially as wives or mothers, and carers? Political protest by many feminist groups continued unabated, but whichever means were chosen, sociocultural changes occurred rapidly during this decade. These continued inexorably despite the backlash and rise of the conservative, new right internationally, characterised by forms of economic liberalism, contrasting with conservative social policies. Similarly, economic liberalism and individualism continued unabated, morphing into neoliberalism by the end of the 20th century.

In the UK, Margaret Thatcher became the first woman leader of the Conservative Party in 1974, and in 1979 was elected the first woman British Prime Minister. She continued as Prime Minister throughout the 1980s, finally relinquishing office in 1992. She was clearly part of what Martin (2013) calls the 'break-through generation', despite her very conservative policies. She resisted but did not rescind a myriad of changes in public and personal lives. Particularly important were legislative changes – in the UK the Abortion Act 1967, Equal Pay Act 1970 and Sex Discrimination Act 1975, setting up the Equal Opportunities Commission (EOC), alongside the Race Relations Act 1976. I do not want to argue that Thatcher was in any sense a feminist, as we argued in *Closing the gender gap* (Arnot et al, 1999), much to Ann Oakley's ire in her review of our work, although she did advance some liberal feminist arguments early in her career, about women's needs for childcare. She, too, became a Baroness as a reward for her contributions to politics, but I am not concerned with women like her, except that she presages the rampant competitive individualism of the 21st century, recognising individual women's professional contributions.

In the US, change was more heavily fought over, although their equal opportunities and 'race' relations legislation, in the form of civil rights, was implemented earlier than in the UK, in the 1960s. Throughout the 1970s there were debates about the Equal Rights Amendment (ERA) to the US Constitution. This was passed by Congress, but required two-thirds of the states to ratify it. The deadline was 1980, and it failed to get sufficient ratification. Part of the reason was the rise of the conservative right in the US, also a backlash to women's rights. Led by a conservative woman, Phyllis Schlafly, it successfully argued against women's conscription to defeat ratification (see Steinem, 2015, p 91). Nevertheless, there have subsequently been major changes in women's rights and involvement in the armed forces, as there have been toward LGBTQi.

Pioneering women were very diverse – politically, in terms of social class, ethnicity and 'race' – and did not agree about their lives and futures. There was no collective view of the waves they wished to make or the kinds of sociopolitical change for future generations. There were major policy gains, many eroded by the neoliberal turn in the 21st century. An influence on subsequent generations is that we now question feminism's new waves, such as third- and fourth-wave feminism.

I contend that feminism has been influential through HE, in two respects. One is the unacknowledged influence on forms of social mobility, given how few women attended university in previous generations. Second is the development of feminist knowledge, through various courses of study, such as women's and gender studies, as well as through feminist social and economic policies. Influencing social democratic public policy-making has been a critical achievement despite the turn away from social democracy, normalising neoliberalism in public policy-making. While individualism in education, social and public policies has never been completely vitiated, its rougher edges were muted by social democratic policies. This is no longer the case, with competitive individualism back on the public agenda.

No permanent waves?

As Nancy Hewitt (2010, p xi) put it so nicely in her edited collection on the waves of the women's movement in the US, punning on the concept of permanent waves for hair curls, there have been 'no permanent waves' since the inception of second-wave feminism in the 1960s and 1970s. She set herself the task of:

> ... thinking about histories of feminism and women's activism over many years. This project ... allowed me the freedom to re-imagine narratives of women's history, women's rights and feminism ... about the adequacy of the "wave" metaphor ... in the United States....The concepts of waves surging and receding cannot fully capture these multiple and overlapping movements, chronologies, issues and sites. (2010, p 1)

I agree that there have been 'no permanent waves' in the UK, like the US or elsewhere, whether we are alluding to hair, air, hand, the ocean or sea. Professor Sue Middleton, from a very modest working-class family in New Zealand, imaginatively thought of waves not as being about hair, but air, saying that 'WLM hit the air-waves just as I was entering graduate school'. Many saw Stevie Smith's poem *Not waving but drowning* as a major critique of the idea as a singular notion. Indeed, when I mentioned this in a lecture to sociology students in Berkeley in October 2014, one student stood up to recite the poem. Another second-wave feminist commented: "No I don't put a label on it. But age and cohort effects are hard to disentangle."

The 1970s were the era of hair waves for those women with straight hair, and straight rather than gay sex. Permanent waves were certainly for heterosexual women to become more attractive to the 'opposite sex', although the terminology of straight and gay was barely on the horizon. Homosexual men continued to be dealt with punitively. The official British pardon over Christmas 2013 of Alan Turing, the senior code breaker of Nazi ciphers at the secret location in Bletchley Park, provides a very clear example of how extreme punishment of homosexuality was in the 1950s. It entailed chemical castration, which, in Turing's case, led to such mental distress that he committed suicide in 1954. This remained hidden until the slow process of change towards more public recognition of homosexuality and lesbianism from the 1960s and continuing into the 21st century, with recognition of gay partnerships and then gay marriage. Most interesting has been the debate in Ireland in 2015, where gay marriage was officially recognised, while abortion and birth control continue to be sanctioned.

Women who were second-wave feminists questioned these social issues about sexuality and the 'compulsory heterosexuality' embedded in social welfare policies. They themselves were pioneering not only in who they became, but where they came from. Their backgrounds were not simply conventionally middle class, as was presupposed. Given the changing patterns and expansions of HE, the majority of the women are 'first generation' or 'first-in-the-family' to go to university. In the UK, the idea of 'first-in-the-family' has taken on very particular meanings with respect to HE policy, and especially the policy of widening access or participation in the 21st century. It has come to mean ensuring that opportunities of university participation are provided for people from socially and economically disadvantaged backgrounds. The British Labour government made a concerted effort to ensure social mobility through HE, with a limited approach that ignored or obliterated the gender dimension, assuming that women in HE are middle class. This is not the case: most women and second-wave feminists are 'first generation' or 'first-in-the-family' – first daughters, first sisters, first from a poor, working-class or even a middle-class family, first from a black or minority ethnic background or as mature (women or married women) students, or first to study a particular subject such as sociology. The lack of public recognition of the implications of opening up women's educational opportunities, especially through HE, is yet another example of everyday sexism or even misogyny.

Newsworthy women honoured as firsts

Two outstanding examples of pioneering women who joined the British Labour Party and rose through the ranks to become women who were the first to hold critical office were seen in the last chapter. Hayman was of a modest social background, while Mallalieu came from an upper middle-class family. Many British second-wave feminists followed the path of becoming involved in Labour Party politics, and over their careers have received similar kinds of honours for their contributions to knowledge as female, if not feminist, social scientists. Of course, this is just one measure of the influence of feminism through HE, and it is fraught with all the complexities of how such honours are achieved and distributed. Nevertheless, it is an important one, although it bears all the hallmarks of the dying British Empire and post-colonialism. But should such honours be spurned? What are the forms of recognition available to women, feminists especially, for their exceptional contributions to knowledge and politics?

Given that we cannot to rid ourselves of the monarchy and hereditary status through our nobility, as we desire, perhaps we need to think carefully about how to subvert forms of privilege. There are many women who are already making such waves, standing up for change in the most unlikely of circumstances, even in our hallowed chambers of parliamentary democracy and in the teeth of everyday misogyny. This shows how complicated and challenging the social and gender order is, and the varied routes that women have taken in making meaning of their lives through work rather than family and being dependent on their fathers or husbands. It also shows how caught we get in the status symbols and recognition criteria of increasingly competitive and status-bound forms of social mobility, if not hierarchy. It is a far cry from arguments about 'sisterhood' and collectivity or collaboration of second-wave feminism. It also shows how important it is to argue for change and recognition at whatever levels we are able to make the case. Of course this may also arouse our envy and competitiveness, as do other forms of the individual forms of advancement. It may not be the egalitarian changes that we desire, and yet it allows us to see what changes may be possible, and how it can be achieved within the current systems of award and achievement. Whether these are harbingers of a feminist-friendly future is clearly another matter.

Perhaps it is the restless and relentless searching after recognition and approval, understanding of insecurity and feelings of 'being othered' that makes much of this seem so poignant and yet importantly purposive. The seeking of professional public recognition, through the very kinds of honours such as senior membership of professional organisations, is another such desire, often not talked about. Alongside this is also the professional recognition of being included in *Who's Who*, 'the recognised source book of information on people of influence and interest in all fields', which, of course, includes all those in receipt of the Queen's Honours and others who have other forms of distinction.

Various organisations have begun to parallel those of the natural science community in scientists wishing to become fellows of the Royal Society (FRS). Initially it was becoming a fellow of the British Academy (FBA) as an equivalent, followed by the creation of the Academy of Social Sciences to provide similar prestige to social scientists. In its origins in the 1990s, the Academy tried to become more egalitarian by creating the title of Academician (AcSS) for both men and women so honoured, and yet trying to create some markers of academic distinction. This was indeed a tightrope activity in trying to develop a community of scholars within the social sciences, including all the diverse and competing disciplines or subjects with different criteria for accomplishment, and balancing the needs and requirements of the various constituent professional organisations. At the same time, there was a strongly felt need to turn the Academy into a publicly acceptable face of the community of social scientists, as a pressure group on a par with the British Academy. This latter organisation recognised the need to include social scientists, and slowly began to compete for membership. While the Academy started out at the turn of the 21st century with a majority of female recipients, over subsequent years this has become a fraught and tense issue. When I chaired the Academy between 2005 and 2009, tensions between different constituencies became increasingly intense, and almost inevitably male domination took over again. A campaign to replace the gender-neutral but somewhat inexplicit term 'academician' by the thoroughly male concept of 'fellowship' was successful in 2014. This is another testimony to how everyday misogyny seeps into organisations, and how difficult it is to remain vigilant, even if intimately involved.

Along my journey, perhaps inevitably, and not without a hint of my own envy, I have had women colleagues who have received Queen's Honours. It is inevitable that, in any system that emphasises individual achievement and success, there will be the consequent downsides of rivalry and envy. All too often these are not acknowledged, left to fester and so distort and deform what small successes can mean for the individual and for the collective as a whole. In this case, this makes meaning in women's working and family lives, but that meaning is often not unsullied by such tensions. While the system as a whole may be unfair, it is also important to recognise the struggles and hard work that many put in to gain such dubious but heartfelt accolades. Of course, the vast majority of women and feminists have either turned down or not received such honours, but may also have made waves in transforming women's lives: through writing, teaching, research, community and collective politics.

The rapid increase of honours given to women in the last decade is because of the transformation of the system, especially through the reform of the House of Lords. The Labour Party, in opposition during the 1990s, set in train a review, and implemented it when it came into office in 1997. The House of Lords Act 1999, by Blair's New Labour government, meant that most hereditary peers ceased to be members, whereas life peers retained their seats. The supposedly social democratic reforms turned out to be modest, and not about women. Altering the balance between hereditary and lifetime peers, represented in the House of Lords, opened up possibilities for some democratisation. The creation of the position of Baroness in her own right rather than as a dependent of a husband allowed for more professional work for women, as a 'working peer', scrutinising legislation from the House of Commons.

In fact, women were not entitled to sit in the House of Lords until the Life Peerages Act 1958 passed by a Conservative government, allowing both men and women to sit as life peers. The first life peers were created as part of the reform of the House of Lords. Inevitably for this patriarchal institution, there was a balance in favour of men: ten men and only four women.

Viscountess Rhondda had campaigned since the 1920s for women to be peers since they had achieved the vote in 1918, and the ability to become MPs. When her father died she tried to take his seat, basing her claim on the Sex Disqualification (Removal) Act 1919, which declared that 'a woman shall not be disqualified by sex or marriage from the exercise of any public function.' Her case was referred to the House of Lords Committee for Privileges in 1921. It was heard the following year and initially accepted, but the Lord Chancellor declined it. She did not want to sit in the House of Commons as she felt that her father – D.A. Thomas, a Liberal MP, who had been ennobled by Lloyd George for services to government – had had no power and she did not belong to a political party.[1] Hereditary women peers were finally allowed to sit in the House of Lords after the Peerage Act 1963, five years after Lady Rhondda's death, but these do not concern us!

The Labour Party reforms changed the system of political representation and scrutiny and how to honour people seen to

---

[1] Lady Rhondda was in a similar position to Tony Benn in that she inherited her father's peerage on his death in 1921, as he had no sons, although in her case, as a woman, she was not entitled to sit in the House of Lords! As a woman she clearly felt rather differently from Tony Benn (see the next chapter).

be influential in local community democracy and civic rights, including having representatives of minority ethnic groups as well as women. Although there is potential for public contributions, there remain limits to what community and local groups can nominate for successfully, as the Queen makes the awards for contributions to British society. The hierarchy of honours remains linked with the British Empire, with the wording for each level being 'for God and the Empire' something of an irony. The most senior level remains a life peerage, with its patriarchal connotations, followed by a Knighthood (Sir) or, in the case of women, Dame (DBE), and below that, gender-neutral categories of Commander (CBE), Officer (OBE) and Member (MBE). The last category has traditionally been reserved for members of local, community groups making noteworthy contributions – derided as 'school dinner ladies' (making school meals) and 'lollypop ladies' (responsible for ensuring children's safety crossing roads en route to school), a sexist put-down.[2] DBE, CBE and OBE are used for levels of specialist, professional contributions to excellence.

These honours may smooth the edges of our sharply divided social class system and provide some acknowledgement of its inherently unequal sexist basis. They do little more than highlight this injustice, showing how some break through from unlikely beginnings, if imbued with a strong sense of chutzpa! The process of recognition of outstanding contribution has long been associated with political parties and contributions to academic or other professions, including to sports, arts, culture, humanities and the social sciences. While nominations are not usually made specifically on the grounds of women's issues or even from women's or feminist organisations, this is increasingly recognised.

In 2015 two young women – fourth-wave feminists – received such recognition for their feminism. Caroline Criado-Perez, a graduate student, received an MBE for her one-woman

---

[2] A close childhood friend of mine, Viv Davies (née Layton), was pleased to receive an MBE for her charity work with disabled young people. She felt recognised as on a par with her successful brothers, a leading glass artist (Peter) and actor-writer (George).

campaign to retain a picture of a woman on bank notes. The other was also a young woman – Laura Bates – who had launched an online campaign about 'everyday sexism' that has powerfully shown the continuing forms of misogyny in our society, despite the claims to the contrary.

The New Years Honours list for 2014 also indicated the immense change for women's lives, even for feminists! But how far it is any indication of gender or social equality is another matter. For many feminists, it remains absurd. As I was writing, Professor Jessica Ringrose, the Canadian feminist educator, wrote on Facebook that she was going to visit the House of Lords to have lunch with a feminist film-maker, Baroness Beeban Kidron:

> TBH these class society things really freak me out!! WHY is someone a baroness? WHY do they work at the House of Lords? WHY does England still even have such an institution? What is the point?!? Obvs. the most important issue I face is what to wear: sateen jeans and a tuxedo blazer. According to Mumsnet (which has directions about what to wear to HoL) this is not smart casual enough but I am NOT wearing a dress! OK that is all for now, update later!

'New Year Honours: women outnumber men for the first time' (Marsden, 2013) was how *The Telegraph* headline put it, adding that 'more than half of those recognised for their outstanding contribution to British society this year are women, up from 34 per cent a decade ago and just 17 per cent in 1974.' What a dramatic reversal in how women's contributions to civic society are perceived, with the pace of change quickening in the 21st century (and the numbers honoured twice a year – New Year and Birthday Honours are not insignificant, being about 1,000 men and women).

Making waves as a woman social scientist

In the past, such honours were given to some exemplary women scientists, as Professor Heather Joshi, a contemporary colleague at the Institute of Education, University College London (UCL), who herself was awarded an OBE in 2002 (for services to women's studies) mentioned to me that her mother was awarded an MBE in 1972. As is evident from her comment, Heather comes from a long line of highly educated and very middle-class women, so there is no sense in which she is 'first-in-the-family' to go to university, making her something of an exception. She has pioneered explicitly feminist approaches to understanding women's lives through her cohort studies. She herself was educated at St Hilda's College, Oxford (in the days when it was still a women's college), and did not need to obtain a PhD having been a high-flying graduate with an MLitt who became a very distinguished economic demographer and statistician, ultimately managing the major longitudinal and cohort studies of women and children. Although she clearly identifies as a feminist, she chose to change her name on marriage (she was a young graduate when she first married, showing the complex interweaving of notions of female independence).

The question of how far women, even university-educated and very middle-class women, can go in changing the rules of the family in terms of marriage, motherhood and work, is also illustrated by her comments. She said:

I was born to parents who were both Cambridge-educated scientists. My mother had a PhD in Zoology. My father just had a polymathic reputation, which took him into the code breaker team at Bletchley, although his day job was as a marine biologist. My mother gave up paid work in 1945, although she never stopped being a scientist. Apart from a couple of years when she taught sixth formers Biology on a part-time basis, she did not "return to work" until 1967. This was precipitated by the wreck of the Torrey Canyon, from which she emerged as a leading international expert on biological and practical aspects of marine oil pollution. She stopped this work soon after my father retired in 1972, but was awarded an MBE for her work. My maternal grandmother was one of the first women to graduate from LSE circa 1905, but her career in paid work was mostly before that. She was a saintly figure who envied me the opportunities my generation had. My paternal grandmother was a conventional upper middle-class lady who doted on my father and objected to my mother taking paid work....

I was also made aware of the contradictory processes, attending a celebratory dinner at Royal Holloway, University of London for the award of an OBE for services to HE to Professor Rosemary Deem, vice-principal for education and professor of higher education management and formerly dean of history and social sciences (8 January 2014). Rosemary had invited mainly close women and feminist colleagues to this important celebration of her achievement. These included the historian of education Professor Jane Martin, the expert on higher education Professor Louise Morley, and the feminist sociologist Professor Bev Skeggs. We had entwined friendships, and were thrilled to be able to celebrate with Rosemary and hear how she made sense of the award that had been announced in the Queen's Birthday Honours in June 2013, receiving it from the Princess Royal at Windsor Castle in the autumn, an event that she posted details of on Facebook.

In her after-dinner presentation she pointed to the importance of women receiving these honours, mentioning the fact of more women in the New Year Honours. Given that the title referred to the British Empire, she suggested it be renamed *British Excellence*. What she saw as particularly important was how she had carved out her career, from relatively inauspicious beginnings as a hard working academic teacher at the then North Staffordshire Polytechnic, through to the Open University, Lancaster and Bristol Universities. A critical thread for her was her commitment to academic professional and research organisations, mentioning the BSA as salient, meeting there colleagues who became critical to her own development. She also acknowledged her commitments to both research, through her membership of national research assessment panels, the Economic and Social Research Council's (ESRC) research grants board, and to teaching and learning through the setting up of the national subject centre for education (ESCalate) based in Bristol. Finally she remarked on working for the profession through editing journals and being aware of the contradictory processes of new forms of open access publication. The pleasures and pressures of being a woman academic, striving to maintain collegiality and professionalism, were uppermost in her passionate account. She hoped that her award would make a small contribution to raising the profile of female social scientists working at senior levels in UK HE.

There is no doubt that Rosemary has been at the forefront of research and campaigning around women and education for over 40 years, with her book on this topic published in 1978 as a first of this genre. She has also been a fearless and tireless campaigner for the Labour Party since the 1980s, becoming a Labour councillor in Milton Keynes when she was based at the Open University. While this award is more than richly deserved, it is, indeed, bittersweet for her, both professionally and personally – her long-standing husband, Professor Kevin Brehony, had died of cancer in October 2013. As an argumentative Marxist historian, especially of children's early childhood education and care, he was not particularly sympathetic to such honours, as she herself mentioned in her talk, although he was immensely proud of his wife. Rosemary herself also acknowledged the complementary, challenging and loving nature of their partnership in her obituary of her husband, published in *The Guardian* (7 January 2014).

Rosemary became a recipient of the British award alongside several other women social scientists, who have also worked tirelessly for the Labour Party. They all have made 'small contributions to raising the profile of female social scientists'. Another prominent recipient is Baroness Professor Tessa Blackstone, who was ennobled by the Labour Party 30 years ago now. She is eminent for having been a university vice chancellor, of two very different institutions – Birkbeck College, University of London, and Greenwich University – and for her manifold public commitments as chairs of boards as well as having served as Minister for Higher Education in a Labour administration (1997-2001). Her achievements, successes and honours are far too numerous to cite here. She, too, started on her journey by studying a topic related to women, although she has not subsequently been at the forefront of campaigning around women's issues: her doctoral thesis topic was on nursery education at LSE in the 1960s. She moved into academia, followed by educational administration in the then ILEA, and for a spell as part of a government think-tank, the Central Policy Review Staff (CPRS). A few years my senior, she was a colleague when I was starting out on my journey as a researcher, back in the late 1960s, first at LSE, and then, while involved in transatlantic educational studies. From a thoroughly middle-class background, although she attended a modest girls' grammar school, she has developed a very self-assured manner, described in Wikipedia as 'patrician' – what a sexist put-down and another form of everyday misogyny! While her choices as a woman have been sometimes controversial – such as insisting on being the Master (not Mistress) of Birkbeck since it would have entailed changing a statute – like most of us academic and professional women, she has never changed from her maiden name, and follows a path of demonstrating individual women's achievement.

Other social scientist recipients include Baroness Professor Ruth Lister, ennobled in 2011, having previously received a CBE in 1999, for her academic policy work on poverty and inequality. Starting off as a policy person, running the Child Poverty Action Group (CPAG) founded by the late Professor Peter Townsend in 1965, it became a key lobby group for transforming children and women's lives out of poverty. Having graduated with a degree in sociology from the University of Essex, Ruth moved from CPAG into academia as a professional sociologist, becoming a professor of social policy first at the University of Bradford, later moving to Loughborough, with a commitment to feminist and gender questions. At a lecture at LSE in 2014, she mentioned that having witnessed her mother's economic dependency on her father, through the household, this crystallised her personal and political views. Ruth determined that she did not want to become dependent, and chose not to get married. This was a choice that many individual women made in the 1970s to avoid the more severe effects of financial and legal dependence on men. She illustrated the developing gendered analysis by mentioning the unequal distribution of household resources and caring work.

This research led her to want to make political interventions and policy change such that she willingly became a Labour peer with responsibility for legislation around care work and parental leave. She argued that since the 1970s, feminism had come on to the political agenda in ways unheard of 35 years ago: the obstacles to change were greater then than now. Her own achievements with social policy changes for women are relatively slight – pathetic actually, as she put it – and she has only managed to achieve tiny victories in terms of legislation. Her work has largely been around the slight change in the terms of parental leave for fathers of newborn children. Indeed, the trend has been towards greater individualisation rather than collectivism for women, but one major benefit has been women's individual taxation rather than a family or marriage tax. She would argue that genuine interdependence is not compatible with unequal gendered power relations.

We, too, have been long-standing colleagues in the field of social policy, our paths crossing through participation in the Social Policy Association (SPA). Ruth, too, shows her commitment to being an independent woman by never changing her maiden name, and her background shares some similarities with my own, raised in a family in the north of England where one of her parents was a refugee from Nazi Germany.

Similarly, the honour of a Damehood has been given to another woman social scientist in 2008 for her work ultimately as vice chancellor of Keele University and involvement in numerous forms of university and research administration – Dame Professor Janet Finch. Initially recognised for her services to social sciences through the award of a CBE in 1999, she went on to excel in her more recent professional career in university politics and administration. She has, at the same time, maintained her strong feminist sociological research on family, education and social policy. She, too, has been a close colleague through our loose network of professional academic work. Indeed, she was extremely proactive in the creation of a national group on the theme of women and social policy in the 1970s, given that her PhD, awarded by the University of Bradford, was on the wives of ministers, subsequently published, entitled *Married to the job* (1983). This led to a rapid rise through the ranks of sociological academe to a senior position at the University of Lancaster, before becoming a vice chancellor. At the same time she was closely involved with her professional association and national research policy and administration. She was the vice chancellor of Keele (1995-2010) while I was working there for six years (1999-2005). Again, coming from modest social origins in Liverpool, but educated first through a scholarship to Merchant Taylors' School and thus a 'first-in-the-family', studying for an undergraduate degree at the then women's Bedford College, University of London, Janet had a meritorious and meteoric career through the groves of academe as a British sociologist. And again, she, too, is best known by her maiden name, although she did have to marry her lifelong partner Professor David Morgan, the family sociologist, in order to become a vice chancellor, yet another contradiction for feminists' continuing role in academia.

Second-wave feminist-social scientists

Many feminists have received an award for making waves as social scientists, although the honour did not usually refer to either gender or feminist questions. Rather, it related to their field of endeavour in relation to social inequality, a measure, perhaps, of the continuing obscuring, or threatening, nature of feminist stances – more misogyny? These include Drs Annette Lawson and Mary Stiasny, and Professors Avtar Brah, Terri Rees and Fiona Williams. The question of how these women got their recognition also illustrates the difficulties that women continue to have in being so recognised fairly. All see themselves as active feminists, formed through their learning and studies within universities, from diverse and modest family backgrounds, being 'first-in-the-family' to go to university. They have had different paths through HE, with Annette and Mary taking more of a leadership and managerial role than Avtar and Fiona, who have tended more to remain in research, while Terri spans both.

Dr Annette Lawson was awarded her OBE specifically for services to diversity in 2004. A distinguished British public policy feminist, she was "the first *girl* in my family to go to university [but] I was born in London to a prosperous landed gentry Jewish family of Sephardi origins." She did not become a feminist:

> ... until I was 50! I thought you could do anything if you worked hard enough – the merit view of life. But was rudely awakened by the way [uni] treated me. It was wonderful American colleagues and friends who helped me into feminism between 1985-88 when we lived in Berkeley and I was a visiting scholar to the then CROW – Centre for Research on Women at Stanford, and at the Institute for Human Development at Berkeley. On the other hand,

I have a memory from when I was about six or seven in Somerset which is significant – I ran in the 100 yards race at the school sports day – remember it was a boys' school. I won with a lot of support from my brother and cousin who ran alongside cheering me on.... But when I was called up for my prize, I heard one of the fathers of one of the boys say "what is a girl doing even running in this race, never mind winning it?" And I always knew my brother as the first born and only son was the favourite and my younger sister who was learning disabled – "slow" was another because of her vulnerability. So I was a typical middle child.... [Annette had already mentioned that she] went to university and won the studentship for the best student in the year in the University of London, two years running, and went straight on to do a doctorate which was immediately published.... After early marriage and childbearing until the youngest of three was three years old, I did not work for money. But in 1976 I became a lecturer at uni. This was an appalling step because I should have negotiated re-entry at, at least senior lecturer level, as a male colleague did at the same time. Never occurred to me, and I was never promoted, yet given huge admin responsibility – senior tutor, graduate studies and chair of department. After the fiasco of leaving uni, I was never successful in getting another academic job (not even called for interview). Partly it was because I had not been promoted and so had the age and kind of career that should have got me a chair, but I imagine my applications were binned as soon as they saw "lecturer". Hence I set up a consultancy mainly focused upon gender equality but also diversity more generally.... I became an activist and was successful at that – chair of the Fawcett Society, and then National Association of Women's Organizations (NAWO), a commissioner of the Women's National Commission (WNC) and its chair....

Dr Mary Stiasny, formerly Pro-Director of Learning and International programmes at the Institute of Education, UCL, was awarded an OBE in the Queen's Birthday Honours awards 2013 for her services to education. Immediately afterwards, she was seconded to be the dean of International programmes at the University of London:

I'm delighted and surprised to be given this award. I have thoroughly enjoyed the opportunities my work has given me to contribute to the world of higher education and beyond. I am passionate about education and developing and improving the experience and opportunities of students, and about internationalising our work. I would also like to thank all my colleagues present and past without who I would not have been able to do the work I have.

Dr Stiasny held various roles in education. After completing a degree in sociology at LSE, and a PGCE at Goldsmiths (where she later studied for a Master's and a PhD), she started her professional life as a teacher of social and environmental studies at Holland Park Comprehensive School. She returned to Goldsmiths to the sociology department as subject studies tutor (for social studies), becoming programme leader for the secondary PGCE within the education studies department, then deputy head. In 1996 her career took her to Oxford Brookes University, where she was appointed deputy head of the school of education. Five years as head of the school of education/school of education and training at the University of Greenwich followed this. She spent four years working at the British Council as their head of education and training before the Institute of Education. Despite this awesome career, she has not been awarded the title of professor, although many male colleagues with far less distinguished pathways have been so rewarded: another example of everyday misogyny? A Queen's Honour may well make that hurt less painful.

She thinks of herself as a second-wave feminist, having retained her maiden name as part of that commitment…

but I hate to think that this might mean we are 'over'…. I think we still have a voice because too many younger women think that the battle is won…. I think that we had less self-confidence about the rights we had, and more anger which was necessary to make a stand since we were less confident – we were learning and realising our voice; but I fear this means that while we were therefore less convinced by the changes and cosmetic effects we saw around us, now women are less aware that things are not as changed as we were told they are…. (Does this make sense? Our conscientisation meant that we saw the smoke screens – now women may not see them....)

Clearly Mary has been aware of the smokescreens in her own career.

The same is also true for Professor Avtar Brah, who is a specialist in 'race', gender and ethnic identity issues (mentioned in Chapter Three). Avtar was awarded an MBE in 2001 in recognition of her research on the questions of ethnicity and 'race' before she was recognised her supreme research qualities and awarded the title of professor. Being a woman from a minority ethnic group has also made it even more difficult to become a professor. Two years ago, there was a media discussion about another one of my participants, namely, Professor Heidi Mirza, entitled 'The university professor is always white' (Williams, 2013). It argued how difficult it was for women academics, and minority women especially, to get the so-called 'top jobs'.

In reply to my question about her feminism, Avtar said:

Yes. I consider myself as a "second-wave" feminist, although sometimes I do not know what this means apart from age. Of course the struggles were different whereas the gains of some of those struggles are taken for granted today by younger feminists. There are few women's studies courses these days. The emphasis is much more on gender as a relational category. Sexuality studies are often now part of gender studies. Perhaps the impact on the neoliberal university is much less.

Professor Fiona Williams of the Centre for International Research on Care, Labour and Equalities (CIRCLE) at the University of Leeds, and now emeritus professor of social policy, received an OBE in 2004 for her work on social inequalities. Her previous roles at Leeds have been director of the ESRC CAVA Research Group on Care, Values and the Future of Welfare and co-director of CIRCLE where she was international professorial research fellow. She also held a part-time position at the Social Policy Research Centre at the University of New South Wales, Australia. In 2012 she was further honoured with the Special Recognition Award (formerly the Lifetime Achievement

Award) from the SPA. Fiona has written widely on gender, 'race' and ethnicity in social policy, and is currently researching the employment of migrant care workers in Europe. On receipt of this she commented: "I feel fortunate to have been part of a discipline that has been more inclusive and less stuck in its ways than many other academic disciplines. I feel this award is a recognition of a critical perspective in social policy that I have helped develop over some 40 years spanning feminist, anti-racist, disability and queer politics: perspective that has been both theoretical and grounded in action and activism."

Fiona is a long-standing colleague of mine. We first met when I was working in Bristol, and while she had a part-time position at the then Bristol Polytechnic she lived in my house, coming over from Plymouth where she lived, on a weekly basis. We found that we had grown up across Ilkley Moor from each other, and around the same time, she attending Ilkley Grammar School, while I went to Keighley Girls. She, too, was 'first-in-the-family' to go to university, although her background crossed class, since, as she says, "my parents started off as working class who became middle class after the war by virtue of my father's progression as a design engineer. I had two elder brothers but I was first to go to university across the whole extended family. Mother was a housewife/artist. My parents were proud that I went to university but they also thought that it would provide me with a good marriage." In this respect, our formal class backgrounds were slightly different, but we both came to feminism at relatively similar times, and shared our commitments to maintaining an identity as independent women through our maiden names.

On discussing the question of her stance on second-wave feminism, she said:

> These days I consider myself more of a "global feminist", that is, concerned with how geo-political relations affect women ... this is the big question. In my own experience, I have moved both with the new waves (especially in taking on an intersectional approach to social division and difference), but held on to the old in that I see gender as still a critical lens with which to view the world.... The Centre for Interdisciplinary Gender Studies at Leeds when

Sasha Roseneil, Jean Gardiner, Grizelda Pollock, and I, among others, set it up were heady days and its interdisciplinarity felt like the apotheosis of feminism in the academy....

Damehood and distinction: what's in a name?

The specific title of a Damehood (DBE) bears with it all the contradictory notions of womanhood with which we have to grapple. In many senses it is a term of ridicule – the pantomime dame – and has been used as a term in songs (see Chapter Three). One recipient of the DBE in the New Year Honours 2015 was Professor Teresa Rees of the Cardiff School of Social Sciences for services to social sciences. She is also a pioneering feminist – although marrying relatively young, she chose to change her name to her husband's (but the marriage was dissolved in 2004), and was awarded a CBE in 2002 for her work on equal opportunities and HE, mainly, but not entirely, in Wales.

Dame Teresa has a distinguished record of research that focuses on inequalities, women and science policy, gender mainstreaming and HE funding, and has been focused on contributing to evidence-based policy in the EU, the UK and Wales. A former Equal Opportunities Commissioner, she received the 'Welsh Woman of the Year' award for 'outstanding contributions to women in Wales', and in 2013 was appointed Director for Wales of the Leadership Foundation for Higher Education. She was pro vice chancellor (research) at Cardiff from 2004-10. She was a member of the National Equalities Panel commissioned by the UK government to study the Anatomy of Economic Inequality in the UK in 2010. She chaired two independent investigations or commissions of inquiry on HE funding for the Education and Lifelong Learning Minister of the Welsh Assembly Government (known as the 'Rees Reviews').

She argues that:

> I am driven by concerns about the outcomes from inequalities and this has informed my research. I am particularly interested in an approach to promoting gender equality known as gender mainstreaming. This is based on the theoretical concept of the "politics of difference", and is about embedding a gender dimension

into policies and processes, systems and structures. It turns the attention away from individuals and their rights, and from groups and their disadvantages, and focuses instead on how policies and practices can, however inadvertently, reproduce patterns of inequality. Gender mainstreaming seeks to promote gender equality in the organisation, its way of doing things and in its culture. I have worked with a range of bodies and governments in Europe and elsewhere to apply a gender mainstreaming approach in the development of governance, science policies, education, training and labour market policies, regional economic development, the "knowledge economy", social exclusion, transport and sport. My interest in inequalities is wider than gender, however, and I was a member of the government Steering Group to set up the Equality and Human Rights Commission, and of the National Equality Panel that reported in 2010 (Hills et al, 2010). I was also a commissioner in the NIACE inquiry on "Learning through life". Most recently my work has focused on women and science policies in Europe, a particular concern of the Research Directorate-General of the European Commission (EC), for whom I have acted as an expert adviser. I was rapporteur for a series of international groups of scientists commissioned by the EC to inform policies on recruiting, retaining and making the most of women in science, engineering and technology in the public and private sectors, and to benchmark national policies on women and science. I also assisted in work on "measuring excellence" for the design of the 7th Framework Programme ... [and as] an expert adviser on a report on structural change in universities.... My third more long-standing area of specialism is labour market analysis, especially in Europe and in Wales. This research has looked at the "knowledge economy", learning societies, adult guidance services, gender segregation, equal pay and the labour market. I completed a five-year EC-funded research project on knowledge economies and regional trajectories in 2011. Fourth, some research has focused on education policy, especially HE following devolution. I was a commissioner on the NIACE Inquiry on Lifelong Learning entitled "Learning through Life", which reported in 2009. The Education and Lifelong Learning Minister of the Welsh Assembly Government invited me to chair two independent investigations on HE funding to assist the National Assembly for Wales develop its policies, especially in the context of devolution of responsibilities for these matters in the Education Act 2005.

Another recipient of DBE in the New Year Honours 2014 was also of my generation. Dr Colette Bowe was awarded the DBE for services to media and communications, having held the post of 'chairman' of Ofcom, a UK regulatory authority, and involved in the Independent Broadcasting Authority (a forerunner of Ofcom) and a range of City bodies. During her career as a professional economist, she worked in Whitehall, City regulation and fund management. She also has been involved in a range of academic organisations, including being a fellow of Nuffield College, Oxford and 'chairman' of the Council of QMUL from 2004 to 2009. This is her alma mater as she went to QMUL initially to study French as an undergraduate from a relatively middle-class Catholic family in Liverpool, back in the 1960s.

Colette and I met as researchers at QMUL after she had finished her undergraduate degree in economics, to which she had transferred, and while she was studying for her PhD. As Colette and I were relatively unusual as women in such a setting, we became friends. We were joined by the now Lady Elizabeth (Liz) Vallance, who was, at the time, a lecturer in politics in the same department. We have occasionally met subsequently although our three paths have diverged greatly. Colette became a very significant figure in the world of business. In February 2013, she was one of the most powerful women in the UK, according to 'Woman's Hour' on BBC Radio 4.

Liz continued as an academic political scientist, writing a major book about women in politics, entitled *Women in the House: A study of women Members of Parliament* (1979) followed by *Women in Europe* (1985). On her retirement from her readership at QMUL, to take up public duties, in 1994, when her husband was knighted, she, too, became involved in university politics, becoming chair of the council of the Institute of Education for 10 years (2000-09). Her husband, Lord Iain Vallance, is an extremely successful businessman, involved in the Liberal Democratic Party, and was first knighted and later elevated to the House of Lords in 2004. Liz, from an unusual Scottish political family in Glasgow, married in 1967, on graduation, and being relatively young, changed her name on marriage, as was the convention at the time. This leads back to the question of how our aims as young and aspiring women pioneers as university graduates have been transformed through the vicissitudes of life. I now discuss the question of how we, as women, are addressed.

A storm in a teacup: being and remaining Miss

As HE has expanded and turned universities into corporate businesses in the 21st century, British universities have developed alumni systems similar to the US. By appealing to alumni, the aim is to provide additional resources for tuition and other services for students, such as accommodation and extra-curricula activities. Requests for donations have been carefully developed in Oxford and Cambridge among others, although they have substantial endowments in the individual colleges and for subject- or discipline-specific needs across the university as a whole.

The universities where I was an undergraduate – Strathclyde and Leeds – began to approach me at the turn of the century, including my being visited by an officer of the Alumni Relations and Fundraising Office at Leeds to discuss a settlement in my will. Interestingly, the term used for the place of undergraduate education is a gendered term – one's 'alma mater'! How motherly or maternal it has been is quite another matter, and I certainly did not feel particularly cosseted by either university, although I did feel that we, as students, were offered chances to channel our creativity, including a sense of our being independent women, struggling towards some notion of women's liberation.

Changing our name on marriage, at the time, seemed to be perfectly normal. Less than a decade later, this was questioned, especially in the WLM. A conscious commitment to sociocultural change has been through our named identity. This is particularly the case for academic feminists, where publication in one's name is essential. Perhaps one reason for not feeling particularly 'mothered' in my case was the fact that at neither university did we have many women as our teachers: indeed, they were virtually absent from the academic staff, although as both social sciences, and subsequently sociology students, women students were in the vast majority. In 'our class of 1966' (to use an American expression), the year that we graduated there were over 50 Honours sociologists, of whom about a tenth were men. Many of my female friends married shortly after graduation, and changed their names on marriage, as was convention. Several embarked on postgraduate study for a Master's or a doctorate, although it was not a necessity for continuing in HE, or for conducting research. At the time, we were not aware of how seismic the changes were going to be in social and sexual/gender relations and employment opportunities. We were offered untold opportunities for paid employment and work while involved with childcare, but our choices and constraints varied according to our particular locales and relationships.

A letter, addressed to me as 'Miss David', popped through my letterbox at home, in the autumn of 2013. It was from QMUL, where I had completed my PhD in 1975. I have only lived at this address since 2002, when I remarried (by coincidence, to a professor of biology at QMUL). The letter was from the Alumni Relations and Fundraising Office asking for a contribution 'to greatly enhance the student experience ... through a range of scholarships, hardship awards and projects which will make a real difference...', and how I would be telephoned by a current student ... to let me know of 'developments at QM and talk to me about how I might support the Fund.'

I was particularly struck by both the envelope and by the letter inside, since I have not been addressed like this for 40 years. It was, indeed, one of our first WLM campaigns to change the language of society, including universities. We wanted gender-neutral or marriage-free adult language, rather than 'manmade language', as Dale Spender put it (1980). A particular campaign at Bristol was to get rid of the term 'chairman' for a 'committee', although it keeps creeping back in – another example of everyday sexism or misogyny. We did not then think about chair for a professorship, since that was so traditionally male it was not on our horizons!

Calling someone 'Ms' rather than 'Mrs' or 'Miss' seemed to have been much more successfully accomplished, and is certainly accepted nowadays by the media. *Ms* magazine, for example, was one of the most successful in the US, founded and edited by the redoubtable Gloria Steinem in the 1970s, a symbol of second-wave feminism in the US. Many women, of course, preferred the title 'Mrs' to 'Miss', with 'Miss' being the term reserved for young schoolteachers.

In addition, many women felt the way that I did, that the term 'Dr' is important not only for establishing one's academic credibility, but also for drawing a veil over one's marital status. When I was at Harvard in the early 1970s I found myself wanting to complete a PhD to stay in international academia. A PhD was not a necessity in the UK at the time, and it was not seen as usual for an economist to do a doctorate. When I asked Maurice Peston at QMUL to convert my research project to a PhD, he asked: "Why do you want one of those?" Although a professor of economics, he did not have a PhD.

Maggie Humm, professor of feminist literature, similarly told me that it was only the belated realisation of the necessity of a doctorate that she started working on a thesis:

> Much later ... when it became clear to me that I could not progress as an academic without a PhD. And also because I had embarked upon a very early form of infertility treatment and fearing lack of success felt that a PhD could become a substitute (to stop people continually asking about my lack of children). I was still an activist and chose to study the US polymath Paul Goodman (poet, anarchist, activist, town planner, novelist, educator, psychiatrist, playwright, political essayist etc) who had been very influential in the left, especially education. My university paid the fees if I registered as a CNAA [Council for National Academic Awards] PhD, so I had an "internal" supervisor....

So, receiving a begging letter from QMUL, with a leaflet explaining quite what the college was doing to enhance 'the student experience' in terms of both curricula and extra-curricula activities, and signed by the principal, was like a red rag to a bull to me. It was declaring that the neoliberal university was much better at accommodating change for undergraduate students than the previously publicly funded university. QMUL seemed not to have recognised how the student population had changed over the last 20 or more years, to include more women and minority ethnic students than the traditional white, male middle-class student. And to be addressed to me as 'Miss' when I had received my PhD from the College, and yet they were able to find my correct home address! So I wrote an email addressed to the principal, explaining my disquiet about their lack of sensitivity to gender issues for students.

After three weeks I had received no reply, and so I sent the correspondence to the *Times Higher Education* for their Letters page, as an example of what I saw as anachronistic. It is, in fact, clearly sexist behaviour in HE today given the predominance of women undergraduates. The editorial team decided that it was of sufficient newsworthiness to publish a short piece on it, which eventually came out entitled '"Miss" no hit with revered alumna', with the byline, 'Eminent professor incensed by inaccurate Queen Mary "begging letter"'. David Matthews, the reporter, approached the College for a comment before publishing his article, and they wrote another letter to me received in the post literally minutes before the copy went to press, 'apologising for the offence caused by the error relating to my title and salutation....' David Matthews reported this as 'human error' rather than the more likely inhuman error in that the letters were machine-generated.

While all of this might seem incredibly trivial – the proverbial storm in a teacup – it is indicative of how change in the gender order in the neoliberal university is only surface deep. This is confirmed by the correspondence following the article in the *Times Higher Education*, the comments online following its publication in the US, in *Inside Higher Ed*, the equivalent publication. I was roundly condemned for not appreciating the efforts of the fundraisers to support my research, and I was seen as self-serving and self-absorbed for making such a fuss out of so little! Only Professor Laurie Taylor, sociologist and author of the satirical column *The Poppletonian*, seemed to grasp the more critical importance of the issue for funding. Entitled 'Dear, oh Dear', he wrote '... It seems that a distinguished former member of our social psychology staff, Professor D.K. Mundayne, recently received a letter from our fundraising officer that addressed him merely as "Dear Cash Cow"', and it was accompanied by a cartoon with a poster saying "What an udder disgrace!"' (Perhaps it is also sad that the term is a sexist one.)

The problems were reinforced by seeing a play recently about Dr Rosalind Franklin entitled 'Photograph 51'. It was largely about her mistreatment as a scientist working on the discovery of DNA in the early 1950s. She was appointed at King's College, London, by Dr Maurice Wilkins, and worked with him on developing techniques to study this. He also worked closely with Drs Francis Crick and James Watson in their lab in Cambridge. A theme of the play was how the three men persisted in calling her Miss Franklin, despite her having obtained her PhD around the same time as them, while they referred to each other politely as 'Dr'. Rosalind repeatedly asked to be called Dr Franklin, and they refused. Although several reviewers pointed out that this was no longer an issue, how wrong they are, as my incident indicates!

Feminist waves

The changes in the zeitgeist from the 1970s to today are clearly complex. While 'feminism' is a term that appears everywhere in the media, its meanings have changed. Patriarchy, sexism and even misogyny still flourish, despite the changes. Liberal feminism, affecting policy change and drawing on some second-wave feminists, has been more effective than more radical or socialist campaigns. Some individual women, including academic women, have been highly successful and influential in their chosen fields. We have seen some notable and influential social scientists, whose influence extends beyond the UK, especially into Europe, although policies of gender mainstreaming remain in doubt. I have concentrated on the UK in this chapter, given its anachronistic system of honours. And there are some international examples of academic liberal feminists of the second-wave receiving similar honours, illustrating how global this process is.

The announcement that 'Senate confirms Janet Yellen as next chair of the Federal Reserve' (Rushe, 2014) was made at the same time as the Queen's New Year Honours, where women exceeded men, in January 2014. Professor or Dr Janet Yellen was confirmed as the first woman to head the US central bank. She had been vice chair, and became the first Democrat to run the bank since the then President, Jimmy Carter, appointed a Democrat in

1979, 36 years ago. She is a professional and academic economist, having worked as a professor at the universities of California, Berkeley and at Harvard University, as well as a spell in the UK at LSE. She is, like many of the women I have discussed in terms of her shared origins (as a Jewish woman), cultural experiences and professional formation, an academic woman, and from the pioneering generation of women as students and subsequently academics.

Our routes have intertwined through the emerging complexity of HE. A year younger than I am, she received her PhD from Yale University immediately after graduation from Brown University in the mid-1960s. She was at Harvard as an assistant professor in the economics department (1971-76) when I was there (1972-73), so we have somewhat overlapping pathways, given that I had gone there from the economics department at QMUL and social policy at LSE. I do not recall having met her in Cambridge, and it is not clear from public statements that she has concerned herself with women's issues *per se*. She is clearly a woman who has maintained her own identity, at the very least through retaining her maiden name, a matter of some considerable note and determination in these politically fraught (yet feminist) times.

Note that Hillary Rodham Clinton (also of the second-wave feminist generation in Wellesley, Massachusetts, becoming a feminist around the same time) kept her maiden name as part of her identity, albeit hyphenated, until well into her husband's first term of office as US President (1993-97). She eventually succumbed to political pressure, although continuing to espouse liberal feminism. She has campaigned on the international stage, including speaking at UN conferences on women. Now known by her husband's surname, she is running for office as the first woman president of the US, having done so unsuccessfully seven years ago. Like Janet Yellen, she has reached a most exalted position within the US political system, albeit when traditional economic systems are quaking under pressures of neoliberal globalisation. Yet another such figure is Christine Lagarde of the International Monetary Fund (IMF), French-American economist and architect of some of the economic and fiscal policy measures taken. She represents professional women who were beneficiaries of the expansion of HE globally, and it is to this generation, born in the 1950s, that we now turn in the next chapter.

FIVE

Cultivating feminists

Beverley Skeggs, well-known feminist professor of sociology at Goldsmiths College, University of London, is representative of the slowly changing zeitgeist of the 1970s, coming into feminism as part of the second generation (born in the 1950s), having learned from her slightly elder sisters. As 'first-in-the-family' to go to university, she is concerned about class and gender in her studies, initially with teaching schoolchildren. As HE expanded, the tendency for women with working-class backgrounds being 'first-in-the-family' to go to university increased, including as mature married women/mother students. Interestingly, too, many began their careers as teachers from either college or university. These feminists born around the Second World War or those from the baby boom era mostly set out with no expectations about becoming academics, forging educational lives in schools, only returning later to HE as mature (married) women students. In the UK, this was a period of unparalleled growth in mature women students that Mrs Thatcher, ironically, codified while she was Secretary of State for Education in the early 1970s by initiating a policy of university expansion for mature students, the majority of whom were inevitably women. Under Thatcherism and Reaganism in the US in the 1980s, women increasingly entered college or university.

The entwined issues of class and gender remain of abiding import for these feminists. Bev Skeggs[1] neatly encapsulates this in the comment she posted on Facebook on 14 March 2014:

> Three men representing the upper (Tony Benn), middle (Stuart Hall) and working (Bob Crow) sectors of the class divide die. So tragic. They all campaigned relentlessly against inequality and made a huge difference to people's lives in many ways, all "speaking truth to power", all uncompromising in their own ways. Their combined struggle is formidable and we really need to keep their legacies alive – from wherever we are, doing whatever we can, whenever we can.

She garnered tremendous support for this statement about these three socially radical men, who, in their different ways, were all sympathetic to feminist as well as socialist ideals.

Crow, Benn and Hall, three men representing the class divide

Introducing how second-wave feminism was cultivated through party politics and university education, I discuss each of the three socialists Bev mentions.

Bob Crow, a British trade union leader, met an untimely death at the age of 52 on 11 March 2014. He was a strong trade unionist, who took his union – the National Union of Rail, Maritime and Transport workers (RMT) – out of the Labour Party because it wasn't sufficiently left-wing. Crow did not benefit from HE, having left school at the age of 16. He was an autodidact, describing himself as a communist/socialist. He

---

[1] Professor Skeggs has received honorary doctorates from Stockholm University, Aalborg University and the University of Teesside (her home town). She is the joint managing editor of the journal *The Sociological Review* and currently holds an ESRC Professorial Fellowship. She was born in Middlesbrough and studied at the University of York (BA) and Keele University (PGCE, PhD). From 1996 to 1999 she was director of women's studies at Lancaster University (with Celia Lury). In 1999 she was appointed to a chair at the University of Manchester. Since 2004 she has been professor of sociology at Goldsmiths, University of London.

was regarded as part of the 'awkward squad', the loose grouping of left-wing union leaders who came to power in a series of electoral victories from 2002. On his death, he was not a member of any political party, but the Trades Union Congress (TUC) Secretary-General Frances O'Grady – the first woman ever to lead the TUC – called him "an outstanding trade unionist, who tirelessly fought for his members, his industry and the wider trade union movement." Latterly, he espoused similar radical political views to Tony Benn, who also became highly critical of the Labour Party in his older age, having been involved from a very young age, becoming one of the youngest MPs in 1950.

Tony Benn was given the freedom of the House of Commons in recognition of his service for half a century (one of only two MPs), whose 16 election wins were the most achieved by any Labour MP (Brivati, 2014).

Both Tony Benn and Bob Crow were active politicians, while Professor Stuart Hall was a distinguished sociologist of political, cultural and 'race' studies. Stuart Hall and Tony Benn were both towering intellectuals who died after long, full lives: Stuart Hall died in February 2014 at the age of 82, while Tony Benn died in March 2014, shortly before his 89th birthday. Both had close connections with second-wave feminism's developments from the 1960s.

Stuart Hall: politics, class, 'race' and education

Professor Stuart Hall met his wife, Catherine Barrett, in 1963 on an Aldermaston march, a demonstration campaigning for unilateral nuclear disarmament (CND) in the UK, and they married a year later.[2] Cath Hall became a second-wave feminist by the end of the 1960s, while also becoming an academic. During the heady days of British WLM, Cath helped organise the first socialist-feminist conference in Birmingham in 1974, a socialist offshoot of the national WLM conferences started in 1970. These were controversial times for the small but rapidly

---

[2]   *The Guardian* online obituary, 10 February, amended on 19 February 2014 to 'Stuart Hall and Catherine Barrett met in 1963, on the Campaign for Nuclear Disarmament march from Aldermaston to London.'

growing WLM, debating the balance between feminism and socialism. Since then, Cath Hall has pioneered historical studies of women's activities in the household, becoming a distinguished professor at UCL. *Family fortunes: Men and women of the English middle class 1750-1850* – co-authored with Leonore Davidoff (1987) – is a classic for family and feminist historians.

Her *White, male and middle class: Feminism and history* is a first study of what has become known as diversity or intersectionality, published as it was in 1992. Together with Heidi Mirza's (1992) *Young, female and Black* and Ann Phoenix's work *Young mothers*, it inaugurated a new wave of feminist studies on gender, class and 'race'. Cath also became editor of the journal *Feminist Review*, established by a collective in the 1980s, providing a platform for critical social commentary, alongside the more contentious *Trouble and Strife*, which was more of a magazine. She later became professor of history at UCL, continuing her historical studies of Victorian Britain and the legacies of slavery.

Together, Professors Cath and Stuart Hall forged a life around radical political, cultural and feminist ideas. This was represented in a celebratory film, made by Stuart's students in 2013, 'The Stuart Hall project'. In it, Stuart described how his associations with feminism had transformed his life in many and varied ways, forever. Obituaries of Stuart McPhail Hall called him the 'Godfather of multiculturalism', describing him as 'teacher, cultural theorist and campaigner, born 3 February 1932; died 10 February 2014', and 'Sociologist who influenced academic, political and cultural debate in Britain for over six decades.'

Tony Benn's connections with feminism are also important. In 1999, he had a plaque made to honour Emily Wilding Davison, the suffragette who was killed fighting for 'votes for women'.[3] It was placed on the door of a broom cupboard in the Houses of Parliament, where Davison had hidden on the night of the 1911 Census so that she could be counted as a Member of the House of Commons when women were still denied the vote! Tony Benn's daughter, Melissa Benn, is an excellent feminist writer, and she, too, is typical of the ripple effects of second-wave feminism. In *What should we tell our daughters?* (2013) she

---

[3]   This incident is a central feature in the film 'Suffragette'.

reviews the state of our knowledge about being a woman in an aggressively capitalist society. Melissa describes her family background, focusing on what made her into a feminist:

> Every woman, whatever her family, whatever her social class, will be able to register the impact of ... changes over several generations. My father's mother, Margaret Eadie, born in 1897 to Scottish "puritan agnostic Humanist" parents and strong supporters of the Liberal party, was not sent to school until she was seven; this, despite the fact that her father was Head of the English Department at Paisley Grammar School, and later Liberal MP. "Had I been a boy he would have sent me to school early and kept me hard at it, but he had no interest in the education of his daughters."[4] (Her father was also profoundly, if puzzlingly, opposed to women's suffrage.) Although used to discussing politics and religion at the family dining table, young Margaret was unable to read or write.... At fifteen she began to think seriously about her future: "Did I want a career or a family? In those days hardly any middle-class women contemplated both. It was felt that the two could not be combined without grave risk of strain for a marriage and neglect for the children." Although a natural scholar with a passion for theological study and discussion, my grandmother "chose" marriage; she did not receive a university education nor was she able to become a priest although she spent much of her adult life tenaciously campaigning for women to be admitted to the priesthood. As the mother of four sons – two of whom died: one in a still-birth, the other of a broken neck, incurred on his last ever operational flight in the Second World War – she never undertook any paid work. To the last, her role as wife and mother came first.

> My own mother, Caroline de Camp, born 1926, the eldest child of a well-off family from Cincinnati, USA, came to adulthood post war; this was a time in which women's beauty, domesticity and fecundity were prized: a period brilliantly dissected by Betty Friedan in *The feminine mystique* and creatively evoked in Mary

---

[4] Margaret Stansgate (1992) *My exit visa*, p 12, (taken from Benn, 2013, p 304).

McCarthy's *The group* or Sylvia Plath's *The bell jar*. My mother completed both an undergraduate degree and Master's ... but there was no serious expectation that she would have a career. Women of this era were not in serious worldly competition with men.... My mother was one of the lucky ones. Her intellectual and work life really took off once we children had left home; she became a respected scholar and campaigner.

Growing up in the sixties and seventies, I was one of the last generation of girls to be schooled at a time when male educational superiority was taken for granted. At the same time, second-wave feminism, led by a generation of educated young women and mothers, gave voice to a brooding sense of existential injustice on a range of personal and political fronts. I was fortunate to have a mother who thought it important to encourage intellectual ambition in girls although there was an unspoken ambiguity about what I might do with my intellect or education.... The period also enabled the rise of a new generation of working class girls to a lifestyle, influence and personal wealth that their forebears would only have dreamed of. I had mixed feelings about the 1980s. I admired, and envied, the new refusal of traditional feminine self-denial even as I disdained so much of the "me first" selfishness of the period. (Benn, 2013, pp 10-12)

Tony Benn: equality and education

The deaths of these three British socialists are important reminders of the controversial radical and revolutionary tendencies over the lifetime of women, especially women of my generation. According to tributes to Tony Benn, he inspired devotion and detraction – love and loathing in equal measure – but for most radicals, he gave inspiration to pursuing radical politics despite controversies. He became more, rather than less, radical as he grew older, finally leaving the House of Commons as an MP, about 10 years before he died, to devote himself to politics, as he put it acerbically. Tony topped several polls as the most popular politician in the UK, and was described as 'one of the few UK politicians to have become more left-wing after holding ministerial office.' After leaving Parliament, he was president of the Stop the War Coalition from 2001 until his death. The new Labour Party leader, Jeremy Corbyn, followed as chair, and there is a Facebook page called 'Tony Benn encouraged me'.

He was a Labour MP for over 50 years, and most significantly for me, he was MP for Bristol South East when I was in Bristol in the 1970s–80s. He was an inspirational figure to the rising Bristol WLM, including our campaigning for him. He was newsworthy in British politics, prior to the 1970s, because of his desire to relinquish the hereditary peerage, which his father received in 1942 for services to the Labour Party. Tony came from a politically active upper middle-class family, with both his grandfathers and his father being Liberal MPs. Tony's father, as Melissa noted, was a Liberal MP from 1906 who crossed the floor to the Labour Party in 1928. He was appointed Secretary of State for India by Ramsay MacDonald in 1929, a position he held until 1931, later rewarded with a hereditary peerage, becoming Viscount Stansgate in 1942. At this time, Tony's elder brother had no objections to inheriting a peerage, given his desire to be a priest. He, as Melissa also noted, was killed in an accident in the Second World War, leaving Tony as heir.

As Anthony Wedgwood Benn, he made several unsuccessful attempts to renounce the succession, the polar opposite of Viscountess Rhondda, discussed previously. When his father died in 1960, Tony was already a Labour MP, having become one in 1950.[5] On 1 November 1950, he was unexpectedly selected to succeed Sir Stafford Cripps as the Labour candidate for Bristol South East, after Cripps stood down because of ill health. He won the seat in a by-election on 30 November 1950. On his father's death, 10 years later, he automatically became a peer, preventing him from remaining an MP. Continuing to maintain

---

[5] Tony's mother, Margaret Wedgwood Benn (née Holmes, 1897–91), was a theologian, feminist and founder president of the Congregational Federation. She was a member of the League of the Church Militant, the predecessor to the Movement for the Ordination of Women. His mother's theology had a profound influence on him, as she taught him that the stories in the Bible were based around the struggle between the prophets and the kings, and that he ought, in his life, to support the prophets over the kings, who had power, as the prophets taught righteousness.

his right to abandon his peerage, Tony fought to retain his seat in a by-election on 4 May 1961 and although disqualified, he was re-elected. An election court declared the seat won by the Conservative runner-up, Malcolm St Clair, who was also the heir presumptive to a peerage. Tony continued his campaign outside Parliament, with the Conservative government eventually accepting the need for change in the law.

The Peerage Act 1963, allowing renunciation of peerages, became law on 31 July 1963. Tony Benn was the first peer to renounce his title, which he did instantly. St Clair, fulfilling an election promise, accepted the office of Steward of the Manor of Northstead, disqualifying himself from the House (outright resignation not being possible). Tony returned to the Commons after winning a by-election on 20 August 1963. From then he campaigned vigorously against such hereditary honours, but in a strange quirk of fate, his eldest son inherited the title of Viscount Stansgate on his father's death in 2014. Interestingly, however, Tony's campaigns against such titular honours led to subsequent reforms of the House of Lords, initiated by Labour in the 1990s (as we saw). When he served in Wilson's Labour government from 1964, the year after his campaign, the creation of hereditary peerages mostly ceased.

Tony would not consider reforms of peerages sufficiently egalitarian and inclusive of all classes, whether men or women. His late wife, Caroline Benn, devoted her life to comprehensive education, being co-founder of the Campaign for Comprehensive Education, famously sending their children to Holland Park Comprehensive, one of the first in the country. She was also a Labour member of the ILEA from 1970-77 and president of the Socialist Education Association. Her husband said of her, "she was my socialist soulmate." Melissa, her daughter, with Clyde Chitty, wrote *A tribute to Caroline Benn: Education and democracy* published in 2004, featuring essays on her life's work on educational reform, and Jane Martin, the feminist educational historian, is writing the official biography.

Political maelstrom of feminism, Bristol-style

The growth of second-wave feminism, from my point of view, was an exciting time in the Bristol WLM in the 1970s. It was a richly creative time with colleagues, both at the University of Bristol and the neighbouring then Bristol Polytechnic, now the University of the West of England (UWE), the name changing from the Further and Higher Education Act 1992, after I had left this most lovely city. Politics meshed with scholarly activities, from local to national politics, to the more radical WLM. These ranged from Wages for Housework, which was heavily contested, to debates on social policies for family allowances, later child tax credits, childcare and early childhood education. A particularly influential campaign was for a university nursery run by a parents' group, known as the University Nursery Parents' Association (UNPA). University opposition was huge and sexist, with many academic men arguing that they preferred car-parking facilities to nurseries, as their wives could look after the children! Caroline New and I developed a strong argument about these facilities in *For the children's sake*, published in 1985, drawing on arguments from many childcare campaigns, and with case studies of different provision across the country.

A founder member of the WLM in Bristol was Ellen Malos (as we saw in Chapter Three), and an interview with her is in the British Library's learning website. She also campaigned and researched areas from domestic violence, women's refuges, women workers' rights to local Labour politics, influencing our political involvement and teaching women's studies through BWSG. I, for example, ran for political office as a Labour Party member in the local government elections in 1977, sadly becoming bottom of the poll! Perhaps this was because I had then to use my married name, recently acquired, which was completely unfamiliar to those who knew me.

Many feminist colleagues were involved in the local Labour politics, subsequently becoming successful Labour MPs, such as Oonagh McDonald, who taught philosophy at the University of Bristol from 1965-76. She was elected MP for Thurrock in the 1976 by-election, leaving Bristol for Westminster in 1976. She became Parliamentary Private Secretary to the Chief Secretary to the Treasury in 1977, followed by being Opposition Spokesman during the 1980s, but at the 1987 general election, she lost Thurrock to the Conservative candidate, leaving politics to become a consultant. Similarly, Dawn Primarolo, who was born in London, studied at Bristol Polytechnic as a bookkeeper and legal secretary, returning to London in 1973. After marrying, she moved back to Bristol to raise her son, a contemporary of mine, also studying for a social sciences degree at Bristol Polytechnic, and later her doctoral studies into women and housing at the University of Bristol. Active in the WLM and the local Labour Party, in 1985 she was elected to Avon County Council, where she was vice chair of the Equal Opportunities Committee. She was first elected an MP at the 1987 general election, and was regarded as a 'hard left-winger', later becoming 'absolutely loyal to New Labour', serving in both the Blair and Brown governments. She remained a Labour MP until May 2015. Finally, Jean Corston arrived in Bristol in 1980 as the local Labour Party general secretary, also actively involved in local women's groups. Her partner from 1980 until his death in 2009 was Peter Townsend, professor of social policy at the University of Bristol, my 'boss' or head of department. Marrying in 1985 in Bristol, Jean went on to study law at LSE as a mature student, followed by becoming a barrister. She was elected an MP for Bristol East from April 1992 to 2005, stepping down at the general election. She was the first woman ever to hold the position of chair of the parliamentary Labour Party. On 29 June 2005 she was created Baroness Corston of St George in the County and City of Bristol. She was commissioned to report on vulnerable women in the British criminal justice system, published in March 2007, subsequently known as the Corston Report, outlining 'the need for a distinct radically different, visibly-led, strategic, proportionate, holistic, woman–centred, integrated approach.'

Illustrating the creative tensions in Bristol, mention should also be made of the work of the award-winning British poet, novelist and children's writer, Helen Dunmore. Educated at the University of York, she, too, arrived in Bristol in the 1970s, where she still lives, and she was also active in the WLM. Indeed, some of her children's books are now included in reading schemes for use in schools.

Becoming feminists Bristol-style, through university education

Feminist developments in Bristol were incredibly creative, energetic and generative of a culture of feminist education. For many, this was a radically different experience from those of the initial generation. Feminist materials influencing student learning and knowledge were co-created with second-wave feminist teachers. The importance of this personal and political learning and pedagogy was threaded throughout. Alison Assiter, now a distinguished professor of feminist philosophy at UWE, born on the cusp of 1950 in a London suburb, was 'first-in-the-family' to go to university:

I went to Bristol University in 1968 and I attended my first feminist group in Ellen Malos' house while I was in Bristol. But I was more active as a Marxist and socialist. I studied philosophy because I loved big questions and arguing! I realise now (after studying counselling!) that arguing with my father was formative for me and taught me to fight for causes.... I went on to do a BPhil in Oxford in philosophy of language, logic and philosophy of science and a PhD in Sussex which was political ... [and it] came out as a book ... so I was using feminist theories then but mainly in an individualist way. I started off being interested in the student movement but mainly Marxist politics and gradually saw the need for feminism.... I was influenced by Simone de Beauvoir and many Marxist feminists, Sandra Harding (later), Sheila Rowbotham, but also by fellow students at Oxford eg, Hilary Wainwright and then later many more.... I gradually incorporated feminism into my philosophical views. This was very difficult because the discipline did not then (and still in some ways does not) really recognise this. It is still a very male and masculine discipline.... Feminism has been very influential both for me and how I have worked ... in as many ways as possible – theories: politics and through taking on management roles in universities ... often being the only woman in the role and trying to carry it out in different ways, sometimes influenced, strangely, by the care ethic.... I was active in feminist campaigns...: I was a founder member of Women in Philosophy, but before that I was reading and thinking from a feminist perspective and trying to incorporate this into philosophy (which was and still is very difficult!).... And I got involved in Radical Philosophy and also activist women's groups and more recently activism against Islamic fundamentalism (through my activities with Iranian women)....

This mix of political, personal and being a 'professional' academic, characterises many of this generation of students from the 1970s. Professor Claire Callender (now professor of higher education at both Birkbeck and the Institute of Education, UCL) was unusual in that both her parents are university educated. She herself went to:

... Bristol University to study social policy as I had wanted to be a social worker. I was "radicalised" at university although family was influential ... subliminally! Mother was very independent and my current partner shares my values ... feminism has been very influential – especially in my personal life and the early part of my professional life – mostly academic interest but some activism eg, helping start a women's training workshop.... It influenced my choice of PhD topic and subsequent research and teaching informed by feminism ... my focus was on women and the labour market so I used Hartman on marrying socialism and feminism and Hilary Land on ... analysing social policy from a feminist perspective....

Another graduate student at the University of Bristol, Professor Sheila Riddell, now at the University of Edinburgh, told me about her modest family circumstances and how she was quite timid about her politics, becoming first a schoolteacher and only later doing a doctorate in education, transferring into HE. She is quite typical of many women, not only influenced by her academic teachers, but also from being 'first-in-the-family'. She is from:

... a lower middle-class family (dad a local authority clerk, mum didn't work from the point that she got married. She had previously worked as an untrained primary school teacher).... Brought up as a Catholic. Rejected the religion at a very young age but kept a sense of social justice. Decided I was a communist and atheist round the age of 11 – didn't go down well *en famille*.... Was a bit wary of women's group at Sussex [university] ... I didn't particularly engage with student politics at university – the politicos were generally more middle class than me. I was terrified of failing and worked very hard. I met my boyfriend when I was 19 and led quite a domestic existence. However, Sussex was infused with an air of questioning and liberalism ... didn't really get into feminism until I was teaching and became pregnant – everyone assumed I would leave my job – I wanted to carrying on working. Feminism suddenly made sense and I read avidly. Started a women's group in Puddletown where I lived [Dorset] and ran girls' groups in school. Went to Greenham Common and became an activist.... My feminism developed in opposition to my mum, who was an Irish Catholic Tory. She scoffed at ideas she didn't understand and when I was a teenager tried to suggest that certain books, ideas etc were not suitable. This made them all the more appealing. She insisted on referring to feminism as "wim lib".... Feminism is hugely influential. PhD at Bristol [in the School of Education] with [now Professor] Sandra Acker as my supervisor was on gender and education. I learned a lot more about feminist thinking and research from her. I attempted to place my experiences within school within a theoretical context. I have branched into other areas since (including disability studies and additional support needs) but always influenced by theories of social (in)equality....

Another storm in a teacup? Everyday sexism and feminism under Thatcher

Many 'education feminists' told me similar stories about how influential their feminist teachers had been, largely for their doctoral studies, and not only in Bristol. This cultivation of feminism through the university was becoming usual as the field of feminism and women's studies began to grow. At the same time, with the expansion of global HE came a right-wing backlash. In the UK this was exemplified by the rise of Thatcherism, with Mrs Thatcher coming to power in 1979, followed by Reagan's rise to power in the US in 1982. There has been an enormous amount of scholarship about Thatcherism and the 'great moving right show', as Stuart Hall dubbed it in *Marxism Today*. The analysis then was of both economic conservatism and social liberalism, with relatively little of feminism in the mainstream critiques. A major re-assessment of *The legacy of Thatcherism* (Farrall and Hay, 2014), arising from a seminar series hosted at the British Academy, also only pays limited attention to women's equality and feminism by contrast with social inequalities and poverty. I was asked to contribute a paper/chapter on family policy, but felt marginalised by the weight of the other contributors and chapters. These, it felt to me, ignored the irresistible rise of feminism under Thatcherism.

Given Lord Geoffrey Howe's death,[6] I was reminded of how difficult it was to comment then on what nowadays we would call 'everyday sexism'. 'Sex and social policy' was the title of a chapter written with Hilary Land about the progress of equalities legislation for women under Thatcher. Published in 1983 in *The future of the welfare state: Remaking social policy*, an edited collection from a Fabian Society seminar (Glennerster, 1983), we commented on the fact that Lady Howe, wife of the incoming Chancellor of the Exchequer, Sir Geoffrey, resigned her post as deputy chairman (sic) of the EOC in 1979, a post she had held since 1975. Lady Howe had become another mature woman student of social administration at LSE where the book was required reading, and sued us for libel. I personally had written the offending sentences about the argument that 'there should not be two breadwinners in the family' (David and Land, 1983, p 144). My mother, among others, could not understand why she found our comments libellous. Surely most normal married women would give up a job on their husband gaining a senior government post?

We were impugning her commitment to equal opportunities by questioning her resignation: indeed, it was a lukewarm commitment. Another storm in a teacup? It was a frightening time, as neither Hilary nor I had much support from the university or the union (Association of University Teachers, AUT), but there was no name at the time for this kind of 'bullying or harassment'. Eventually the publishers settled out-

---

6 Obituaries in *The Guardian* and *The Observer*, 11 October 2015.

of-court with the Howes. Copies of the book were recalled, and the offending sentences removed before further copies were published. We had been radicalised and feminised by this incident of everyday sexism.

Being 'radicalised' and 'feminised' through critical and political education was a major theme for all of us. Like Sheila, many budding feminists were from working-class families, and mothers when they returned to study. In 1986, I moved to London to what then was South Bank Polytechnic, later becoming South Bank University in 1992, subsequently London South Bank University. I was appointed head of a large (by university standards) and multidisciplinary social sciences department. It already had a reputation for feminist work, conducted variously by Dr Dulcie Groves and the late Dr Mary McIntosh, both of whom had left.

By this time, I, too, was a mother with primary-age schoolchildren, for whom the University of Bristol nursery had been vital. Juggling my children's educational lives with my own feminist and 'managerial' work proved far more complex than I had anticipated, leading to major controversies with colleagues. 'Prima donna inter pares', borrowing the title from an article I had read about Mrs Thatcher, was about my personal struggles in managing feminist and other social scientists (David, 1989a). This provoked colleagues to question whether I should have aired these issues in public rather than 'keep it within the family community of academics'. Academic departments harboured political and professional debates about feminist studies!

Setting up the inaugural Social Sciences Research Centre (SSRC) with students and colleagues proved relatively less troublesome. During this time, I had several doctoral students who told similar stories of becoming feminists through their education and being mothers. For example, now Professor Rosalind Edwards, of the University of Southampton, who subsequently became director of the SSRC, told me that she was born in Brighton and moved to London, only to return to live in her paternal grandmother's house with her partner and five children:

I went to Brighton Poly. I was 30, with five children. My partner and I had moved down to Brighton from London about six years earlier. I did social administration as I wanted to be a social worker at the time and that seemed to [be] most obvious route. Really wanted to do sociology at Sussex University but going to a university rather than poly seemed rather intimidating at the time.... We are a middle-class Jewish family though not practising very much.... I had a vague knowledge of feminism from my late teens, but I think that I only considered myself a feminist once I started studying with the Open University (OU) prior to going to Brighton Poly [a new university]. I can remember challenging some of the lecturers at the OU summer school on the second level course I took because I thought that some of Barthes' (who we were studying) ideas were sexist.... I then went to LSE for an MA and to South Bank to do my PhD on "mature women student returners".... Feminism has been a part of my learning and life – relationships within my family and my academic career.... I used to have debates with my own parents and actually fell out with my parents-in-law because they thought that I was turning their son into a wimp (he did washing up and childcare!). If my husband hadn't been supportive I think we would have split up. I brought my children up with knowledge of feminism.... I hope I've made some contribution to academic feminism. I've not been involved in much activism. I don't feel good about that last bit.... Lots of women influences – too numerous to mention them all. Socialist-feminist ideas. They were influential because they spoke to me.... I've been part of a women's workshop since my PhD days. It's still going – now led by younger career researchers – and I'm still part of it....

Diane Reay, now professor of education at the University of Cambridge, was also a doctoral student with Ros, arriving as another example of Ros' work, as a mature woman/mother student, but in this case, from having been a primary schoolteacher to do a doctorate. Although Diane was of my generation, like many other second-wave feminists, she initially became a (feminist) schoolteacher. She, too, was from a working-class background and 'first-in-the-family' to go to university, developing her feminist persona through her studies:

I went to Newcastle to read politics and economics because my father thought English, which was my first choice, led nowhere! And we were both very interested in politics. Economics was by default. I then did a PGCE primary course at Newcastle College of Education.... I was a feminist in my teens but doing economics with all-male teaching staff and an all-male student cohort apart from myself strengthened my feminism.... I was always a feminist and was involved ... in pacifism and CND in a very male university when I was a student. I was arrested because I invaded the rugby pitch in Newcastle ... when South Africa was playing. I was in [the] Socialist Workers Party and it was very macho and not at all feminist and I was disciplined for inappropriate dress ... saw that as part of my feminism ... very male and on economics course where I was the only woman ... very difficult and aware of feminist issues.... I got an economics essay back saying why was I writing about gender ... 1970s activism in a residents' group.... I have always tried to live a feminist life and work in feminist ways, but more specifically I was involved in FAAB (Feminists Against Academic Bollocks) for a number of years [in the early 21st century] and intervened in academic debates through performance and parody. I have also always fought for improving the rights of women, both in schools and universities. As a schoolteacher in the 1980s I was a member of the anti-sexist working party, and we agitated to improve the situation of girls in schools and produced anti-sexist learning materials. We held girls-only conferences and taught girls-only groups in mixed-sex schools. As an academic I was actively involved in improving the rights and conditions of researchers – nearly all women – and am still trying to improve the conditions and status of researchers [in Cambridge].... It is now a totally different world – I entered under Thatcherism. I think it has got worse....

Heidi Safia Mirza, now a professor at Goldsmiths College, University of London, with Bev Skeggs, was appointed at South Bank while I was head, and jointly supervised Diane's thesis with me. She, too, was a very young mother as an undergraduate student and 'first-in-the-family' to go to university. She had been radicalised by racism before feminism, saying:

I went to an all-girls' school in Trinidad, which was quite high achieving in a gendered way. High-achieving girls didn't mean careers for girls; it meant good wives for husbands! The school was started by my grandmother, about 30 years before I had gone there. So there was a tradition of education among the women in the family. My aunts in Trinidad were all teachers – so there were strong female "role models" in my early life – but they lived very traditional lives in a very patriarchal culture. Growing up in Trinidad I was very influenced by the black power movement in the early 70s – I remember seeing Angela Davis on the TV – speaking confidently to crowds and raising her hand in a black power salute. I thought she was amazing. We had an attempted coup on the island – black power was an empowering political vision and a crucible for my postcolonial/black feminist thinking. When we came back to England in 1973 we lived in Brixton and I went to the local school. The racism there was incredible. I was determined to show the teachers and the girls in the school that I was as good as them, if not better.... I do think I was racialised before I was feminised! That came later at university when I got married. It was so important to get a place at university that was funded!... If I was growing up today I would not have that chance. It was an opportunity that was there for everybody. HE was being opened out for the working classes, and for girls as well, and it was seen as a natural progression. When I graduated ... it was very racist times in the UK, with the National Front in its zenith. It was very hard to get a job, and on top of that, I had a young baby. I had got a first for my dissertation, so I sent off to Goldsmiths College sociology department and I got an ESRC quota award in 1981. This amazing opportunity changed my life! My PhD thesis was a small-scale ethnography of young Caribbean girls like myself in a London school. Because of my experience, I wanted to write about interplay between career choices and educational structures. So in a way, the thesis was about my own life, it was a process of exploring the practices of racism and exclusion that I saw around me. *Young female and Black* became a best-selling book with Routledge. It was a carthartic thing to see it in print. I am amazed it did so well. At the time it was very exciting for me ... [but] there was a lot of sexual harassment of young women students by male lecturers in universities ... a group of women academics ...

got together to speak out about their transgressions ... but ... no one would ... risk everything.... At least as women we felt some safety in numbers and found common ground and solace with each other. I began to learn about feminist theory from them. In 1985 I worked in Thomas Coram as a part-time researcher with amazing feminists like Ann Oakley and Ann Phoenix.... My life chances shaped my feminism, which then spilled over into my academic development. My marriage was very pivotal for me as a black/postcolonial feminist. I got married in my first year of university when I was 19, and I had my daughter as I was leaving in the third year. In fact, I was very pregnant when I sat my finals! My husband was a very devout Muslim, and I wasn't! I converted to Islam during the time of the first Muslim uprisings in the 70s. There was a growing anti-imperialistic movement among the African and Middle Eastern students at university. For the first time I really felt I had a cause. I became personally politicised and wore a headscarf (hijab). Ironically, for the first time in my life, I understood about dignity and respect for women – that is, not to be seen as a sexualised object, but to be myself. So ironically I became feminised through Islam.... My degree built my confidence as a woman which I had not got at school ... there was a lot of passion and activism in what I was doing. Rayah Feldman was a part-time tutor ... who supervised my dissertation ... on women's issues ... we later worked together at South Bank – I was bowled over by the opportunity to be there! I met such wonderful feminists who have become lifelong friends and colleagues!

University education and American feminism

The American feminist Wendy Luttrell, now a distinguished professor at the Graduate Center of New York University, also told me that it was through her university that she had been radicalised and feminised, as she was one of the first generation in her family to go to college:

I was born in Chicago, Illinois, USA, in 1953.... Because of my mother's aspirations (for herself and her children) she raised us as Methodists and then Presbyterians as we became more and more comfortable. This is relevant in the sense that some of my earliest activism and interest in social theory came from my involvement with the church – my "confirmation" in 1966 included reading E.P. Thomson's *Making of the English working class* which was transforming, and being involved in the civil rights movement when living in Kansas City, Kansas. My politicisation was in conflict with my parents who were conservative Republicans.... I went to the University of Pennsylvania in Philadelphia in 1971, drawn to their new interdisciplinary urban studies programme. I was in the first cohort of this programme, and I was, in general, fascinated by cities, immigration issues, ethnic/"race" relationships. I had a "work-study" fellowship that enabled me to attend, and was partially supported by my great aunt "Doll", who was excited by the possibility that the first Luttrell would go to college. She sent a cow to slaughter and gave me the proceeds. My work-study job was in the library where I shelved books 20 hours a week. I would say I was first introduced to a collective sense of feminism in my first year in university when I became involved in the anti-war movement and met older women activists who recruited me into their women's circle. I then became part of the "women's centre" group that organised two things: a "university without walls" that would teach courses about women and women's contribution to society and demand various things of the university, including better lighting on campus (there had been many rapes on campus), a childcare centre and the first official "women's studies" course. I enrolled in this women's studies course on Virginia Woolf and admit I found it boring. English wasn't my subject, sociology was, and it hadn't yet any faculty offering women's studies. In junior year I went to Boston, Massachusetts, to work in one of Jonathan Kozol's "free schools", and became involved in a socialist feminist group that met at a women's bookstore in Cambridge, Massachusetts. And after I graduated, I became involved in a women's community education centre.... I was part of a larger community of women in Philly who were involved in women's healthcare, rape crisis centres, domestic abuse centres, women's legal services and women's educational access and learning centres.... I sang in a women's choir, and there was an underlying tension between gay and straight women, in all these various activities. I co-founded the Women's College Program, and after working there for two years, went off to University of California, Santa Cruz, to study

sociology. I didn't really envision myself becoming an "academic"....
I more or less backed into becoming an "academic" – and would
say that my feminism has influenced every life and career choice
that I have made along the way. Mostly I would say my feminist
"activism" has been more local than global, always finding myself
involved in organisations dedicated to improving women's lives,
and that my feminist academic contribution has been equally
theoretical and practice-based.... I have a PhD in sociology from the
University of California, Santa Cruz. My three areas were "family,
community studies, gender".... When I arrived, I was part of a
small cohort of 10 students, one of whom was my ex-husband.
I was called into the department chair's office and told that he
was worried about letting a married couple into the programme,
warning me that I would not be taken seriously as a scholar if I were
to get pregnant. While this was an explicit message, the implicit
message among the women faculty was that they were all single
or married without children – having a child in my second year
of graduate school was very unusual at the time. I would say that
my feminism was both strengthened and questioned by virtue of
what I think was becoming aware of a certain kind of "careerism"
within the academy that required women to forgo having children
at earlier ages in order to succeed. Issues of family–work "balance"
– a misnomer in my mind – have been central to me personally,
professionally and intellectually all my life.... I always use feminist
work in my own teaching – starting with the very first adult literary
classes I taught in 1977 – using Tillie Olsen, for example – and
developing an adult literacy curriculum using women's own life
stories....

Feminists teaching for a change

I now want to turn to look at how education clearly has the
power to transform lives, through its ripple effects. How might
we design feminist pedagogies to enhance this? I have chosen an
illustrative story of ongoing commitments to feminist education,
by the American Frinde Maher, now a retired professor of
education, living in the US. She is clearly a second-wave feminist,
telling me that it took her a while to become:

... a feminist after university and after 10 years of high school history teaching, at the same time that I began my college teaching career. Although I had been in a consciousness-raising (CR) group in the late 1960s, it didn't really take – I spent the 60s as an anti-Vietnam war activist and a socialist revolutionary who thought that the women's movement was secondary to the workers' movement to overthrow capitalism. Since the early 1980s, until 2008, I was a college professor of both education (which meant that I trained secondary school teachers) and women's studies. My college, Wheaton College, was an all-women's college until 1988, and the faculty benefited from grants from the government and private foundations to include study of women into the curriculum. The study groups that these grants sponsored for faculty became my introduction to feminism as theory, history, pedagogy and activist practice. I joined the ranks of academic feminists as soon as I came to Wheaton and because my field was pedagogy, or classroom practice, my research field became feminist pedagogy.... *The feminist classroom: Dynamics of gender, race and privilege* sought to influence fellow academic feminists to see the classroom as a site of feminist activism and feminist knowledge-making.... As a college professor, I always taught and did research from a feminist perspective. My classroom was always discussion-based and collaborative, as has been much of my writing. Both *The feminist classroom* and *Privilege and diversity in the academy*, our second book, were researched and written with Mary Kay Tetreault.... Feminist pedagogies have been at the base of my research and teaching for many years. Since the 1990s, however, I have been equally interested in the progress that women and people of colour have made to become members of the professoriate. *Privilege and diversity in the academy* is based on research done at three American universities to find out on what terms, in what departments and disciplines, based on what kinds of policies, have these "newcomers" joined the faculties. We interviewed over 100 people at the University of Michigan, Stanford University, and the University of Rutgers in Newark. We found out that a "hidden curriculum" of racism, sexism and classism keeps people out of academic careers and that explicit hiring policies promoting diversity are necessary.... The publication of this book has led me to visit colleagues in South Africa for many years now, especially going to the University of the Western Cape, which is a formerly "coloured" university outside of Cape Town. There, my colleague Beverly Thaver is doing similar work on "deracialising" the formerly all-white professoriate at South African universities, and we have collaborated on research and presentations on our results.... In the work for our second book we have found that there has been a lot of change at the policy and official level, differing by department and by institution. Day care centres, maternity leaves, more flexible tenure policies and explicit policies to hire women and minorities are much more common now, although still few and far between nationwide. Some places, like the University of Michigan, are much more progressive in this regard than others.... Studies and gender studies, to use the new turn of phrase, can influence the modern university by sticking to the feminist agenda of international equality and international rights, for women, but for everyone.... I ... have students from all over the world doing important feminist work in local settings. An example – the student who worked in a women's health centre in Mongolia, whose official policies on abortion were much more progressive than anywhere in the US right now.... I think that the future of the university depends on courses, curricula and subjects that are neither the liberal arts of the past nor the instrumental "career"-based subjects of the current day. Right now in the US universities are increasingly divided between elite schools, both private and a few public, for the few who can afford it, who are being trained in the liberal arts and "critical thinking" to run society, and the rest of the public university system, which is being systematically starved of funds and increasingly made to focus on narrow training for careers in industry and technology. Feminists can call for and enact a new liberal arts curriculum, based on history, literature, psychology, sociology and the sciences, for and about the many and not the few, for and about working people in the US and Britain, but also South Africa and Indonesia and Somalia and Yemen, to bring the concerns of women in each and all of these places together in conversation – a conversation in which Western privilege and exploitation, women's as well as men's, is fully acknowledged and dealt with. Academic feminism is fully up to this task, although, as always, it will take a social movement outside the walls of the academy, which I am not sure is there right now. I think HE must be public and widespread, and that public funding should be its basis. The US should follow the *old* tuition policies in the UK rather than the other way around, and both countries should expand, of course, rather than constrict access as they are doing now. It is a hard time for the academy, for feminism, and for academic feminism. Time for another women's movement!

Ripple effects of feminism

It is clear that there have been many routes into feminism, in transforming women's lives and turning them into passionate pedagogues, concerned about social and gender justice above all. While some of these routes have remained primarily political, other routes for later generations and cohorts have been more clearly through diverse forms of education and the desire to transform it and the wider society to be more equal, more egalitarian, less exclusive and elitist.

I want to end on a personal note, introducing my dear friend and a former colleague, the American feminist educator, Kathleen Weiler, to a current colleague, Jessica Ringrose, who is professor of gender and education, originally from Canada. When I mentioned to Jessica that Kathleen was visiting London, she was incredibly excited to meet her, as she had used Kathleen's educational and feminist work when she was working on her doctorate, back in Canada, some 10 years or more ago. Somewhat like a star-struck teenager, she came over for dinner, clutching Kathleen's edited collection *Feminist engagements* (2001), and begged her to sign her copy.

Both were very touched by this small act of feminist engagement. Perhaps even more interestingly, Jessica had introduced me to a feminist high school teacher from New York who also happened to be visiting – Ileana Jimenez. Ileana, who definitely sees herself as a third-wave feminist, proudly wearing the t-shirt, was also excited to witness this small act, and more importantly, to learn of all the earlier feminist work that had been done for and on behalf of teachers in school, work that she had not encountered before, despite being a very prominent feminist high school teacher in the US.

We turn now to consider the resurgence of feminism among women who were born in the last 40 years, to see what kinds of waves they are making – political, social and educational.

SIX

A feminist resurgence

There has been a dramatic resurgence of politically engaged and public feminisms in the 21st century. The encroachment of capitalism into ever-increasing forms of digitisation, sexualisation and pornification of the culture has enabled both feminist and other, including misogynistic, critiques. The 'selfie' generation is a good way to typify the impact of this kind of competitive, individualistic and 'academic capitalism'. The question is whether this is one new generation or several competing and contested approaches to the new public order of global neoliberalism. Is it similar to or different from previous generations? The very notion of resurgence implies the idea of an ocean or sea waves – it is as if a new wave is emerging during the early 21st century. Feminism is used online, in the media, politics and in HE. But what precisely does it mean to call oneself a 'feminist' today? Are there different tendencies, or *Fifty shades*, as Appignanesi and her colleagues (2013) put it?

It seems to me that feminism is everywhere and yet nowhere influential or powerful. It is everywhere in the sense that some politicians claim the term, such as, most recently, Justin Trudeau in his Canadian election victory (October 2015); yet it remains anathema for some. In October 2014 in the UK some politicians wore a t-shirt saying 'This is what a feminist looks like', including the Prime Minister David Cameron, in celebration of the Fawcett Society's campaigns over 150 years. But I feel that this was merely window-dressing and not at all serious. So in some senses, it is still nowhere.

When I went to Brighton to give a public lecture entitled 'Higher education: A feminist critique', the young man who introduced me was very pleased that I claimed to be a 'feminist academic activist'. This was in contrast to their previous speaker, in the lecture series on 'What should universities be?', namely, Lord David Willetts, the Conservative politician whose ideas I was contesting. The purpose of my lecture was the influence of different waves of feminism on HE in the past and present. When I was starting out, the term 'feminism' had been abhorred, and it took me some time to claim the term. I recall specifically why I did so, as mentioned in Chapter Three. And I claimed the term proudly as it was indeed an epiphany or an Eureka moment for me.

In this chapter I want to engage with some of the younger generations of women scholar activists with whom I have worked. These range from feminists from my recent European-funded research project into challenging gender violence for children and young people to friends and colleagues around the GEA and other HE settings. I have written about the implications for educational policies in a mainstream text, *A feminist manifesto for education* (David, 2016: in press). Here, however, I want to muse about the impacts that I, among others, have had on feminist activism in the academy and in the wider world. Have we contributed to the resurgence of feminism and, at one and the same time, the backlash against women's impact on social change? In my study *Feminism, gender and universities* (2014), I referred to these women as my third cohort – women born between 1965 and 1980 – who learned their lessons from earlier generations of second-wave feminists. I want to consider their feminism, and how our interactions have changed my views and approaches, just as I and others may have influenced them.

Subsequent generations of younger feminists may consider themselves third-wave, as I mentioned Ileana Jimenez doing, and she is of the age of this third cohort, or even fourth- or fifth-wave feminists, if the wave analogy remains apposite. My young 'fourth-wave' feminist colleague, Emily Henderson, critiquing my study, mentioned how her 'generation' was missing from my study, although she appeared in the photograph on the cover. She linked this to her own work, *Gender pedagogy: Teaching, learning and tracing gender in higher education* (2015), published while still completing her doctorate.

As I was putting the finishing touches to my study, I wrote in the *Times Higher Education* about my stories of three generations of second-wave feminism (David, 2013). I had a range of passionate replies, including one on the website, which endorsed my cohort analysis, recounting her own epiphany in going to Greenham. Catherine Harper wrote on 9 February 2013 that:

> I'd fall into the third group of women. Background in rural Northern Ireland during the Troubles, politicised in the context, but "found" feminism via CND, animal rights and the NI peace movement. Went by boat and train to Greenham Common and had my "epiphany". Self-defined feminist ever since: it colours everything I do, and as I've become older I've realised just how vital that "awareness" is, both of the continued inequalities for women in academia and beyond, but also how tied to other inequalities – LGBTQI, race, ability, age – feminism is. It's the full flavour of my life, and recently I've adopted a "presence, voice, partnership, principle, persistence" mantra as a way of ensuring I (with a capital 'I'!) maintain it proactively. I've always been very moved by other women's stories of their "personal political" struggles, and the piece above was very good to read.

I was recently asked by one of my colleagues, Fin Cullen, to review a book for *Women's Studies International Forum*. I accepted because it seemed a quick way of getting up with the latest international work on feminism, especially among younger generations, and so it proved. *This is what a feminist slut looks like: Perspectives on the SlutWalk Movement* (Teekah et al, 2015) is about how viral feminism went in response to comments by Toronto police constable Michael Sanguinetti in January 2011. The four Canadian editors mention in the introduction that he argued that:

> ... women should stop "dressing like sluts" in order to avoid sexual violence, although it is pertinent to note that founders' always saw Sanguinetti's comments as merely emblematic of a broader rape culture deserving of protest. (Teekah et al, 2015, p 6)

They illustrate the similarities and differences between waves of feminism, drawing on the work of women of my third cohort. Jessica Ringrose's work with Emma Renold (2012) gets an important mention for their powerful analysis, drawing on the third-wave feminist, Judith Butler, of what is called 'feminist politics of re-articulation'. The word 'slut' is reclaimed from its negative imagery and rehabilitated (Teekah et al, 2015, p 3). They state that:

> Feminist organising has often solidified around particular rallying points. The first wave of the women's movement gained traction around organising for women's right to vote and the push for Prohibition. Likewise, the women's movement of the 1960s and 1970s gained solidarity looking at abortion and women's rights within both familial and employment roles.... Despite both legal and substantive gains for women, however, women of every age, sexual orientation, race and class continue to experience sexual violence. While all women, gender non-binary folks, and trans folks are at risk of violence, this threat is greater for women in particular locations, especially women of colour and with disabilities. SlutWalk responded to the epidemic of violence, but it did not emerge exclusively in response.... (Teekah et al, 2015, p 3)

They then try to argue about whether SlutWalk represents 'the fourth, fifth or sixth wave', saying:

> ... in many respects, SlutWalk appeared to be uniquely contemporary feminist actions. The passion of the movement and its specific manifestation in the gleeful spectacle which ensued drew on the camp sensibilities that are often ascribed to "third wave" feminism... It remains too soon to truly assess the long-lasting impact of SlutWalk on the face of feminism. It is our supposition, however, that SlutWalk has the capacity to live on as a pivotal event in feminist engagement, especially for young women.... Nonetheless, SlutWalks may have, in their capacity to shift complacency, moved a generation. (Teekah et al, 2015, pp 7-8)

Before moving on to the stories of feminists who may consider themselves beyond second, third or even fourth wave, I briefly review the contested nature of a feminist resurgence in the media.

Rise of feminist activism in the 21st century

Examples of the welcome new rise in feminist activism can be found in British media, with *The Guardian* and *The Observer* newspapers leading the way. It seems that we, as earlier generations of feminists, have been highly successful, at least in some media, but is this really the case? How extensive and enduring has this success been? A new magazine, *Feminist Times*, modelled on the 1970s British feminist magazine *Spare Rib*, was inaugurated with great controversy about its provenance and approach in 2013. One of its instigators, Charlotte Raven, wrote to celebrate its publication (2013). Articles entitled 'Feminism is offensive', with the byeline 'The attempt to rebrand the women's movement is a sure sign that we are doing something right'[1] and 'We still need angry voices', 'Whatever its name, a new feminist magazine is needed more than ever'[2] appeared together, alongside other articles that either ignore gender or relegate it to an insignificant question. So women's and feminist voices are often seen as rather frightening, a symptom of media misogyny about women's place in the public sphere.

A new British lobbying organisation, which also mirrors earlier feminist campaigning in the 1960s and 1970s, has sprung up, known as UK Feminista, led by Kat Banyard, campaigning for legal and media transformations with a set of new 'demands'. Everyday Sexism, led by Laura Bates, is another British example of such online and media action. These two young women, former students, have also written about the issues and their campaigns (see Banyard, 2010; Bates, 2014a). There are many feminist journalists such as Laurie Penny and Bidisha, also both former students and younger than my third cohort. These women are usually seen as 'fourth-wave', by contrast with third-wave feminists such as Naomi Wolf and Naomi Klein in the US,

---

[1] *The Guardian*, 8 October 2013, p 34.
[2] Ibid, p 13.

and Natasha Walter in the UK – women who make sexuality explicit, such as LGBTQi in politics.

An intriguing reversal of the role of HE in contributing to feminist engagement is Caitlin Moran, a young British journalist on *The Times* without any formal education, and certainly not any university education, starting off as a journalist aged 16 and now of the third cohort's generation. She published a very feisty and successful book, *How to be a woman* (2011), paying homage to its feminist inspiration, Germaine Greer, recreating feminist political commitments rather than a more measured academic feminism. This led her to develop a TV series entitled 'Living with wolves', with a feminist edge and theme, and to her becoming a feminist icon and stand-up comedienne.

A most exciting campaign to have a woman reinstated on English banknotes, in the wake of the controversy to remove the only woman from them, was launched single-handedly and successfully by Caroline Criado-Perez in 2013. She described how she used new media such as Twitter and Facebook to get her campaign heard speedily and vocally, while at the same time studying for her Master's degree at LSE. She, too, has certainly learned her lessons from her feminist teachers extremely well. She represents a welcome new face of feminism for the 21st century, although her campaign was for a very modest issue, the face of women in the banking or economic system!

Are the women of these younger generations – the 'daughters' of second-wave feminists – aligned with radical and socialist feminist critiques, or have the ripple effects turned into new waves?[3] What is particularly noticeable is the transformation in feminist knowledge rather than feminist values: how these women build on feminist wisdom, gleaned by previous generations. Education is particularly important here: knowledge and ideas mostly learned at school, college or university, illustrating women coming of age, during the expansionary period of global academia of the 1990s, in which gender issues and feminism in academia had achieved a legitimate, if not inclusive, space and place. These women have tended to raise

---

[3] Suzanne Moore, a feminist journalist, wrote 'Generation Y and their parents deserve better' in *The Guardian*, 21 March 2014.

lesbian and queer issues to the fore, linked especially with the post-structural work of Judith Butler, known as 'genderqueer'. Questions of diversity, identity and ethnicity seem to be more urgent and pressing. The women I had conversations with were passionate and had a strong sense of the continuing importance of feminist education, of a vital task yet to be accomplished. Academic women's place remained subordinate and not assured, and some argued that, as the renowned feminist Hester Eisenstein (2009) would put it, feminism has been 'seduced' by corporate models of action, belief and goals. 'Socialist-feminism has lost out to this seduction.'

This comment is confirmed by another example of feminist resurgence from the US. Sheryl Sandberg is chief operating officer of Facebook, whose new book was published in the UK with great fanfare in the spring of 2013. Entitled *Lean In: Women, work, and the will to lead*, it develops an argument, ostensibly supported by the older 'liberal' US feminist Gloria Steinem, to help women stop sabotaging and limiting themselves in the workplace. Sheryl is a Harvard-educated economist, who went on to work with the former president of Harvard University, Larry Summers (who resigned in 2008 over his comments about women's brains being smaller than men's). She has had a meteoric business career, becoming the most senior woman at Facebook at a relatively young age, itself a young organisation for the digital media age. She has thus imbibed the spirit of capitalism and liberal feminism with a vengeance, and now writes to advise women on how to take a leaf out of her book. What is clear is the paradox of hyper-capitalism, with such a woman at one of its helms, and the attempts still to use new social media as a platform for feminisms. *The Guardian* and its sister Sunday paper *The Observer* devoted several pages and column inches to interviews, reviews and comments on this phenomenon. The journalist Maureen Dowd (2013) wrote:

> She has a grandiose plan to become the PowerPoint Pied Piper in Prada ankle boots reigniting the women's revolution – *Betty Friedan for the digital age*. She wants women to stop limiting and sabotaging themselves. Sandberg may mean well ... but she doesn't understand the difference between a social movement

and a social networking marketing campaign. People come to a
social movement from the bottom up, not the top down. She has
co-opted the vocabulary and romance of a social movement not
to sell a cause, but herself.... (emphasis added)

Let's now consider how influential second-wave feminism has
been in educating new waves of feminists, and how creative
these new generations have been in opening up issues, at least
for public scrutiny, even if the solutions, educational and/or
political, seem far off. These women are far more diverse than
previous generations, as HE has expanded and drawn in yet more
women who are first-generation and working-class, but also even
more mobile internationally than previous generations, as Terri
Kim and Rachel Brooks,[4] also two of this generation/cohort,
have shown. Women's lives in academe, particularly, but not
only, as students, may be more subject to sexual harassment and
violence than hitherto. How is it that women's lives in education
and HE are more unsafe, risky and hazardous than for previous
generations, when so much more explicit feminist education
has been taken seriously? Is it that these issues are particularly
threatening, and threatening to male authority and power?

I now want to illustrate the continuities and changes in the
feminist activist and political work of this generation, using
some of the stories from good friends and colleagues of mine.
They are all feminists struggling with working in neoliberal and
austere times, especially within global academe.

Educated to become feminists

Carolyn Jackson is now a distinguished professor at Lancaster
University, and has been chair of the UK's GEA. She has done
some very exciting work on 'lad cultures', especially in HE. I
have known Carolyn since she was a young graduate student over
20 years ago, when she was thinking about her own experiences
in HE. I found her comments very moving about when she first

---

[4]   Terri Kim from South Korea, and now a reader in HE at the University of
East London, and Rachel Brooks, professor of sociology, at the University
of Surrey.

became aware of feminist issues, given that she came from an unusual family background where she was 'first-in-the-family' to go to university:

> This is a tricky one to answer. Doing A-level sociology I certainly became interested in feminist issues, and developed a passionate interest in issues about in/equality, women's roles, employment etc. This was developed much further at university. In the first year at Lancaster students studied (and still do, for the most part) three subjects. I did psychology, education studies and sociology, so actually covered quite a bit about gender, inequalities and so on. I did a women's studies module in year 2, and tended to take option modules that focused on gender/sexuality. So, in a nutshell, the answer is probably from A-level onwards, although I can't recall when I started thinking of, or labelling myself as a feminist. Very influential activism through protest marches ... and women-only events....Women's studies (WS) was very strong at Lancaster when I was an undergrad. WS permeated my sociology and ed studies first year courses. Some -psychology tutors were also involved in WS, and so adopted what might be called a critical approach to psychology. I did my third year dissertation on gender and language ... on graduating from my undergraduate degree I applied to do a WS MA at York and WS/sociology MA at Lancaster, but didn't get funding.... I got an 18-month job as a research assistant working in educational research at Lancaster on a project on motivation. I registered to do a PhD part-time but didn't do much. At the end of the contract I trained as an ambulance person, and did that for about nine months. I left as I was offered funding to do a PhD, at Lancaster, which I did....

Carolyn is very explicit about the importance of sexuality to her feminism, with her partner also being an academic at the University of Manchester, and one of my second rather than third cohort: "Penny and I have been together as partners since 1996, and working with Penny in various ways has been influential and important...." Together, they told me about how they are both heartened and depressed by current changes, both in academia and more widely, illustrating the views of feminists across the generations. They both see themselves as continuing the traditions started by second-wave feminists, but are reflective of the new generations who find the struggles in HE more, rather than less, difficult today. I have known them both for about 20 years, since they were embarking on their academic activist careers:

> The rise and fall of WS is notable ... we seem to have come full circle from an attempt by individuals to inject WS into department provision, to a more coherent set of provision coordinated by centres, and now back to more disparate efforts of individuals in departments. Again (although there are clearly still some very important networks within institutions, especially relating to research), the argument that WS teaching is now "mainstreamed" is not entirely convincing. Wider politics – there are questions about the ways in which university EO policies are/are not translated into practice – there appear to be large gaps between them. [Here] I [Carolyn] am committed to the anti-harassment network (which was set up by feminists) and have seen that it does some important work. However, I'm also aware (and have sympathy with) criticisms that university points to such networks as evidence of its commitment to tackling bullying and harassment, but the network is staffed by volunteers (mainly women), is largely unresourced, and arguably in some cases allows the institution to avoid tackling some deep-rooted issues ... both of us note with dismay how many UG [undergraduate] students see no need for feminism as they believe girls and women are "successful and can do anything". Most have usually shifted position by the end of our modules, thankfully. However, it's a struggle getting them to see beyond their original notion that feminism is no longer needed. It was both heartening and depressing that there was "a reclaim the night" march in ... last month. Heartening in that it was organised, and reasonably well attended, by young women. Depressing that we still need them.... Our worries are that with the new fee regime students will choose traditional subjects (already evident from what we gather. Certainly applications in many social sciences are down, except in areas such as law and history) at the expense of sociology, gender and WS, education etc. Also, there will be an emphasis on STEM areas. This is likely to have a disproportionate impact on women academics. How do we fight this? Also there's

a worry that increasing pressures in HE mean that feminists have
less time and energy to keep fighting....

Professor Davina Cooper, now at the University of Kent, is also
an influential feminist lawyer. She was a student in Bristol where
I first met her, back in the 1980s. She comes from a middle-class
intellectual London Jewish family. She, too, has developed her
feminism from the second wave, but has been very creative in
developing new ways of studying issues, especially on LGBTQi,
and at the same time, being very politically engaged. She also
became a feminist when:

> I was about seven and I became very conscious of the different
> ways my brother and I were treated, particularly at school, but
> also in wider family circles. My first response was to try and
> pass as a boy. I got short hair, refused to wear dresses, was very
> stroppy, and people often thought I was the boy and my brother
> the girl, which I rather liked. My aim was to challenge people's
> common-sense assumptions and different treatment by making it
> impossible for them to sensibly gender us. But after about a year, I
> realised that this strategy reinforced a kind of sexism – that I was
> only being treated "better" because I looked like a boy. I stayed
> looking "boyish" 'til my teens, but I reclaimed a girl identity on
> the premise that nothing could be read off or determined by
> it.... My twin sisters (who were 12 years older than me) were
> probably the biggest influence on my feminism growing up. And
> Our bodies, ourselves. Their copy was in the house, and I devoured
> it in my last year of primary school, worrying over the merits
> of different contraceptions, home or hospital births in a kind of
> abstract, after-school leisure hours kind of way.... I moved from
> Bristol to do my undergraduate work in law at University College
> London, followed by a PhD at Warwick, starting at LSE, and then
> transferring to Warwick. I wanted to explore the potential of the
> local state to act against the status quo, what happens when public
> bodies try to promote a sexual politics that counters dominant
> forms of heterosexuality. It was very informed, at least at the
> beginning, by structuralist Marxism on the one hand, and social
> feminist work on the other – the idea that public bodies could
> only with difficulty, and only temporarily, work against dominant

social relations. I had several supervisors including Terry Lovell (the feminist sociologist).... Feminism has always been an important part of my politics. As a kid my focus was the "fairness" of gender equality and freedom, but later I was very influenced by feminist organisational norms – the bottom-up participatory politics of women's movement ways of doing things – the importance of culture and intimate relations as well as public and material ones ... the way my feminism developed in my late teens was completely caught up politically with identifying as a lesbian. Didi and I got together in 1989. Our politics haven't always been completely in step, but they've taken shape dialogically in relation to each other.... I've tried to bring both the form and substance of feminist approaches into how I work. I'm sure not always successfully, although it's been easier in environments where feminism had some legitimacy – on the council and in the research centre I was involved with (Arts and Humanities Research Council [AHRC] Research Centre for Law, Gender and Sexuality). Far harder being a feminist as a magistrate, where I was told my encouraging nods, when defendants and witnesses were speaking, and even my shoes, were quite wrong!

Feminism as a life-saver

Domestic violence has been an everyday experience for many women for many years and generations; it is only through feminism that it has come on to the public agenda. A young émigrée from the US, now Professor Penny-Jane Burke, at Roehampton University, was self-taught, and expressed this poignantly, passionately and powerfully:

I was born in New York City – raised and grew up in West Hollywood, California – parents professional artists, no university, father graphic designer, mother freelance illustrator ... became a feminist during university (as a mature student at Middlesex after an Access to HE course) mainly through my own reading ... good experiences taught me about inclusive pedagogies ... poor teaching practices taught me how not to teach!!... After my undergraduate degree, I was encouraged by my friend's partner (who was doing his PhD at the time) to carry on with my work at MA level – I was passionate about women's access to HE and he thought that I should look in to doing an MA – I did – and discovered the women's studies course there.... I got a studentship to do this (otherwise I don't think I could have managed it financially).... Feminism has been crucial to my learning – indirectly and explicitly – eg, when I was in a women's aid refuge I first explicitly encountered feminism and this was a life-saver in terms of understanding and making sense of my traumatic experiences of domestic violence – and also learning about my rights and my position as a woman – this was strengthened at university when I started to read feminist theories for my coursework – theory has been more directly influential to me than activism which has not been a significant part of my history/experience (although I have participated in "activism" in more modest, localised ways).... My parents never really understood what I was doing or why – always felt/feel I was a disappointment to them because I was not an artist – my husband comes from a working-class background and we married before I started the Access course – but he has always believed in me and supported my feminist perspectives and so his emotional support has always been important – I had three boys (when I started my degree I had a one year-old son, a four-year old son and an eight-year-old step-son) – so I always felt I was moving across two completely different worlds – and trying to develop a way to be a feminist mother ... developing an identity as a feminist was tied directly to developing an identity as an academic – the two were completely intertwined – but I often felt "not good enough" – especially as I came to it so late and did not experience any of the activism of the 70s and 80s or of second-wave feminism – the experience of escaping domestic violence was also key in my sense as a feminist and my passionate commitment to challenging assumptions about domestic violence and understanding it as tied in with patriarchy (and not "battered woman's syndrome").... Initially black feminist writers or feminist theorists of 'race' – so Angela Davis and bell hooks really caught my imagination early on (this is partly because of their passion and the power of their writing, but also because I have always felt "Other" myself, and have a lot of different ethnicities in my family background, and have been extremely committed to challenging racism since a young girl) – later on it was people like.... Bev Skeggs [mentioned in Chapter Five] because of her work on gender and class – and Nancy Fraser because of her work on social justice ... while I was doing my PhD I had a post at a further education college to develop and run a course called "Return to study" – I created my own women's studies Level 2/3 course as part of that this was collaborative in the sense that I wanted to develop "collaborative pedagogies" with my students – but I didn't have the chance to work with anyone else....

Feminism in the 'psyche' of the university

While most of the women I talked to have a melancholic take on the future of global academe, Penny-Jane is less gloomy:

Feminism has been highly successful and so there is no doubt that its influence remains even with increasing levels of global neoliberalism shaping and reshaping the university – feminist influences remain as a resource for legitimate challenges to the assumptions of the "neoliberal university" and are often taken up (not always acknowledged though) by critical scholars – feminism has entered into the "psyche" of the university – I feel – in such a way as to make certain things unspeakable – keeping a check on issues of equality – but of course this is always under threat and it is also being overshadowed by the instrumentalism, "marketization" and neoliberalism of the contemporary university – the university, though, is not a homogeneous unit – actually there are universities and differences between them – so that there are some spaces that are more influenced by feminism than others – it is crucial that younger feminists protect and develop those spaces.... I believe that feminists must be strategic and must be highly committed to influencing new spaces, new subjects, new students and new professions in and beyond the university – which is what drives me to do the research I do – feminist pedagogical practices have an important role to play in negotiating this process – in creating spaces of resistance and innovation – and in challenging new spaces that might erode the progressive, critical, transformative, subversive, empowering spaces that feminists have managed to create in and beyond education.... Feminists must be strategic about this – we live in an era where everything – even education

– is being driven by "the market" – therefore feminists must create curricula that speak but simultaneously subvert those markets – women's studies might not be as "marketable" as it was a decade or two ago – so there need to be creative ways – and empathetic and responsive ways – to understand the perspectives of young people and their concerns but to demonstrate to them the relevance of feminist insights – this takes careful thought and lots of creativity ... there is an assumption that more women means more equality – but of course women can behave in oppressive, inequitable, competitive, individualist, self-serving and damaging ways just as men can – the importance is that feminist practices influence academia and wider society – however, at the same time, women must not be marginalised because they are women and/ or because they do not perform in certain hegemonic masculine ways – I think there are continuities with young feminists shaped by second-wave feminists, but inevitably reshaping the terrain in relation to the contexts in which they live and face challenge – as HE changes, feminists will find ways to respond/subvert/challenge those changes that threaten agendas for equality and social justice ... with new technologies breaking down the constraints of communicating with feminists in other parts of the world, the focus on collaborating across different trans/national contexts will become increasingly important – however, this is not really different from contestations over time – feminist standpoint theory teaches us that our feminist perspectives are always shaped by our social contexts, influences, generation, ethnicity, class, sexuality etc. As new forms of feminism emerge, they will do so in relation to the particular social issues, conflicts, contexts that are also emerging – younger feminists are as committed to this as ever, I believe. I have every optimism that new forms of feminism will continue to struggle against the emergent problems of the time and place – including, for example, issues about the increasing levels of poverty in certain parts of the world, new and environmental concerns, war and conflict and ways to promote peace, and many other ongoing and emergent issues.... Feminism has a key role to play in the struggle to defend public forms of HE, struggles over access to HE as well as challenges ongoing and new inequalities in HE. This is an ongoing struggle – clearly we are facing new challenges – one of the key concerns is to find ways to work together and to undermine rampant individualism, which will always undermine activism and the struggle for change and transformation....

Another American émigrée, Dr Kelly Coate, now at King's College, London, and from a middle-class family, has a similar story about learning about feminism at college. She is far less sanguine than Penny-Jane about the future:

I first learned about feminism in North America when I was very young, whereas my journey through European feminist thought has developed as I have matured. For me, then, these two geographically oriented distinctions are part of my own life history and I cannot disentangle the geographical locations from my experience of my journey through different times in my life.... (Davis and Evans, 2011, p 79). I went to Northwestern University, in Chicago to study liberal arts, and undertook some women's studies during my undergraduate degree [all of which she found] ... a powerful experience.... [While there] in the library, reading around some of the recommended texts for another module, I discovered *The female eunuch* (Greer, 1970) and experienced a life-changing moment.... My personal revolution, then, initially happened almost entirely in my head. I read books and selected as many feminist courses that I could squeeze into my programme.... This was a time of profound learning that was precious and now evokes nostalgia; the time to read, think, deeply explore new ideas, to have my ideas challenged and developed, and to enjoy learning how to employ feminist theories to most aspects of life... (Coate, in Davis and Evans, 2011, p 81)

She came to London on graduation, originally for a brief trip, but found herself staying and undertaking various relatively short-term administrative jobs in universities, and later for the FWSA. During this time she decided to take an MA in gender and society at Middlesex University, and then moved:

... to undertake a PhD in the history of women's studies ... as I was finishing my PhD and looking for a starting point for an academic career, I fell more into doing mainstream HE research rather than feminist research. The funding for HE research often went to the men, and I was employed to work on a number of research projects with high-profile male academics. The environment was anti-feminist, really, and in some cases the contributions I tried to make in terms of highlighting gender within research were deleted. Now looking back on it, and after reflecting on everything that has happened, I think the male research teams I worked in were exceedingly patriarchal and anti-feminist. It wasn't just a chilly climate because it was more nuanced than that: there was patronage of a few women, exploitation of a few others, and hostility towards most other women. As it became increasingly difficult to bring a feminist perspective into collaborative work (the few bids I worked on with other feminists weren't funded), I had to find a way to remain being a feminist academic. I remember when one female colleague told me I needed to get out from under the men to find my own voice, and she was right. In the meantime, I was very preoccupied with trying to support students with allegations of serious sexual harassment against one of these men and it was a very difficult time. [The late] Diana Leonard helped me a great deal, but even now, after about six years, I am still angry about how effectively we were silenced and dissuaded from pursuing a formal allegation (I often think we should have just gone to the police). Some of the responses we got from the university when we tried to pursue formal allegations of sexual harassment were unbelievable....

Her comments about her struggles around this, both personally and politically, are courageous, telling me:

...one legacy I left behind is that there is now, in that university, a formal policy concerning harassment of students (there were only staff policies in place prior to our case) ... an academic can be accused of serious professional misconduct (and possibly criminal behaviour), but if his research record is considered important, he will be kept on by any means possible.... I now see my role as a feminist academic to be mainly one of offering support to other women academics and trying to make universities less sexist places to work. My [then] ... university has the worst promotion rates of female academics in Europe ... and I've been involved in various initiatives around that. We ... set up a University Women's Network and a Gender Research Consortium. We probably need to revive the idea of a "glass ceiling" network because I know a number of women ... (myself included) who have hit it. I think I have a number of good women around me (in this institution and beyond) who will continue to offer amazing support and inspiration. But it is hard working in a patriarchal institution and continually feeling the disadvantages of being a woman. I honestly believe that there are male academics here who can't quite accept the idea that women can be scholars and leaders....

Kelly, whom I have known since my FWSA days, has gone on to be a marvellous model scholar-leader, developing a funded project on mid-career women, with Camille Kandiko Howson and Tania de St Croix (2015). Funded by the Leadership Foundation, they looked at the under-representation of women at senior levels in HE, and focused on how women feel about being at mid-career stage, as well as the thorny concept of prestige, and how gendered a concept it is.

The luxury of doing something I enjoy

Fin Cullen, mentioned above, has a most interesting perspective, seeing herself as a 'second-and-a-half' waver. Since she is young enough to be my daughter, she cannot be of the second wave, but agrees more with this political perspective than subsequent third- or fourth-wave perspectives, although she is very familiar with those, too. She told me how much she enjoys her teaching and research, and sees teaching as a political act, although she, too, has a pessimistic perspective:

On a disciplinary level, feminist thought has revolutionalised many subject areas completely. However, I note how institutionally based the changes were, and how like the tide some of the earlier-won battles have slowly become eroded. For example, the demise of university-based crèche and childcare facilities. Indeed, I know of several UK campuses that have child-free policies, with no children allowed on site. A pain for many student and staff parents. There still remains a massive lack of parity in many institutions, in relation to promotion and career trajectory. Put simply, the impossibilities of combining a healthy work–life balance is an enduring issue … [but] the luxury of being able to do something I really enjoy. It is a tough balancing act … as a (fairly) young academic in the past I have often found myself making tea and cleaning up at union and departmental meetings. It often appears patriarchy is still alive and well in many institutions…. I have a painful relationship with what passes as some continuation of the earlier radical activism. At feminist (activist) meetings I have been shouted down … and realised that I am tired of orthodoxies. The thrust of much activism seems predicated around dogmatic certainties, that scholarship has supported me in questioning. I can't, perhaps, go back. Yet I like the energy and innovation of the activist space, in contrast to the sometimes-stultifying spaces of academia where the feminisms debated become increasingly abstract and reified. Hurrah for our ability to theorise and contemplate, but we must not lose sight of the activist, policy and practice space too…. I am not sure where feminism can take us next. The move of a gendered analysis into the mainstream in many disciplines left women's studies, then gender studies programmes floundering, and maybe our success is also our loss. I think there was something very powerful about those women's studies programmes, but also, at the same time, the increased marketisation of HE makes such spaces incredibly difficult…. Yet, the rise of neoliberal forms of academic employment risks unpicking some of the battles partly won of prior decades. The modern university with its long hours, child-free zones and lack of crèche facilities, is, for example, not a mother-friendly space. The notions of contrived collegiality in and across departments is unrecognisable from the mutuality present in feminist collaboration I have previously experienced. The pernicious individualising thrust of HE settings remains incredibly masculinist, and often makes me consider my future within such a field. I note that I am sounding exceedingly gloomy. The marketisation and potential privatisation of the rest of the sector means an increased proletarianisation of the HE workforce. I fear that this means many female academics will be pushed into evermore casualised, low-paid, teaching-only contracts in low-status institutions. So what role has feminism to play? As always, a space to critically organise and think and teach against the grain, even if only to enable these newly casualised (or redundant) feminist academics space to consolidate and perhaps re-enter the academy when the HE reforms fail to "work" and there is a return to what the university is for beyond narrow market-driven ideals.... I think that new and existing forms of feminisms will come to the fore in dialogue with "Western" feminism – and problematise the kind of colonialist rhetoric used by some governments from the Global North to make sense of their continued subjugation and dominance. At this juncture with the global economic crisis, I'm also not sure that the global power axis will remain in the US, and the shifting dynamics of economic and cultural dominance over the next decades may mean that contemporary taken-for-granted civil rights may need to be re-negotiated and reclaimed in many cultural contexts.... The marketisation of HE makes me wonder what kinds of spaces there are for the myriad of feminisms that inhabit the academy. In my rather marginal area – the deprofessionalisation of youth work will leave the practice hollowed out. Indeed, the competency-based route has little space for engaged epistemological debates around gender equity. Instead, a light-touch, "diversity-lite"-based kind of paper exercise may take the place of engaged and thought-through analysis of gender relations, heteronormativity and feminist pedagogy. The current proposals for teacher education would point in a similar direction. This all sounds rather pessimistic, but the instrumentalist thrust of neoliberal education policy will push, I believe, feminist work to the margins, and/or concentrate it in elite institutions.

Women's studies as a life-changer

Finally, I turn to Jessica Ringrose's story. She is both a friend and feminist colleague. Jessica persuaded me to go on a SlutWalk with her back in 2011, and I have only recently recalled that her involvement was deeply personal as the origins were in her doctoral 'alma mater'. She did her doctorate at York University in Toronto, and it was here that the police constable advised women (students) to avoid dressing like 'sluts', with his comments immediately going viral. Two hundred SlutWalks were organised internationally, with one in London. I found myself going on this with Jessica. Although I was of two minds, I am pleased that I did so as I thoroughly enjoyed both the spectacle of waves of feminism and its revolutionary fervour.

Jessica also told me that she, too, became a feminist:

> ... at university though saw feminist trends in mum retrospectively. I come from a Canadian military family – father was an officer but my parents divorced when I was 11, and so my main experiences are having a single mother with a meagre income. This meant that I first went to college as we couldn't afford university, failed that and so then went to university the following year, the University of Victoria, in my home town. I started in English literature because I was good at writing, hated it and then switched to sociology because I was brilliant at it and finally I took a minor in women's studies, which changed my life in the second year of university.... Feminism has been hugely critical to my learning since my undergraduate days ... shaping every facet of life from decision to delay marriage and definitely shaped decision to delay childrearing.... Mum has been very influential in supporting my education and not adopting the traditional mothering role of nurturer.... Women's studies was central to my learning and development as an academic.... My PhD was on anti-racism in women's studies, defensiveness of white feminism, issues of intersectionality, problems of contradiction and wanting to relate as "feminine" and nurture the relationality problems explored by Gilligan and Brown, manifesting and problematic learning dynamics for feminist pedagogies ... and so it continues to have a massive influence and is the reason for continuing to live abroad for the feminist gender and education community in the UK....

The university, a misogynistic control mechanism

Jessica is also very critical of working in the neoliberal university, agreeing with Penny-Jane about the ways that feminism is both in the psyche of the university, and in our own:

> For me, academic feminism represents a set of painful conflicts and contradictions that are important to confront and face as part of a project of understanding where we are in the contemporary

HE institutions at this moment for those of us that make a living in this industry. The fundamental paradox we are faced with is age-old. Feminism, at its most basic, purported to offer a shared understanding of oppression of women and a political platform to fight against this. The idea of a shared vision is exclusionary and even violent in its imposition; however, if it does not address differences among women, as non-white, non-middle-class women, non-Western have been pointing out to exclusionary liberal feminist reformers for a very long time. Beyond these inherent problems with a singular feminism, being a "feminist" in academia or at various stages of one's schooling career contains the essential paradox that schooling and education equals competition. From the outset, insertion into the schooling machine means you are competing for grades, status, reward, resources. Scholarships and studentships and later positions and grants and even the courses that you can teach about feminism or gender when you have a job are all competed for. When you are inserted into the academy, you must compete to secure and maintain any position of power. This means that you are in competition with your "feminist" colleagues. It is a war zone, rather than some idyllic place of shared ideas and mutual respect in working towards the common goal of gender equality. This is the basic scenario that we have to take as our starting point to forge genuine recognition of ourselves and of others (Benjamin, 1998), with the thorny couplet of "academic feminism". We have to confront the deeply divisive nature of the power hierarchies, structures and discourses that mediate our relationships with our female (and obviously male) colleagues in academe. We need to work to manage this competitive conflict in ethical ways – through a feminist ethos – that would require somehow addressing how taking up positions of power means negotiating a phallic mantel of control that does not need a gendered body: confronting the displacement of male power from the male body – that women can wield their exclusionary power the same as men, and why would we expect differently? An unproblematised notion of "academic feminism" actually sets women up to fail if it does not teach us how to confront and manage these complexities of masculinist control, power and division through which the university and its constituents operate. That being said, there are possibilities for forging ethical alliances in the university if the ethics of feminist academe are confronted in reflexive ways. There is also potential for engaging in research through feminist methodologies and theories and shining light on the vast web of gendered power relations connecting us.... This marginalisation of feminist politically oriented research is also a paradox in relation to desires for "objective" science and social science.... Spaces outside academe may prove the most freeing and thought-provoking for feminists working inside the academy. Social media has made networked online feminism a growing source of information and support, although, as well, another space for competitive hierarchies that must be managed by academics engaging with or "plugging into" this wider feminist assemblage (Ringrose and Renold, 2012). The UK GEA is one such academic forum, run through the voluntary actions of its members and executives rather than officially supported through university funding, for instance. Thus feminisms' most radical potential may be connected to the thinking of academic feminism, but takes flight outside the institutional walls. This is evident in the range of amazing feminist action and protest happening around the world in various sometimes controversial ways, from the internationally viral SlutWalks to the protest group Femen, who bare their breasts in a bid to get exposure from a media apparatus consumed by commodifying the female form and parts (breasts especially). There is a wide range of inspiring young feminists who are organising on Facebook, Twitter and via other networks to raise awareness of the issues related to sexism and girls and women's rights, but also issues related to masculinity, heterosexism and LGBTQ and queer activism and thinking. The US blogger Feminist Teacher has over 5,000 Twitter followers, and there are other groups like Youth Twitter Feminist Army who are actually using Tweets to challenge sexism at school. There are highly committed teachers in the UK who are organising to fight repressive educational tactics, including the curriculum revisions that have removed a concern for social wellbeing, including sexual and relationship education, from school. These groups spring up and mobilise partly through social media, with Feminist Fight Back's S-word event geared at challenging the problems with current UK sex education an example in point. The challenge for academic feminism is to watch, learn and listen from these important ripples of activity, action and challenge to power from outside the academic pulpit. When older feminists reproduce a generational melancholic and typically Oedipal and maternal narrative of suggesting girls and young women are simply succumbing to sexism, or failing to live up to the opportunities paved through earlier feminist struggle, they are missing the point entirely. They are failing to recognise the different forms of engagement and feminist life forms that are becoming in the world – even *gasp* if they do not call themselves feminist!!! Indeed, the biggest challenge for us academic feminists is to use the magnificent powers of critical analysis that we have generated through our time in academia to try to see and possibly connect with *the feminist waves that are continually churning up in the world.* And this is not just in some first-, second- and third-wave analogy, but rather in the repeated rhythms of everyday discussions, negotiations and actions through which gender and sexual power relations are unfolding and sometimes being contested and transformed. (emphasis added)

Jessica has managed to mention all the contentious wave analogies and exciting feminist resurgences in this comment, including making mention of Ileana Jimenez. She has shown how complex and contested in academic, educational and public spaces the 'wave' analogy is.

I now turn to Ileana's story to illustrate the exciting continuities and changes in feminist resurgence. Ileana is a New York high school teacher, daughter of Puerto Rican migrants to the US, and founder and sole blogger at Feminist Teacher, her own unique platform. She stayed as a paying guest in my home for five weeks in 2014, and opened my eyes to the exciting ways in which feminism was on the resurgence in schools and colleges in the US. It was she who told me of Obama's White House Task Force, although she was cynical about how far it might go with its recommendations, and whether anything would be done, in the end, to combat campus and school-based sexual assaults and violence. We became feminist friends, and she has come to regard me as her feminist 'soul mother', writing moving comments on her Facebook page.

We had met through Jessica, who had organised a panel on feminist critiques of education at the American Educational

Research Association (AERA) annual meetings in San Francisco, in April 2013. Jessica had planned a panel to discuss different generational and international feminist critiques of aspects of education. There were five very different presentations that came together in interesting and imaginative ways to provide a comprehensive picture of feminist education and educational critiques, with a feminist discussant from Canada – Marina Gornick – creating a picture of how influential feminism was becoming in education in the Global North. My presentation was about my study on the passionate pedagogies of second-wave academic feminists, while Professors Jane Kenway and Debbie Epstein (also from my generation) provided examples of elite girls' schooling in several Commonwealth countries, linked to the former British Empire. Jessica and her colleague, Emma Renold, of Cardiff University, gave an intriguing presentation about the young people they had interviewed for their study of contemporary schooling, and in particular, their feelings about learning to be young women and men, and the prevalence of sexualisation in their lives. Dr Victoria Showunmi, also from UCL's Institute of Education, gave a presentation about the diverse secondary school children she had interviewed about their feelings on racism, sexism and classism in their lives. Ileana gave a most lively presentation about her work with her diverse male and female high school students, talking about how she explored their learning lives through literature as well as outside the classroom.

Like many of this cohort, she is the first generation into HE and, through her education, has become totally committed to feminism as a politics and as an education. While the daughter of a New York police officer and secretarial mother, and raised a Roman Catholic, she became enamoured of feminism, initially at high school, and then totally immersed at Smith College, Massachusetts. She, too, wrote quite spontaneously about her 'feminist epiphany'[5] happening in high school and at Smith, and has since blogged and written similar materials as part of her teaching:

---

[5] See http://feministing.com/2010/11/06/the-feministing-five-ileana-jimenez/

Viva la feminista ... summer of feminism. Finding my Latina feminism[6]

If it weren't for some Irish white guy, I never would have become a feminist. When I read James Joyce's *A portrait of the artist as a young man* in my senior year in high school, it changed my entire life. Never before had I read a novel that spoke to me with such intensity. The main character, Stephen Dedalus, was repeatedly teased and picked on the playground. I was teased and picked on the playground with names like spic and nigger. Here was a boy who wrote poetry hidden underneath the covers. I wrote poetry with big words that no one in my family understood. Here was a boy who questioned the Catholic Church and went off to college to proclaim non serviam, or "I will not serve" the church, and instead became an artist, a writer, and a thinker. At 18, I also questioned the Catholic Church and went off to Smith to proclaim my own destiny as a queer feminist writer and thinker. But while I read Joyce, I kept asking: Why isn't this character a Puerto Rican girl living on Long Island via the Bronx in 1993? And why haven't I ever read a book with a Latina protagonist who shares my story? When I finished reading the novel, I was on a mission. I was determined to find books with female characters that would reflect me back to me. Through my research, I discovered second wave feminism, and in particular, the literary criticism written by white feminist theorists during that time. I'll never forget ransacking the public library bookshelves and finding Kate Millett's *Sexual politics* and Sandra Gilbert and Susan Gubar's *Madwoman in the attic*. Reaching across dusty books, I also encountered French feminism in Simone de Beauvoir's *The second sex*. Finding these books in my local library was like finding my own heaven. I was so enamoured with my discoveries, I was convinced I was the first person to read these works. Through these critics, I learned about old school feminist novelists like Colette, Erica Jong, and Sylvia Plath. I devoured Judy Chicago's memoir, *Through the flower*, and cried when I saw images of her famous Dinner Party celebrating forgotten women in history. Still though, these were all white women writers and artists. Where

---

6 See www.vivalafeminista.com/2010/09/summer-of-feminista-finding-my-latina.html

were the Latinas? Where were the women who could tell me how they reconciled their Latina identity with their burgeoning feminist ideals? I couldn't find them while I was in high school. Instead, I wrote a 20 page paper in my AP English class comparing Joyce's exploration of gender, sexuality, and his vocation to become a writer with women writers exploring their own gender, sexuality, and artistic vocations: Chicago's *Through the flower,* Jong's *Fear of flying*, and Plath's *The bell jar.* When I finished writing my paper, I promised myself that as soon I arrived at college, I would find not just Latina writers but in particular, Latina feminist writers. That summer of 1993, I watched Ruth Bader Ginsberg get grilled and then confirmed by the Senate Judiciary Committee. It was the first time I had seen a female justice get seated to the highest court. I remember falling in love with Ginsberg, and it was her chutzpah that inspired me to go with my gut to transfer from Boston University to Smith when I arrived in Boston that fall. As soon as I arrived at BU, I took a Peter Pan bus out to Smith and landed an interview. By that January, I transferred to Smith and enrolled in Nancy Saporta Sternbach's Latina and Latin American Women Writers class. I wasn't supposed to be in that course, as it was only open to juniors and seniors. I was so determined to get in though, that the night before the class started, I called the professor at home! Dios mio, the things you do at 18! It was in that class that I found Cherríe Moraga. I'll never forget opening my very first course reader with its hot orange cover and black binder rings. Inside were excerpts from *Loving in the war years*. Reading Moraga's words was magical. It felt like I was reading a journal I had written in my heart but never knew how to write. Her words, "My brother's sex was white, mine was brown," exploded off the pages. Moraga gave me the strength to see myself in all the ways that I lived as a light-skinned Puerto Rican woman who was also brown, queer, and feminist. I recognised in her words my own struggles and doubts, my own anger and frustration. I also found hope that through writing, we Latina feminists could not only find our own voices but also find each other's, no matter what risks we took to find them. I learned from her that we need to commit to each other as Latina feminists, not by shouting non serviam, but instead by lending a hand to one another and saying a tu servicio.

Continuities and changes in the waves of feminism

Ileana is a most energetic and exciting feminist teacher, and has been extremely creative in trying to embed feminist ideas into the practices of high school teaching in the US, almost unheard of for the UK. She has also been very creative about her own college education, and inspired by many formative feminists from Smith College, whose work she follows closely. Smith has been home to many feminists and radical women (see Chapter Two). As I was originally penning this, it was the week in which Gloria Steinem turned 80, and there were major birthday celebrations, including her trip to India. Sylvia Plath, the feminist poet, was also a student at Smith, and Ileana was excited to have lived in her house at Smith and to be able to find plaques to her in Primrose Hill, London (where she committed suicide).

Ileana also told me that Margaret Mitchell, author of *Gone with the wind*, had been at Smith. And by coincidence, this same week in 2014 was the anniversary of the film, and my dear former colleague in BWSG, Professor Helen Taylor's book, called *Scarlett's women: Gone with the wind and its female fans* was reissued to commemorate the 75th anniversary, with a new, updated introduction to her critically acclaimed 1989 study (Taylor, 2014). Now professor emerita of English at the University of Exeter, Helen Taylor (2014, p iv) wrote that: 'Our 21st century world looks very different from that of 1939, and there is a challenge to discuss, let alone celebrate, *GWTW* in the year *Twelve Years a Slave* justly won its Oscars. But there is still a need to understand and explore the extraordinary success of Margaret Mitchell's novel and David O. Selznick Jr's film, particularly for women readers and audiences.' Margaret Mitchell's novel was published in June 1936 and has sold 25 million copies, been translated into 27 languages, and won the 1936 Pulitzer Prize; the film premiered on 15 December 1939 and received eight Oscars, and has been called the greatest movie ever made.

This reflection on a feminist critique of Margaret Mitchell brings together both the continuities and complexities of feminism today by comparison with its past, recontextualising feminism in a much more ambiguous, ambivalent and anxious world. As a parting gift to me, Ileana gave me a book of poems and essays by Judith Viorst, a second-wave American feminist, originally published in the US in 1968, with the inscription that 'You are the hippest woman over 30!' Entitled *It's hard to be hip over 30* and republished by Persephone Books in 1999, it illustrates Viorst's ambivalent views of the WLM, which some may now share, but I don't, with the following extract from her poem 'A Women's Liberation Movement woman':

> When it's snowing and I put on all the galoshes
>
> While he reads the paper
>
> Then I become a
>
> Women's Liberation Movement woman.
>
> And when it's snowing and he looks for the taxi
>
> While I wait in the lobby
>
> Then I don't. (Viorst, 1999, p xii)

SEVEN

Feminists on campus

It is clear that feminism is now in the eye of the storm of neoliberalism and 'academic capitalism', a term that the US feminist Sheila Slaughter invented almost 20 years ago to illustrate how entwined HE is with advanced economic systems. The term is now seen as a classic, with my colleague, Sir Peter Scott, professor of HE, mentioning this in his presentation for the new, well-endowed Centre for Global Higher Education (CGHE) (Havergal, 2015). This term has already lost its feminist edge, as CGHE has become the main source of research for British and international HE policies: neither feminism nor gender feature in the 15 or more projects planned for the next five years. When asked about this, Professor Simon Marginson, director of CGHE, mentioned his gender sensibilities, and how this would be threaded through all the projects. This absence or lack of specificity is yet another example of everyday misogyny in universities today.

In this chapter I explore some evidence of feminist contestations on university campuses, given how important HE is to all of our economic, personal, political and sociocultural lives today, as part of the zeitgeist.

First, I set the scene by demonstrating contested notions about gender equality in HE between feminists and neoliberals, with neoliberals arguing that, with the achievement of formal statistical equality in terms of students, there is no longer any issue to contend with. This is misogyny masquerading as metrics, to paraphrase my colleague Professor Louise Morley of the

Centre for Higher Education Equity Research (CHEER) at the University of Sussex. I then muse about examples of feminist contestations over sexual harassment among students, training students to challenge sexual violence, and between feminists as academics or students. Some of these latter are very unfortunate media debates between waves of feminists on campus, showing how feminism *per se* has been brought into public disrepute. Yet feminist campaigning has successfully exposed sexual assault or harassment, 'rape culture' or 'lad culture' on campus, although policies remain woefully inadequate, not only for students, but also for women and feminist academics.

The development of global HE in expansionary times has transformed women's involvement as both students and academics, but recent moves towards neoliberalism and austerity have altered how feminists can take action within the academy, as Jessica Ringrose and others have already intimated. The old liberal–humanist arguments about how universities are spaces for creative thinking and allow for academic freedom and/or freedom of expression are being eroded as austerity bites. Even more importantly, new quasi-legal notions of radicalisation are also having an impact on campus cultures, and constricting and confining sociocultural debates. Indeed, the now annual and ever more popular Feminism in London (FiL) conferences are distancing themselves from academic institutions. In 2015 the conference location was moved from my institution to an American-style two-day conference in a central London Hilton hotel, illustrating the contradictions.

The notion of 'gender equality' contested

UNESCO's *World atlas on gender equality in education*, published in 2012, is the clearest example of the international commitment to global gender equality in education, including HE. It provides a vast amount of statistical information about where women and men are *as students* across the globe, relating the information to international criteria. It provides corroborating evidence of the point made by Sheila Slaughter, that education is a vital ingredient of economies today. Indeed, its title illustrates how normal the issue of gender equality has become. The notion has been captured by governing neoliberal elites, and changed to a modest goal of 'access and inclusion'. Feminist notions of the transformation of power relations are no longer embedded in the idea of gender equality.

As we saw at the end of Chapter Two, the UNESCO report shows how there has been an enormous growth in student numbers, with the headline: 'Women now account for a majority of students in most countries [and this is part of] an increased of around 500 percent in enrolments over less than 40 years (1970-2009).' They go on to say that 'female enrolment at the tertiary level has grown almost twice as fast as that of men over the last four decades for reasons that include social mobility, enhanced income potential, international pressure to narrow the gender gap … [but] access to higher education by women has not always translated into enhanced career opportunities, including the opportunities to use their doctorates in the field of research' (UNESCO, 2012, p 75).

This sober statistical international publication shows continuing gender inequality in employment, even for the most highly educationally qualified. So, while 'the female edge is up in tertiary enrolment through the master's level [it] disappears when it comes to PhDs and careers in research' (UNESCO, 2012, p 107). They also say that 'Even though higher education leads to individual returns in the form of higher income, women often need to have more education than men to get some jobs…. Women continue to confront discrimination in jobs, disparities in power, voice and political representation and laws that are prejudicial on the basis of their gender. As a result well-educated women often end up in jobs where they do not use their full potential and skills' (UNESCO, 2012, p 84). Clearly there is much that remains to be done to transform the gendered power relations in global HE and beyond, as misogyny continues to rule.

European policies are frequently strongly in favour of gender equality, not on social grounds, but for economic competition and business innovation. At a gender summit in 2011 about research in Europe, Robert-Jan Smits, EC Director General for Research and Innovation, argued that: "The promotion of gender equality is part of the European Commission's strategic approach in the field of research and innovation. It contributes to the enhancement of European competitiveness and the full realisation of European innovation potential."

The EC produced specific statistics on gender equality in 'science', where science is the umbrella term for research across all subjects and disciplines in universities. Their nicely named *She figures: Statistics and indicators on gender equality in science* (European Commission, 2009) provide evidence and indicators on gender equality in universities during the 21st century: 'The *She figures* data collection is undertaken every three years as a joint venture of the Scientific Culture and Gender Issues Unit of the Directorate-General for Research of the European Commission (EC).' They showed the proportion of female students (55%) and graduates (59%) exceeded that of male students.

Another example is in the US, by *The Chronicle of Higher Education*, the magazine for academia, in a special issue on 'Diversity in academe: The gender issue' (2012). As the editor noted: 'It's well known, for example, that female undergraduates outnumber their male counterparts ... the undergraduate gender gap is especially striking among black students ... women are advancing in the professoriate as well' (Mooney, 2012).

She figures 2009 painted an interesting picture: in the preface to the report, Janez Potočnik, a Slovenian politician who served as European Commissioner for Science and Research, stated that 'while there are equivalent numbers of women and men working in the field of Humanities, only 27% of researchers in Engineering and Technology are female. And what about researchers' career progression? Women account for 59% of graduates, whereas men account for 82% of full professors. Do you find that hard to believe? Check out chapter 3.' He then presented the case for more action by policy-makers:

> *She figures 2009* tells us that the proportion of female researchers is actually growing faster than that of men.... The figures are encouraging but the gender imbalance is not self-correcting. *She figures* is recommended reading for all policy-makers, researchers, teachers, students, and for parents who share a vision of a democratic, competitive and technologically advanced Europe.

The report argues for serious action to make gender equality across all science and research more of a reality:

> Women's academic career [sic] remains markedly characterised by strong vertical segregation: the proportion of female students (55%) and graduates (59%) exceeds that of male students, but men outnumber women among PhD students and graduates AND academic staff. The proportion of women among full professors is highest in the humanities and the social sciences. The situation thus appears more favourable for the youngest generations of female academics but the gender gap is still persistent.

Yet another source of statistical evidence is the Association of Commonwealth Universities (ACU), which brings together all 54 countries of the Commonwealth and its 500 universities. On its website it argues that: 'Today's ACU combines the expertise and reputation of over 90 years' experience with new and innovative programmes designed to meet the needs of universities in the 21st century. HE is more international than ever before: the market for students and staff is a global one ... academic reputations are based on global connections.' Gender equality is not a prime objective of ACU, but it does have a unit committed to developing gender equality in leadership and management in HE, established in 1985, as the ACU's gender programme. It set itself two important objectives of assisting in the development of a Commonwealth-wide gender network to provide moral, professional and intellectual support, and a database of women who are, or might be in the future, leaders.

Media storms about gender equality

There is no one organisation that provides comprehensive figures and statistics in the UK. Although UK government departments collect statistics about schooling and HE, these figures are published separately, and do not provide a comprehensive public account of the situation as regards gender or other equalities. The Social Mobility Commission, set up by the UK coalition government in 2010 and chaired by Alan Milburn, following from his work as tsar of social mobility after he had been a

Cabinet minister in the previous Labour government, did not either. Milburn had originally chaired a committee to report to government on progress towards social mobility in the graduate professions, where the committee had identified a continuing glass ceiling for women in 2009. In 2013, as chair of the statutory Commission, he dropped gender from its concerns, and returned to concentrate solely on social class and poverty.[1]

But there are several sources of evidence providing the detail that confirm the overall moves towards gender equality in numbers of students in the UK, while gender inequalities among academics remain rampant, as they do internationally. For instance, Universities UK (UUK) set up a unit to gather gender statistics, initially named as its Equalities Unit, in the early 21st century.[2] This built on and paralleled the Women's Equality Unit, set up under the New Labour government, in the Cabinet Office in the late 20th century. The government's Equality Unit was moved between departments and administrative units over a 10-year period, and was eventually abolished by the UK coalition government in 2010, despite its excellent work in providing a forum for women to develop a strong network of feminist researchers and campaigners.[3] UUK's unit has also been transformed over the last decade, in line with neoliberal tendencies. Although continuing to be financed by public funds across the four nations of the UK, it is no longer under the umbrella of UUK, but has become an autonomous organisation, renamed the Equalities Challenge Unit (ECU). In its current guise, it provides detailed evidence about equalities in HE in annual reports that gather statistics across various social groups including gender, ethnicity, disability and age, bringing them together as 'multiple identities'.

ECU's mission statement in 2014 confirms its neoliberal tendencies: 'We support universities and colleges to build an inclusive culture that values the benefits of diversity, to remove barriers to progression and success for all staff and students,

---

[1]   As reported in newspapers on 18 October 2013.

[2]   Nicola Dandridge was chief executive in the first decade of the 21st century, and was then appointed chief executive of UUK.

[3]   Professor Claire Callender was one of the first heads of this unit on secondment from her university post.

and to challenge and change unfair practices that disadvantage individuals or groups.' This is elaborated as: 'We believe that the benefits of equality and diversity and inclusive practice are key to the wellbeing and success of individuals, the institution's community, the competitiveness and excellence of institutions, and to the growth of the sector in a global economy... [and its] needs...' This indicates just how limited gender equality is within the priorities of the ECU, despite the fact that they have created a series of equality charter marks, including on gender equality. For instance, one now includes: 'Addressing gender inequalities and imbalance in the arts, humanities and social sciences, in particular the underrepresentation of women in senior roles.'

The ECU's statistics show how normalised gender equality for students has become that it hardly bears comment, with almost 57% of students being women, while gender inequalities remain rampant in the academic labour market. The ECU shows high median and mean gender pay gaps among levels of staff in universities. For example, three-quarters of UK national staff in professorial roles and two-thirds of non-UK national professorial roles were *white males* in 2014.

A headline in the *Times Higher Education* (Grove, 2015) illustrates how this is continuing: '"Striking" inequalities in higher education fuel gender pay gap', with the byeline 'UK's female academics paid an average of £6,146 less than men, report finds.' This is a report from ECU for 2015, and shows that:

> ... female academics ... are less likely to have a permanent post and more likely to be part-time or employed on a teaching-only contract.... Among academic staff, women make up just 22.4 percent of the cohort ... noted that there are 86,590 female academics in the UK, an increase of 26,445 on 2003-04. The number of men has risen at a slightly slower rate, meaning that women now constitute 44.6 percent of academics compared with 40 percent ten years earlier.

In 2013, less than a quarter of women were (full) professors (2905) out of a total of 15,320, and proportionately more are on fixed-term rather than open-ended or permanent contracts. There remain far more women on part-time contracts than men, almost two-thirds or 34,705 out of 63,665. Thus, over the last 15 years, while the proportion of academics in UK institutions has barely increased, women have increased relative to men, although largely remaining in subordinate roles.[4]

As another instance, for International Women's Week in March 2014, the *Times Higher Education* published a major piece entitled, 'The numbers don't look good, guys', inevitably, perhaps, written by one of their male staff reporters, David Matthews, and addressed to their male readership, as the title implies. Indeed, the whole tenor of the piece is that it is men's right to have better opportunities than women, a form of a laddish or misogynistic culture, perhaps? The byeline of the piece was 'UK women are in the majority at almost every level of study', and David Matthews demonstrated this by an array of facts and figures, and commentary from an entirely male set of interviewees (2014, pp 24-5). One, Jürgen Enders, professor of HE at the University of Southampton, was quoted as saying that, 'Boys getting outperformed in education by girls reflects an international trend, also found in the UK.' Asserting that 'Boys, you have been outplayed', Matthews then asked, 'are there any crumbs of comfort for men in these figures, or are they simply being comprehensively beaten by women in the classroom? The rise in female participation is happening during "a period of declining graduate premium" – at least in the UK, according to Professor Enders. This raises questions about the benefits of higher education for women, and [about] boys eventually finding other routes to attractive jobs and salaries.' The article ended rather lamely, by demonstrating, 'the fact that just one in five professors in the UK is female [is] all the more jarring – universities have become places where the students are largely female, but the academics mostly male.'

As part of the same issue, but not linked together by the editors of the THE, another article addressed that very question of how to redress the balance of gender equity among academics, by looking at 'a new book published for International Women's Day [which] argues that women will achieve their full potential

---

[4] See www.jobs.ac.uk/careers-advice/working-in-higher-education/1379/ statistical-overview/

within universities only once we rethink what we mean by "success"' (Matthews, 2014, p 16). This book is based on the challenges that University of Cambridge women academics face in their professional and personal lives, and how these disadvantage them in a sharply gender-segregated HE, where it is clear that women are regarded as not as important as men. The book is threaded through with examples of the struggles that women in science, technology, engineering, mathematics and medicine (STEMM) face, as well as distinguished women within the humanities and social sciences.

A particular cause célèbre was that of Professor Mary Beard, a Cambridge classicist who was subject to a barrage of misogynistic insults and abuse following a television appearance a year previously on a popular BBC programme, namely, 'Question Time'.

This book had followed from a report from the University of Cambridge's gender equality champion, Dame Athene Donald, who had argued for structural changes in academia to tackle inequality, especially, but not only, for women in scientific careers (*Times Higher Education*, 20 February 2014, p 10). Indeed, it is clear that these problems are endemic in HE today, and the *Times Higher Education* argued 'Gender equity: must do better', since a major workforce survey had shown that 'discrimination against women persists in the UK academy, even in institutions that have been recognised for their good employment practices' (*Times Higher Education*, 20 February 2014, p 13).

Showing their liberal feminist tendencies, however, both Mary Beard and Athene Donald leapt to the rescue of Professor Sir Timothy Hunt, FRS, who got himself into hot water with a lecture to female science journalists at the world conference of science journalists in Seoul, Korea, in June 2015. He had made derogatory remarks about women in science, and especially in science laboratories, that immediately went viral. The provost and president of UCL, Professor Michael Arthur, wrote the following comments in the weekly staff newsletter, illustrating how contentious Hunt's views were, and justifying a commitment to gender equality on socioeconomic grounds:

UCL was the first University in England to admit women on equal terms to men. Equality between the sexes is one of our core values, yet this past fortnight our commitment to women and to women in science has been challenged, our reputation put under pressure and we have been part of an intense and uncomfortable media storm. The trigger for this was remarks about the place of women in science made by Sir Tim Hunt. I don't intend to repeat or re-analyse who said what, where or when, and thereby provide more fuel for media speculation. I will simply restate that when on the 10th June Sir Tim sent in his resignation from his honorary position with UCL, as Provost I sanctioned acceptance of that resignation in good faith on the basis that it was his personal choice as the honourable thing to do.... What good can come of this episode and what ultimately is the big picture that UCL should now focus its energies and efforts on? Equality, diversity and the greatest good for the greatest number are enshrined in our Benthamite origins. Those values hold true to this day and we constantly try to live up to them.... To a significant extent, we, like many other universities, have failed to achieve the level of equality and diversity that we aspire to. We have been self-critical in this regard and have identified the need to do better as a key part of our strategy, UCL 2034. We are making slow (some would say glacial) progress on gender equality and are working hard to tackle racialised inequalities (perhaps an even more complex issue) head on. Women now make up 33% of the senior academic and professional staff in grades 9 and 10.... In other words Equality and Diversity is not just an aspiration at UCL but informs our everyday thinking and our actions. It was for this very reason that Sir Tim's remarks struck such a discordant note. Our ambition is to create a working environment in which women feel supported and valued at work. To be frank, a reputation for such helps us attract the very best women to UCL, including women in science. Athene Donald's blog contains some excellent practical suggestions for what we should actually do to improve things for women in science, all of which I agree with. There have been many calls for me to reverse my decision to accept Sir Tim Hunt's resignation from his honorary post at UCL, but there have also been very significant representations to me not to do so, including, but not only, from women in science. Our view is that reversing that decision would send entirely the wrong signal and I have reason to believe that Sir Tim would also not want that to happen. An honorary appointment is meant to bring honour both to the person and to the University. Sir Tim has apologised for his remarks, and in no way do they diminish his reputation as a scientist. However, they do contradict the basic values of UCL – even if meant to be taken lightly – and because of that I believe we were right to accept his resignation. Our commitment to gender equality and our support for women in science was and is the ultimate concern.[5]

In the public eye: student life on university campuses

Clearly, students, and women students especially, are very much in the public eye, through the media. HE is now a central facet of our lives, reaching as it does, nowadays, huge swathes of the population in the UK as elsewhere, such as other countries of Europe, the US and the developing world. A particularly intriguing but arcane fact for the UK is that the future King and Queen – Prince William and Princess Kate of Cambridge – met as undergraduate students at St Andrews University, a sign of massively changing times whereby the Prince was allowed both to be a student and to consort with a commoner, albeit one whose family had amassed a considerable fortune, but through a marketing company, in keeping with increasingly neoliberal times! And their son, Prince George, will be, if he goes on to inherit the title, the first King to be the son of a male *and* female graduate! In further evidence of these changing times, Prince William returned to postgraduate study at the University of Cambridge in January 2014. So, even within the ancient system of the monarchy, HE is increasingly becoming a feature, a process started perhaps by Prince Charles, who himself was the first in line to the throne to graduate. He was part of the beginnings of the process of expansion of HE in the 1960s, the implications of which, in terms of women's complexly changing personal, social and professional lives, are still being worked out.

---

5   See more at www.ucl.ac.uk/news/staff/staff-news/0615/26062015-provosts-view-women-in-science

Student life and life after university has also become a fundamental part of popular culture – the zeitgeist – in the Global North, with films, novels, newsprint and television series, as we saw in Chapter Six. For instance, *Fifty shades of grey*, the best-selling salacious novel of all times, published in 2012, opens with two young female Canadian students about to graduate. The book is about young women's sexual fantasies that involve sexual subordination and lust, rather than love, described as 'mommy porn'. Nevertheless, the author E.L. James reverts to the 19th-century habit of not revealing her forenames, acknowledging the ongoing misogynistic nature of public life. Since the book was originally published, we should perhaps then not be surprised by *The Guardian* report (28 February 2014, p 5) entitled, 'Staying power: *Fifty shades* sales pass 100million', that the book which is 'about the 27 year old billionaire Christian Grey's seduction of … the college student Anastasia Steele … has surpassed all previous book sales…. More than 27m of the books by E.L. James had been sold in the UK and Commonwealth countries…. More than 45m copies in the US…. The first novel of the trilogy … has spent 100 weeks on the *New York Times* bestseller list.' Moreover, a film based on the book has been made, and James has written a sequel to the trilogy about Grey's own sexual fantasies that, many argue, amounts to sexual or gender violence, and his behaviour, in real life, would be subject to criminal prosecution.

As the books were written by a woman, who has become a multi-millionaire, it is claimed that these women's sexual fantasies must be acceptable. But are our sexual fantasies moulded by the particularly abusive and violent culture that is being re-created within our increasingly competitive society for the global race to the top? Many feminists have argued that they contribute to 'mommy porn' or sado-masochistic gender violence, but whichever, Lisa Appignanesi, together with Rachel Holmes and Susie Orbach (2013), edited a book entitled *Fifty shades of feminism*.

Appignanesi (2013) justified their use of the term in a media article entitled 'How *Fifty shades of feminism* dragged the F-word out of the shade'. She argued that 'fifty million women readers can't be altogether wrong … [but] our times are still embroiled in misogyny … so it is fifty women exploring what feminism means to them today.' All the contributors are former students and feminist journalists, professionals or academics. But they do not attend primarily to the increasingly overt nature of a sexualised and laddish culture on campus, particularly, but not only, among students.

Yet this has been subject to an increasing amount of feminist research, to try to make campuses safe for students and for others. It has also been to develop policies to deal with sexual assaults, harassment and a rape culture. A particularly crass instance of this attempt to make campuses safe for women was the comment made by the Toronto police constable, referred to earlier, about women not dressing like 'sluts' (Teekah et al, 2015). As the cover of the book argues, 'in April 2011 ... a protest responding to slut shaming and victim blaming culture, exemplified by a recent event at Osgoode Hall Law School at York University, in the name of campus "safety"....'

Such issues of campus safety are, however, only just beginning to be part of developing more inclusive gender policies internationally, and in response to recent feminist campaigning. Indeed, British policy responses remain very muted by comparison with North America, although there have been some recent institutional responses through developing lessons in 'sexual consent' for incoming undergraduate students.

Protecting students from sexual assault: President Obama's White House Task Force

US President Barack Obama took the question of campus safety very seriously in response to the White House Council on Women and Girls that reported on college sexual assault in early 2014. The report, entitled *Rape and sexual assault: A renewed call to action*, found that 22 million American woman and 1.6 million men had been victims of sexual assaults, with a poor criminal justice response due to police bias and inadequate training: 'No one is more at risk of being raped or sexually assaulted than women at our nation's colleges and universities....' This was widely reported in US media with the *New York Times* (24 January 2014): 'Acting a month after he gave the Pentagon a year to show it had cut down on the number of sexual assaults in the military, Mr Obama summoned cabinet officials and senior advisers to a meeting to review progress more broadly against rape and other sexual attacks throughout society. But the focus was on problems at college campuses....' Similarly, the *LA Times* (24 January 2014) reported on how:

> President Obama launched a federal task force ... to combat sexual assault on college campuses, telling the estimated one in five women who are victims, "I've got your back." Flanked by senior members of his Cabinet at the White House, Obama said he expected recommendations from the group within 90 days. He credited an "inspiring wave of student-led activism" that has cast a spotlight on the issue in recent years.

Interestingly, there was very little comment about this in UK media or politics. Martin Pengelly reported for *The Guardian* (2014) that 'President Barack Obama used his last weekly address before his State of the Union speech to appeal for action over what he called "the crime, the outrage, of sexual violence".'

On 22 January 2014, Obama announced the setting up of a White House Task Force to protect students from sexual assault, to deal with rape and sexual assaults on college campuses, and also covering elementary and secondary schools. To quote from the memorandum: 'Because rape and sexual assault also occur in the elementary and secondary school context, the Task Force shall evaluate how its proposals and recommendations may apply to, and may be implemented by, schools, school districts, and other elementary and secondary educational entities receiving Federal financial assistance' (The White House Office of the Press Secretary, 2014). It is also worth quoting this to show how far-reaching the terms of the announcement were, and how the President sought to involve very senior members of his administration, including the law, to support his actions, although, in the final analysis, the report was only to be advisory:

> The prevalence of rape and sexual assault at our Nation's institutions of higher education is both deeply troubling and a call to action. *Studies show that about one in five women is*

a survivor of attempted or completed sexual violence while in college. In addition, a substantial number of men experience sexual violence during college. Although schools have made progress in addressing rape and sexual assault, more needs to be done to ensure safe, secure environments for students of higher education. There are a number of Federal laws aimed at making our campuses safer, and the Departments of Education and Justice have been working to enforce them. Among other requirements, institutions of higher education participating in Federal student financial assistance programs (institutions), including colleges, universities, community colleges, graduate and professional schools, for-profit schools, trade schools, and career and technical schools, must provide students with information on programs aimed at preventing rape and sexual assault, and on procedures for students to report rape and sexual assault. Institutions must also adopt and publish grievance procedures that provide for the prompt and equitable resolution of rape and sexual assault complaints, and investigate reports of rape and sexual assault and take swift action to prevent their recurrence. Survivors of rape and sexual assault must also be provided with information on how to access the support and services they need. Reports show, however, that institutions' compliance with these Federal laws is uneven and, in too many cases, inadequate. Building on existing enforcement efforts, we must strengthen and address compliance issues and provide institutions with additional tools to respond to and address rape and sexual assault. Therefore, I am directing the Office of the Vice President and the White House Council on Women and Girls to lead an interagency effort to address campus rape and sexual assault, including coordinating Federal enforcement efforts by executive departments and agencies (agencies) and helping institutions meet their obligations under Federal law.... The Task Force shall be co-chaired by designees of the Office of the Vice President and the White House Council on Women and Girls. The functions of the Task Force are advisory only and shall include making recommendations ... and consult[ing] with external stakeholders, including institution officials, student groups, parents, athletic and educational associations, local rape crisis centers, and law enforcement agencies ... providing examples of instructions, policies, and protocols for institutions, including: rape and sexual assault policies; prevention programs; crisis intervention and advocacy services; complaint and grievance procedures; investigation protocols; adjudicatory procedures; disciplinary sanctions; and training and orientation modules for students, staff, and faculty.... (emphasis added)

The Huffington Post provided a moving and graphic story from a former student, Malika Saada Saar, who wrote:[6]

In the '90s, a group of students scrawled the names of rapists on the walls of a women's bathroom at Brown University. It was not done to create a witch hunt. It was done as a desperate act to bring accountability to the assailants. We were desperate because Brown University, at that time, failed to construe rape or assault committed by other students on campus as a crime. The administration responded to the assailants as boys acting out, who were, at most, asked to take a semester off. Since then, Brown University has taken significant strides to render sexual assault and rape a crime for which individuals must be held accountable. But very few colleges and universities have done the same. The result is that, almost two decades later, a culture of impunity thrives on college campuses. And, of course, the incidents of sexual violence have therefore increased. This week, the White House Council on Women and Girls released a report on college sexual assault that revealed the following facts:

- One in five students has been assaulted; and
- Assailants are often serial offenders: Seven percent of male students in a study cited by the report admitted to committing or attempting rape – and nearly two-thirds of them admitted to committing these assaults multiple times – six on average.

It is incomprehensible to me that college and university campuses remain unsafe places for young women. How is it that in 21st century America, when more and more women are entering

---

6 President Obama's Task Force on College Sexual Assault, Tweeted by Malika Saada Saar; see www.twitter.com/rights4girls

institutions of higher learning, we are still so vulnerable to sexual violence? How is it that rape culture is so comfortably a part of our college culture? But while violence against women continues unabated, something important did happen yesterday. President Obama named the issue of violence against women on college campuses and used the power of his office to denounce these acts as crimes for which the perpetrators must be prosecuted. I was especially struck by these words from President Obama: "We need to keep saying to anyone out there who has ever been assaulted – you are not alone. You will never be alone. We've got your back. I've got your back." I thought back to being 19 at Brown and feeling so small and scared to speak out against the policies that protected those who committed rape and assault. All of us who were part of that movement at the time, victims and allies alike, felt so alone in what we were asking of the university. Nobody in power had our back. I am now a mother to a little girl who, years from now, will enter one of these institutions of higher learning. My husband and I are working hard to give her the best opportunities so that she may go to a college of her choice. My heart breaks at the thought that she too will enter college without the freedom to be safe from violence. I cannot accept that her story, or the story of any young woman, might be an uninterrupted narrative of victimisation, regardless of her educational status and accomplishments. I am prayerful that the White House Task Force to Protect Students from Sexual Assault will break the inevitability that to be female is to be at risk for violence, especially on a college campus. But, we only get closer to that reality if our colleges and universities adopt the necessary policies to end an entrenched, historic tolerance of rape and assault.

Similarly, Facebook, Twitter and other media were awash with posts about sexual assaults on campus. The following autumn I found myself in the US giving lectures on three college campuses about my study, *Feminism, gender and universities*, and about my EU Daphne-funded study of education and training to challenge gender violence among children and young people, directed by Dr Pam Alldred. This latter Gap Work project conducted in four countries – Ireland, Italy, Spain and the UK – was still in the process of completion, but it clearly spoke to the concerns about sexual assault and violence on campus. We had tried to develop education and training in universities to challenge gender-related violence (to include homophobia) by working with education and youth professionals, who themselves work with children and young people (Alldred and David, 2015). While the participants in my lectures to first, sociology undergraduates at the University of California, Berkeley, second, to academics and administrators of the Diversities and Equalities Unit at Dickinson College, many second-wave feminists, and third, to graduate students and Faculty in Education at Penn State, State College, Pennsylvania were very varied, all told me about the importance of dealing with campus sexual assaults. I was told about the 'HALT sexual violence on campus' campaign in California for the month of October, and joined a small demonstration at the Sather gate entrance to Berkeley at the end of my lecture. How fitting it felt to be able to campaign again.

I was also reminded of being in California for the first time some 45 years ago, when I was given a massage in the Berkeley Hills for my birthday by some proto-feminist friends, but pre-dating the notion of waves of feminism. The masseuse invited me to have music while she was treating me, and suggested several pieces, including the ocean. I did not then appreciate that the American word for the sea was the ocean, and asked for this! It was both relaxing as the waves were lapping on the beach, and stirring for the gentle change it invoked. And perhaps that is what is still stirring in California and the rest of the US.

On the other hand, many also told me how contentious the question of dealing with campus violence continued to be, especially given the increasing involvement of the legal profession in the US, such that it was becoming a big industry to deal with such questions on campus. Indeed, as Ileana had predicted, commissioning the report was clearly important to raising consciousness of the issues of sexual assault, leading to new forms of protest such as Sexual Assault Awareness Month (SAAM) becoming a more regular public feature. Nevertheless, the report is only advisory, and has remained contentious.

A particularly poignant example of this is the student Emma Sulkowicz, who became the face of 'college rape'. It is poignant because issues of 'sexual consent' are so hard to substantiate.

Emma claimed that, in 2012, a fellow student had raped her in her dorm room at Columbia University, NYC. Paul Nungesser, a student from Germany, claimed, through his lawyer, that the sex had been consensual. After the school found him 'not responsible', Emma began carrying the mattress on campus, vowing to do so until she graduated or he left. Indeed, she carried the 50-pound mattress around campus for two years, including for her graduation or commencement ceremony in May 2015. Supported by her parents, *The New York Times* also reported that Columbia's President Lee Bollinger turned away as she crossed in front of him at commencement. She argued that she was not just going to throw the mattress away, and that a New York museum might like to keep it.[7]

The culture of 'laddism'

While there is far less media or political debate and fanfare about campus safety and sexual assaults in the UK, several of my feminist colleagues have done very important work on looking at the rape and 'lad culture' on campus. Their work is becoming more important to developing new policies and practices, while at the same time, it has been subject to contestation by other feminists. Two among my third cohort of feminists in the UK have done similar work on the changing sexual culture of university campuses. Interestingly, both have doctorates in the sociology of education, supervised by second-wave academic feminists.

Now director of the Centre for Gender Studies at the University of Sussex, Dr Alison Phipps is a feminist sociologist with expertise in sexual violence, particularly among students. After completing a BA in political theory and history at the University of Manchester, Alison went on to do an MA there, and moved to the University of Cambridge to undertake a PhD in the sociology of education, specialising in gender. This is where her political and research interests began to take an explicitly feminist focus, and she gradually became involved

---

[7] See www.nydailynews.com/new-york/columbia-u-anti-rape-activist-graduates-mattress-tow-article-1.2228061

with the FWSA, becoming its chair during 2009–12. She moved to studying sexual violence on university campuses, including undertaking a major survey of students and sexual violence for the National Union of Students (NUS) in the UK, reported in 2010. This was entitled *Hidden marks*, a lovely play on words about gender in HE. She has since published widely on the topic, and presented papers with Isabel Young, a colleague, in national media and in academic circles. In a presentation at the British Educational Research Association (BERA) in September 2013, and since published, they wrote:

In late 2012, we were commissioned by NUS to conduct qualitative research on "lad culture" at UK universities. This functioned partially as a follow-up to the *Hidden marks* survey (NUS, 2010), which had revealed a high prevalence of sexual harassment and violence against UK university women. "Lad culture" was ... indicative of the persistence of gendered structures and cultures in HE. Our research aimed to provide a qualitative examination of the phenomenon ... and interviews with 40 women students. Our report, entitled *That's what she said* (Phipps, 2013), was launched by NUS on International Women's Day 2013. Our participants were recruited from Higher Education Institutions, students' unions and student groups across the UK.... The majority of respondents were undergraduate students aged between 18 and 25, but some were postgraduates and two were over 30. All were cisgendered women, although some expressed ambivalence in relation to their gender identities. Almost 80 per cent identified as heterosexual.... Giving an insight into the social context of laddism ... most defined their ethnicity as white British and described themselves as middle class.... For our participants [laddism] was primarily found in the social sphere ... a key site for the operation of "campus culture" ... laddish values and behaviours were thought to dominate here, especially extra-curricular activities and nightlife ... with sport and alcohol.... Laddish behaviours included misogynist banter, objectification of women and pressures around quantities and particular forms of sexual interaction and activity. One described ... a member of the rugby team dressed in a vest reading "Campus Rapist" on the front and "it's not rape if you say surprise on the back".... Two-thirds of our study participants talked about sexual harassment, describing it as a normal part of university life and as at least partially produced by "lad culture". As one ... said: "I don't know anyone, any of my female friends who haven't had some kind of encounter that was harassment whether it be verbal or physical since they've been at university".... The discomfort expressed by many of our participants was less bound up with sex than with sexism, confirming suggestions that "lad culture" may in fact merely represent "sexism with an alibi".

Carolyn Jackson at Lancaster University (mentioned earlier) has had a similar educational trajectory: it is only recently that she has moved to studying campus sexual violence, having previously been concerned with 'laddism' in schools. Her evidence and arguments are equally concerning, given the political context that student 'lad culture' has become a national issue, arguing that: 'The phenomenon, often associated with the website Unilad, has become a catch-all term for anything from boozy boisterousness to casual misogyny and even sexual abuse. But despite numerous media reports on laddism, universities still have little idea of how widespread its effects are' (Wiseman, 2013). In a paper with Steve Dempster, a colleague at Lancaster, and Lucie Pollard, at the University of Greenwich, entitled, '"They just don't seem to really care, they just think it's cool to sit there and talk": Laddism in university teaching-learning contexts', they argue that:

Over the last 2-3 years there has been a sharp increase in the UK in the number of concerns voiced about "laddism", "laddish" or "lad" cultures in higher education. Drawing on a project that explored laddism on a sports science degree in one university, this article explores constructions and understandings of laddism in HE, particularly in teaching-learning contexts. Undergraduates suggested that laddish behaviours in teaching-learning contexts included: talking and generally being loud; being a joker; throwing stuff; arriving late; and being rude and disrespectful to lecturers. Mature students (men and women) and women were particularly critical of these behaviours, and resented the ways they negatively impacted on their learning. The impacts of laddism on the lads

> themselves and on others are explored, as are the ways in which
> laddism is challenged. (Jackson et al, 2015)

Carolyn has begun to work on a new study with Vanita Sundaram of the University of York, and presented a paper at the GEA conference in June 2015. Here they talked about "'Lad culture" and HE: exploring the perspectives of staff working in HE institutions'. This important paper illustrates different perspectives of feminist academics and other staff in relation to dealing with gender and sexuality in the classroom as much as in the student cultures on campus, an attempt to understand how to develop more critical perspectives in relation to teaching particular subjects as much as to do with how students interact away from the classroom. Nevertheless, Professor Gill Crozier, a second-wave feminist, contended that the concept of 'lad culture' was concerned more with questions of racism than gender. She argued that the concept was racist in that it was exclusive of black and minority ethnic students in that they did not see themselves as 'lads', it being a term exclusively for white men/boys!

Alison Phipps has also extended her studies and has been commissioned by Imperial College, London, to undertake a study of 'lad culture' and sexual harassment at a largely science-based institution. She has also become involved in an extension of the EU Daphne-funded study that I conducted with Pam Alldred (Alldred and David, 2015). Given my ageing sensibilities, I have now withdrawn my involvement in continuing to develop education and training for professionals involved with gender-related violence. However, Pam, Fin Cullen and Alison are now about to start another EU-funded study, this time to educate and train university academics and staff on gender-related violence and sexual assaults. This, again, will be a multi-nation study in Europe to develop a greater understanding and policies for HE institutions around sexual assault, bullying and harassment. How much this is still needed and how much I cheer them on, with their sophisticated and complex feminist take on third-wave feminism and beyond.

However, there are some glimmerings of change at the policy level, while there is some measure of 'zero tolerance' for a 'lad culture' at some elite British colleges. For example, for 'Freshers' week' at LSE in the autumn of 2014, the rugby club produced leaflets that described women students as 'slags, sluts and mingers', and these were circulated around the school. The director of LSE, an American sociologist, Professor Craig Calhoun, immediately withdrew the leaflets, and insisted that the rugby club be denied a presence for a year at the LSE. At a public lecture to the Academy of Social Sciences that same week, he described first, his job as an 'administrator' (to use the American term for a senior university official), and how he had had to deal with this issue of 'sexual bullying'. He then went on to discuss the impact of the social sciences in government and politics, the invited theme of his lecture. Here he 'parked' the question of sexual abuse and harassment, let alone gender equality, and lectured as if there were no current issues to contend with!

In other words, all the policy and media focus is on students, and especially the dilemma of a 'lad culture' or sexual assaults. Here, however, there have been a few attempts to develop a new approach to sexual consent on campus, with a number of British universities developing a policy for their own institutions. For instance, a leader in *The Guardian* (20 October 2015, p 32) entitled 'Sex and the student body – Consenting adults: it's all about respect', argued that:

> ... a documentary about sexual assault and rape on US campuses [was] being screened across British universities this week. Ahead of it, students will see a film made by *The Guardian* that reports on the attitudes to and experiences of sex and consent at UK universities. The US film tells the stories of women who became victims and then, in their own words, survivors of rape and sexual assault. It could have been made in the UK... For many female students, sexual experiences range from the unwelcome to the forced. Yet support for those who are assaulted, even when rape is involved, is too often inadequate.... The rise of lad culture, and the heavy drinking that often goes with it, is often blamed for women's experiences.... The head of one Cambridge college ... emailed all students ... I fear that these bullies will leave the college and become unethical pariahs like insider traders.... [as if!]

Other Cambridge colleges and other colleges have developed a practice of providing information and lessons in 'sexual consent' for all incoming undergraduates. This is a welcome start, but it is not enough. Far more important is education, from cradle to grave, to change the culture and the zeitgeist of sexualisation, to ensure that all learn about respectful lifelong relationships that should be maintained. This is barely happening. There is virtually no concern at all about the fact that women are still subordinate within the staffing of global HE. As we look across the echelons of HE, women become more and more rare, most especially for black and minority ethnic groups. The *white male* remains legitimately in power in HE. Indeed, this is now a policy challenge for the UK's government to uphold unabashed and without shame.

Feminists need to continue to build the knowledge and evidence base to counter the arguments that are increasingly made in political arenas about individual women's successes and achievements. At least the opportunities for doing this kind of work within universities and in other educational arenas have increased, as is clear from the above two illustrations of the work of Alison Phipps and Carolyn Jackson, among others.

The influence of misogyny on the neoliberal university

However, the arguments that Jessica Ringrose and others have made about the culture of universities are evidence of how hard this is. For example, Professor Sandra Acker, now emerita at OISE, University of Toronto, argued that misogyny is increasing with the increasingly stark performance-oriented university. She said:

> The university seems to be changing without much input from feminists and it is interesting to see how little attention to gender HE research pays. I have seen umpteen co-edited books with chapters on different countries *vis-à-vis* some aspect of HE such as accountability or governance. Gender is hardly ever featured. Perhaps we could say that "maleness" has influenced the neoliberal university in its relentless focus on performance, competition, achievement.... Women's studies courses were both stand-alone

and part of the curriculum of other disciplines, especially in the humanities and social sciences.... Women's studies departments are closing and there is little scope for experimentation. Looking at the current situation, women academics and doctoral students are better represented than they were in the past; women are a high proportion of those in contingent positions ... differences between disciplines continue; women's responsibility for children still makes a big difference to their career chances, especially combined with labour market changes that make certain jobs scarce and often part-time and short-term. Although there are some prominent women politicians, politics remains a male-dominated pursuit. Changes can be seen in the arts, in professions like law, medicine and pharmacy. In reflecting on my career some of the themes that stand out are changing technologies ... (huge differences in the last 40-50 years); the rise of the research culture; changes in the academic job market; the changing university (neoliberal, global); increases in women's representation and feminist methods, theories and curriculum in certain fields; the rise of other aspects of equity.... Another point is the changing relationship between students and faculty (staff), related to change in the student (and staff) body (more diversity), to student "consumerism" and perhaps to feminism. When I was a doctoral student we didn't even call our supervisors by their first names, let alone expect them to be endlessly available and inclined to mentor us. We did not get extensive comments on chapter drafts or instruction in how to publish.... I think our generation [of feminists] mentored each other and then went on to mentor new generations.... But probably more important was the "peer mentoring" and the simultaneous growth of many other women in the same stage of life with similar interests.... Younger doctoral students and faculty now get much more help and advice. However, the academic world into which they try to go is less open, less forgiving, and expects constant, intensified productivity....

Similarly, Professor Louise Morley, using *She figures*, argues trenchantly about how what is now called 'new managerialism' and the so-called 'leaderist turn' in HE are subverting and reinforcing the 'rules of the game' in misogynistic ways. She provides "an international review of feminist knowledge on how gender and power interact with leadership in HE ... to unmask the 'rules of the game' that lurk beneath the surface rationality of academic meritocracy', arguing that:

> ... curiously, in a culture of measurement and audit in HE, women's representation in different roles and grades is not always perceived as sufficiently important to measure, monitor or map comparatively. The Centre for Higher Education and Equity Research (CHEER) at the University of Sussex had to construct its own tables. The data that do exist suggest that women disappear in the higher grades, ie, when power, resources, rewards and influence increase.... The highest shares of female rectors (vice chancellors) were recorded in Sweden, Iceland, Norway, Finland, and Israel. In contrast, in Denmark, Cyprus, Lithuania, Luxembourg and Hungary, no single university was headed by a woman when *She figures* reported in 2009.... This under-representation reflects not only continued inequalities between men and women, but missed opportunities for women to influence and contribute to the universities of the future.

She concludes that, 'we need new rules for a very different game' (2013, p 2). It is abundantly clear that gender equality is a highly politicised and contested notion in HE today, given the changes towards neoliberalism and its impact on women's participation in global (and academic) labour markets. While there has been huge transformation in women's participation as students, especially undergraduates, in HE across the globe, this is *not* matched by a significant change in women's participation in academic labour markets, as I have tried to show with various statistics for Europe, the UK and the US, and qualitative examples.

The expansion of global universities has gone hand-in-hand with new systems of ranking and socioeconomic relations intensified through business and marketing strategies. This intensification is particularly the case in terms of the culture of student and academic life, whereby sexualisation has become increasingly marked. So, while it is true that there are far more students nowadays and the majority are women, this does not mean that there is more than formal equality in terms of 'the numbers game'. This is controversial, as the 'numbers game' is a mask for continuing power plays, whereby the 'rules of the game' remain misogynistic.

The situation is even more alarming for women from black and minority ethnic backgrounds, made abundantly clear in the *Times Higher Education*, following its report about ECU figures for 2015. These statistics also show that 'the numbers of black and ethnic minorities in the UK academy have shot up, but they remain under-represented at senior levels.... When Baroness Valerie Amos began work as the new director of the School of Oriental and African Studies (SOAS), University of London it was a landmark moment for UK HE.... For the first time a black woman in charge of a university. In fact, Amos is the first black Vice Chancellor full stop' (Grove, 2015). Baroness Amos was formerly a Labour government cabinet minister, and UN ambassador, but does not come from academia. She was professionally involved in local government and in the equalities units and administration.

Grove goes on to demonstrate and highlight the difficulties that black and minority ethnic staff continue to face, particularly women. He quotes Kalwant Bhopal, professor of education and social justice at the University of Southampton, who is not surprised by the level of so-called 'academic flight' given her studies interviewing black and minority ethnic staff about their frustrations with working in academe. These comments have also been expressed by other feminist academics, such as Sara Ahmed, professor of cultural studies at Goldsmiths, Ann Phoenix, professor of child studies at my institution, and Farzana Shain, professor of education at Keele University. This frustration is best expressed by Professor Heidi Mirza, former colleague, now at Goldsmiths, and working closely with Sara Ahmed.

The 'hideously white' place of academe today

The question of feminist ethical practice becomes far more difficult in forbidding times, going far beyond the traditional notions of 'informed consent'. Indeed, the notion of informing, or being informed, takes on contradictory and paradoxical meanings. What now constitutes civil liberties in a cyber-world is also difficult.[8] While the beginnings of academic feminism were felt as stressful within social democracy, this is much more the case in academe today. Heidi expressed the dilemmas of being in and out of academe and its deformed nature extremely appositely:

As a feminist professor I find the academy a very stressful space now. The individualism of the neoliberal culture means there isn't a lot of sharing or camaraderie in universities any more. To stay on top of the food chain – which you are as a highly visible black woman professor – you have to keep producing. There are high expectations and it is exhausting. There's a sense in which you never feel complete and you always feel that the knowledge you are chasing is illusive. Especially now, with the internet where there is so much new information. I've talked to other senior female academics and there is a feeling among them of being a fraud or an interloper in the academic space – which they often attribute to their class or gender – and in my case, ethnicity.... In the specialist field that I work in, which is about the intersectionality of "race" and gender in education, my peers are small in number and getting smaller in the age of austerity where there are so few new appointments and promotions. Many minority ethnic women are choosing to leave HE as racism is as entrenched as ever. Despite the raft of equality policies and legislation they see no future there. HE in Britain remains a 'hideously white' place, (like the BBC!) – there are still only 1.3% BME [black and minority ethnic] staff in HE. In the context of policies on widening participation in HE, and the continued lack of equity in access, particularly for working-class black and white young people, "diversity" has become an all-consuming discourse. However, black women's experience at the institutional level is still very much shaped by the power of whiteness in such places of privilege. Being a body "out of place" in white institutions has emotional and psychological costs to the bearer of that difference. Many just leave.... Feminism is as important today as it has always been. Global gendered and raced

---

[8]   I wrote this before the news of Edward Snowden, the US so-called whistle-blower, and his evidence about the official and secret uses and abuses of the internet were made public (2013).

inequalities are as entrenched as ever. Patriarchy and religious fundamentalism still dominates the majority of women's lives globally. Violence against women is endemic and trafficking of women and children is on the increase. Global capitalism depends on the exploitation and sweatshop labour of women from the Global South. It is important to continue to develop our theoretical and activist thinking about the universal interconnections between "race" and gender inequality and its integral relationship to educational opportunities in HE. Ultimately it is feminism that is still – after all these years – at the vanguard of these outrageous justices against women.

Gender segregation versus gender equality and radicalisation

Indeed, yet other examples of contestations on campus include pressures, at least in the UK, from particular religious groups that may be in the process of what is being called 'radicalisation' to maintain particular religious identities that include gender segregation in lectures and by public speakers. Back in the autumn of 2013, the chief executive of Universities UK, the organisation of university chiefs, who had previously been chief of the ECU, backed calls for public speakers to be able to ask for gender segregation in their lectures. A particular male Muslim speaker had asked for women who wished to attend to be confined to the back of the hall, and, after discussion, this was given official backing. (This is a little like the way Orthodox Jewish women are required to sit behind a curtain in communal prayers in synagogues.) Rendering women subordinate is clearly acceptable today, although a similar decision surely could not have been made on the grounds of 'race', ethnicity or religion: Jews, gays and blacks at the back, would surely have been outlawed?

This kind of development is not confined to the UK. A similar decision was made by a university in Canada, with the *Times Higher Education* headline announcing 'York sticks by "no women" promise to male student', and the byeline was 'Human rights invoked in guaranteeing female-free seminars' (30 January 2014, p 18). In this case, too, it was because of the male student's religious beliefs that he was able to ask not to have women students in his sociology class. What an intriguingly odd place York University in Toronto is becoming! And yet, this is where Lorna Marsden, author of the wonderfully evocative title and inspiring essay, 'Second-wave breaks on the shores of U of T', started out. I, too, flirted with the idea of becoming a dean there almost 15 years ago, with several dear feminist friends and colleagues there: namely, Professors Deborah Britzman, Alison Griffith and Alice Pitt. And I have already mentioned that Jessica Ringrose conducted her doctorate there. What a sure sign of the changing times of feminism. Perhaps another friend and colleague from New Zealand speculates rightly about the changing forms of feminism in the new world order.

The Twitter/Facebook phenomenon

Sue Middleton, recently retired as professor of education at Waikato University in New Zealand, put the changes in a different light, arguing:

> I don't think today's young women are any better off than we were. They have their own issues to deal with eg, sexualisation of little girls; new forms of alcoholism; compulsive consumption (consumer throwaway culture).... This generation's politics are quite different – their "organisation" is via Twitter and Facebook and their activist "groups" are "virtual". The decline of the "public" and the protection of "education for democracy" are my major concerns. The Twitter/Facebook phenomenon reshapes and possibly renames feminism.... Their activism is online. They belong to green/socialist rather than explicitly feminist networks. Feminism always accommodates to new conditions and "our" feminism won't work for "their" contexts.... The emerging feminisms will be based in the Arab/Islamic world, in India and POSSIBLY (but not necessarily) China as the consequences of its one-child policy come to the fore. Western young women seem to have inherited a terrible situation – required to have careers to pay basic bills and not being able to choose to spend time with children. Young girls seem to see equality as "getting as drunk as the boys" and having indiscriminate sex. This isn't what "we"/I fought for. The West has lost its way....

Finally, I turn to another media storm, this time between waves of feminism. Here we witness not just waves breaking on the beach, but very choppy and stormy waters, in which some feminists may feel themselves drowning. Certainly, feminism is being renamed and may need to be reclaimed in new ways, a point to which I return in my final chapter.

Second-wave feminism meets fourth-wave feminism in a university media storm

Germaine Greer, as we have seen, is one very public face of (second-wave) feminism, and is very media-savvy. While I was finalising this book, an angry debate went viral about her being 'no platformed' by Cardiff University. She had agreed to give a public lecture on 'women and power' in November 2015. The women's officer and several thousand feminist students signed a petition objecting to her lecturing, for her 'misogynistic views towards trans women'. This provoked outrage from some older second-wave feminists, who argued on the grounds of free speech that she had a right to be heard, while younger third-wave and beyond feminists were equally apoplectic about her being given a platform. It may be welcome that feminism is being debated in public, but it seems to me very sad that this narrow and ultimately destructive debate is being had in the media about the academy. It turns feminisms into self-hatred and ultimately illiberal positions. And yet, we are still trying to maintain a place and space around the table of academe.

After discussions, Greer agreed to go ahead with her lecture, having initially pulled out, although she has not made any public concessions. Inevitably, the media have made short-shrift of this, with *The Observer Profile* calling her 'still fiery, still outspoken: the feminist lioness', and with the byeline, 'The formidable writer is again embroiled in a protest over her views – but she's never been a stranger to controversy and there's no doubting that she has brought zest and vigour to our intellectual lives.' That said, Bedell (2015, p 31) also argues that 'it's now more what she does – putting herself out there – that is admirable than what she says.' All that is to decry the importance of her second-wave feminist writing over the last 35 years. Indeed, she has been a very public face of second-wave feminism, with her abilities to translate academic feminism into everyday understandings in the media as many on the London 70s Sisters email list acknowledge and even praise.

Defence of her position in arguing against transgender or trans women being acceptable in places reserved for women was presented in the media by Dame Athene Donald, the gender equality champion of Cambridge and 'Master of Churchill college'. Her title illustrates her liberal gender equality sentiments. She wrote an article entitled 'Greer's views may be controversial but she has the right to be heard', arguing that universities should be the bastions of 'free speech', and also says that Germaine has:

> ... form in speaking out against trans people. Nearly 20 years ago she objected to the fact that Newnham (then and now an all-women's college in Cambridge) was admitting as a fellow a woman who had transitioned from male to female some years previously. Newnham went ahead anyhow and that individual remains a fellow of the college.... The idea of "no-platforming" individuals by student bodies just because the invitee might express disagreeable – as opposed to illegal – views seems to be spreading. This is not an action likely to encourage sensible debate. It smacks of censorship.... Let us make sure our universities thrive as places where robust discussions can be heard and the fundamental principle of freedom of speech continues to flourish.

Other (second-wave) feminists have been 'no-platformed' for their views of trans women, and also for views around prostitution, with prostitutes now often named as 'sex workers'. For example, the feminist journalist Julie Bindel was also no-platformed by the University of Birmingham for her views. Intuitively I agree with the defence of academic freedom and free speech, but I have also been persuaded to feel that this continuing commitment to gender binaries, such as men and women, boys and girls, helps to make issues around sexuality, homosexuality and transgender or transqueer far more difficult to debate dispassionately. There are many questions that now need to be raised and debated in safe places and spaces about feelings about gender and sexuality that are only just being opened up for debate. It is indeed curious that Germaine Greer, who was one of the first second-wave feminists to question the stranglehold that definitions of womanhood and sexuality had on our lives, should now be questioning new forms of being a woman, although it is interesting that it is men transitioning to women who tend to become more powerful in cis women circles. Women who transition to men, as, for example, the case of Jack Monroe, cookery writer, campaigner and social commentator, seem to have a more difficult time. Writing under the headline 'We're all a bit non-binary inside. So why do we segregate by gender?', she said 'I don't want to slot into a male/female box: I was raised as a girl but now I just want to be myself. It's time to dismantle the gender constructs...' She concluded her personal testimony and plea by stating that, 'if that threatens you, have a long hard look at yourself and ask why my ovaries-and-testosterone combo makes you uncomfortable. Gender constructs need to be deconstructed for all of our sakes – that's feminism, and I'm not waiting around for Germaine Greer to catch up with us all to do it' (Monroe, 2015, p 39).

EIGHT

Feminist fortunes

As we have clearly seen, the 'F-word' has become centre-stage in global, international HE and media debates, even if it is still not taken seriously in British party politics. In this final chapter I want to reflect on the changing meanings of feminism in the context of changing public and political discussions about how we women should live our lives. These also take place in a massively transformed socioeconomic system towards global 'academic capitalism', that is, a system in which HE and gender, women and/or feminisms have a place and space, even if this is not as powerful a place as we, as feminists, would like to claim. The 'selfie' generation neatly encapsulates the ideas of self-reflection in public and digital media. Indeed, now inevitably being part of that generation, with my constant use of my iPhone, I want to review what has changed, and what I now feel about the sociocultural and political changes in women and men's lives. How influential have we, as feminists, really been, and where might we go from where we are now, using feminist ideas and concepts?

I draw together the threads of the argument that I have been making about gender, women, equality and social justice to weave a complex picture of the changes with respect to men and women's lives in families, education, in universities and in the public worlds of politics, the economy and work. I provide some contemporary illustrations of how second-wave feminism, and some of the articulate, public policy feminists who have been my subjects throughout the book, have been continuing to strive for policy change and activism in an increasingly hostile and neoliberal global world. I consider feminist fortunes, to paraphrase the lovely title of the socialist-feminist political philosopher Nancy Fraser's (2013a) book, *Fortunes of feminism: From state-managed capitalism to neoliberal crisis.*

Fraser argues that, from her perspective as a second-wave feminist, second-wave feminism has gone through three acts, much like a play, and I tend to agree with her: from the WLM as 'an insurrectionary force' to shifting 'its attention to cultural politics just as neo-liberalism declared war on social equality' to now, 'as neo-liberalism has entered its current crisis, the urge to reinvent feminist radicalism may be reviving' (Fraser, 2013a, p 1). These do not necessarily map onto the waves of feminism that I have considered in this book, but do encapsulate the waves of political contestation to feminisms in its moves from patriarchy, through sexism, and now, into everyday misogyny.

In this last case, we are now in what might be thought to be the denouement, although there is some hope for a different world with a future for feminist activism. In many national political respects, we have witnessed a return to traditional relations between men and women in terms of power, prestige and oppression, marriage, female economic and social dependency, childcare and education, despite all the wider socioeconomic and cultural transformations. Many of the social welfare protections and systems for the prevention of sexual abuse, neglect or violence developed in the last 50 or so years have been overturned as we have moved from a political system of social democracy back to a more root-and-branch form of economic neoliberalism. I want to revisit some of these contradictory issues – women more publicly present and yet still unequal and relatively powerless and at increasing risk of male violence or everyday misogyny.

It is indeed something of a paradox that feminism, as a notion, has become part of the current zeitgeist, although it is heavily contested among different currents of feminism. How do the current debates about feminism, as, for instance, in the one about Germaine Greer in the UK, or Hillary Clinton, in her bid to become US president in 2017, map on to the views and values of second-wave feminism that we shared as an aim for sociopolitical transformations? Since the debacle about Germaine Greer, the London 70s Sisters email list has carefully discussed meanings of feminism, ranging from the old radical feminism, about lesbianism, and also socialist-feminism, about our traditional critiques of patriarchy and male power in personal and political relationships, to new forms of male power through the 'manufacture' of gendered identities, where being a woman or a man cannot simply be seen in binary terms. Indeed, subsequent debates about feminisms from the 1970s were about its intersections with class, 'race' or ethnicity and sexualities, interlaced with dealing with sexual or gender violence.

Intersectionality, to use a rather ugly expression, has taken many international and cultural forms, but is particularly important for our understandings of intergenerational and intercultural forms of feminisms, as well as increasing inequalities within and between nation states in an increasingly globalised world, a world where new market niches are sought for capital, including sex and sexualisation, and the medicalisation of gender. The possibilities for breaking down gender binaries, especially the bodies that we inhabit with our minds, are infinitely more varied now than in the past: transgender, trans woman, transsexual.... And generations of feminists have varied takes on these contested and contestable issues.

So what precisely is the feminism that I wish to reclaim from the current turbulence or maelstrom of ideas? How is it that the backlashes to our educational and energetic feminism have become so embroiled in everyday misogyny? Indeed, is this the right concept for the current conflicts against feminisms of whatever hue, or is the notion of neo-patriarchy, linked with neoliberalism, to use the socialist-feminist journalist Bea Campbell's (2013) notion, more apposite, given my abiding concern to think through feminisms linked with socialism as a way forward? In my view, misogyny is a helpful term because it draws on psychoanalytic concepts about how the structures of society (based on notions of normal gender relations) are embedded in our unconscious perspectives, or our psychic lives, and are what Caroline New, my dear feminist friend and colleague called, being 'like the air we breathe'. These ideas also help me to think through issues about my everyday living and to distance the ideas from the purely individual and personal. As we have seen, the term 'misogyny' is now used in popular social media, and even in party politics in some countries such as Australia and New Zealand.

On the other hand, some deeply personal incidents also influence both my feelings and my thinking. For instance, my dear little dog Harry died aged not quite nine, of a congenital heart murmur, a condition of Cavalier King Charles Spaniels. A mighty feminist friend and colleague, Diana Leonard, had bequeathed him to me five years ago, when she was dying of cancer and he was not yet four years old. In my mourning for her 'foppish dog', I am reminded of my mourning for her, and ponder what advice she would want to give me and countless other feminists now: about feminist strategies for a more socially just world, developed through educational scholarship and activism. She would surely applaud the way radical feminism has come to the fore while decrying the continuing feminist contestations on campus. She often remonstrated with me for my lack of attention to lesbianism in my work. What would she and other feminist friends and colleagues who have passed away advise, women such as Diana's early feminist associate, the late Sheila Allen, who also bravely fought for women's rights together with anti-racism, and the late Professor Sue Lees, who fought so bravely for a better understanding of sexual harassment and therefore sex education for girls and young women? And what of Irene Bruegel, who, in her later years, insisted on bringing together feminist economic strategies with questions of sociopolitical justice, concentrating on the plight of Israel's occupation of Palestine and refugees, laced with her own personal history of being the daughter of Czech Jewish refugees. And what of the late Jean Anyon of the US, who shared these visions and argued, like Hester Eisenstein (2010), that socialist feminism had lost out to the corporate business seduction of feminism or the dangerous liaisons between feminism and corporate globalisation?

It is indeed somewhat heartening to hear and read the plaudits to another avowedly public feminist figure, who bravely fought, the late Professor Lisa Jardine:

Lisa Jardine, who has died aged 71 after suffering from cancer, was the leading British female public intellectual of our times. She could properly be called a polymath.... But more important to her than her impressive intellectual achievements – her research, her essays, her fascinating books and stimulating broadcasts – was the opportunity to show a generation of women who came after her that it was both possible to succeed at work and many other things as well... Lisa's guiding principle was that knowledge should be shared.... She was a vocal feminist in the 1970s, and that fervour never left her. In many of her books she sought out the female influence on national, literary or scientific events. But at heart she could not help being a bit of a Jewish mother....

She did not see herself as a feminist theorist, but her engagement with feminist interpretations led to her *Still harping on daughters: Women and drama in the age of Shakespeare* (1983)....

All her life she was a champion of fairness, which lay behind her support for comprehensive education, the NHS and for generations of women in all walks of life. (Kennedy et al, 2015)

Lisa's life and her feminist values of fairness, intellectual rigour and yet the sharing of knowledge and zestful vocalisation of campaigning for a better future encapsulate some of the issues I wish to highlight. By combining my intellectual and personal interests, as part of my wish to transform lives, especially the lives of other women and those with mental health issues, I volunteered to be a trustee of the Women's Therapy Centre (WTC) almost a decade ago. This has been a most exciting and difficult journey for all involved, illustrating ways in which misogyny continues to bear on the lives of some of the poorest women – British citizens, asylum-seekers, migrants and refugees, victims of rape and sexual abuse, young mothers – despite our fighting for them. Just as I was finalising this conclusion, a wonderful piece of poetic justice occurred, giving me slight hope for better feminist fortunes, even within an increasingly misogynistic and global neoliberal world.

Feminist poetic justice through therapeutic interventions

As chair of the trustees of WTC I became involved in planning celebrations and fundraising activities for its 40th anniversary in 2016. This is together with other trustees who range across the generations of feminist politics, including, in particular, Professor Sasha Roseneil, who is both an eminent feminist sociologist and group psychoanalyst, and with Professor Susie Orbach. In 1976, Susie Orbach and Luise Eichenbaum established the WTC in Islington, London. It has grown enormously in public stature over the last 40 years, as a beacon of feminist psychotherapy, especially through the work of Orbach, Eichenbaum and other feminist psychoanalysts such as the late Sheila Ernst. But the current reach of the organisation is very limited given the culture of austerity, and public policy cuts to social welfare and health services for women, which are continuing and getting worse by the day.

I had become enamoured of feminist psychoanalysis back in the 1970s, initially through undertaking some psychotherapy while at Harvard in the early 1970s, where it was freely available as part of the institutional health service. On my return to the UK, I continued to read about and to have some individual psychotherapy. I particularly liked the work of Nancy Chodorow, whose book, *The reproduction of mothering: Psychoanalysis and the sociology of gender* (1978), spoke to my twin concerns, at the time, with feminism and the sociology of motherhood. As already mentioned I tried to weave these two into *The state, the family and education* (this book was re-issued in early 2015, something of a measure of its continuing relevance, linking together ideas about governance, women and education). From the 1970s, I toyed with feminist psychotherapy in both my professional and personal life, including using Chodorow's (1989) *Feminism and psychoanalytic theory* and Janet Sayers' (1991) *Mothering psychoanalysis.* In particular, as already mentioned, I followed the feminist scholarship of Juliet Mitchell with colleagues such as Ann Oakley and Jacqueline Rose, although it was not always easy to present a clear path through to policy analysis and political campaigning. More recently, combining psychic understandings with sexual and social relations has become more commonplace in feminist work and campaigning. Jacqueline Rose's psychosocial scholarship has become more erudite, with, for example, *Women in dark times* (2014), and less easy to relate to feminist activism, *per se*, although she, too, has become active in our campaigning about social justice for Israel and Palestine.

The WTC was founded to provide psychoanalytic psychotherapy to women. This kind of professional psychoanalytic support for women with issues about their mental health was not available elsewhere in England, and only rarely available in the US, where both Susie and Luise had undertaken their psychoanalytic training. Five years later they established the Women's Therapy Centre Institute in New York City.

The WTC quickly became unique in its second-wave feminist critique of women's issues, by providing individual support for women's mental health through professional psychological services, influential especially for individual women's work. *Fat is a feminist issue,* written by Susie, was published in 1978, as the first ever critique of how women's feelings become wrapped up in issues about their women's bodies. It became a self-help manual for women who were compulsive eaters. This bestselling book was quickly followed by a second version. In 1982, Susie and Luise jointly wrote *Outside in… Inside out*, about women's psychology based on their work at the WTC, with an expanded version called *Understanding women* published in 1983. Having started out as Freudians, they provided a critique of Freudian orthodoxy and biological determinism, centring on a radical reappraisal of the mother–daughter relationship, and how the family and social context creates women's sense of themselves. They built a model of women's psychology, illustrated with case studies, and discussed the consequences in terms of psychological problems – such as depression, phobias and eating disorders – commonly affecting women. A companion volume called *What do women want* was published in 1984, highlighting the fact that women are brought up to understand men's emotional needs, but men are not brought up to understand women's, leading to a crisis in the relationships between men and women.

Their work sparked both my personal and professional interest, and I note with some pleasure that my sister Anne bought me a copy of *Bittersweet* for my birthday in 1987, since it was about 'sisterhood and networking [and] the emotional tangles which are presently causing havoc in women's relationships with each other.' On the back cover of this book Orbach and Eichenbaum argue that 'women have travelled a long way since the heady days of early feminism in the sixties and seventies. Both in public and private, their expectations are better defined, their needs better understood, their commitment to each other better appreciated. But this is only the first stage towards self-realisation, since their very real achievements often result in feelings of rage, envy and inadequacy directed not at men but at each other'.

Since then, Susie in particular has become a public intellectual through her professional and journalistic work, including, famously, being the late Princess Diana's therapist. She has established a range of campaigning groups such as Antidote, an organisation committed to developing emotional literacy in private life, and Endangered Bodies, around women's bodies. Although she has moved a long way both personally and intellectually from the WTC, since its early days – becoming a 'post-heterosexual', as she puts it – she remains deeply committed both to its next 40 years and its survival at this conjuncture. So she, too, has become involved in our 40th anniversary celebrations and fundraising strategies.

It is a piece of feminist poetic justice that we have been offered premises at LMU to hold our celebratory conference in December 2016. These are now called The Old Bathhouses, and are in London's East End. It just so happens that these premises were the former purpose-built premises of the Women's Library (mentioned in Chapter Three). As Dr Anne Summers, Chair of the Friends of the Women's Library, put it in a letter to *The Guardian* entitled, 'There is a museum of female emancipation: The Women's Library':

> The Women's Library, whose original collections were those of the female suffrage petitioners of 1866, is an accredited national museum as well as a library and archive, and its contents cover changes in women's lives from the 18th century to the present day. It was forced to leave its purpose-built and Heritage Lottery-funded premises in London Metropolitan University in 2013, but now is housed at the LSE.... (Summers, 2015)

Indeed, the way that LMU 'forced' the library to leave its premises was deeply misogynistic, arguing that it was not paying its way, and yet keeping the buildings for LMU's own commercial use, buildings that had been designed by a feminist architectural collective called Rooms of Our Own, led by Wendy Davis. This had sparked a long and contentious campaign to Save The Women's Library, which was ultimately unsuccessful, in these days of ruthless competition between universities for market capture. LMU was at the time a so-called 'failing university' in London, whereas LSE was a premier elite college, and one that wanted to capture elite women, too. The move to locate the Women's Library in one of the premier social science collections in one of the more elite universities in the UK does, however, send out the message that education and HE *are* vital for policy and political change.

As part of the contested public debate about LSE and the Women's Library, the newly appointed director of the LSE library in 2014, Elizabeth Chapman, wrote:

> ... one of LSE's greatest assets is that we are a campus university, located in the centre of London, and throughout the transfer we have been open about keeping all of the library's collections together in a single location ... and the Women's Library reading room will be accessible to the public throughout the year. LSE is undoubtedly different to previous locations for this collection – we host a vibrant and immensely popular public lecture series alongside our world-renowned taught courses. These differences will be explored to their fullest potential as we bring out the best in this unique collection for a wider audience than ever before. (Chapman, 2014, p 33)

These sound like sterling and promising words.

I turn now to consider some other feminist reflections on where we are today, with an important one held at LSE for the inauguration of the Women's Library in its new premises, and the other at the British Library, for International Women's Day in 2014. Both feminist conversations contain many of the threads about changing forms of feminism and political action that I have presented throughout this book: balancing feminist activism and keeping misogyny at bay.

Women, money and social inequalities

Professor Mary Evans, LSE centennial professor at the Gender Institute, hosted and chaired the conversation at LSE, on behalf of the Women's Library, which was about women, money and inequality. There were two speakers – Professors Emerita Diane Elson and Ruth Lister – who were, with Mary, all part of the WLM morphing into second-wave feminism. All have been social scientists since the 1960s, but also involved in feminist activism, through WLM. As we saw earlier in Chapter Four, Ruth is now a Baroness and strives to develop social policy issues in the House of Lords, developing a gendered political and social analysis of the issues in the UK, from women's economic dependency through to women and children's poverty. More recently, she has been involved in the House of Lords debate about tax credits, in which the House of Lords successfully blocked the Conservative Chancellor of the Exchequer's (George Osborne) plans to cut back public spending on poor working people, largely women, a point to which I return later.

A key point that Ruth made was that women's lack of power and control over resources led to economic violence such that women's freedoms were curtailed. Indeed, women in economic dependent relations could become trapped in violent and abusive relationships: *the so-called power of the purse and force of the fist!* This led to her wider intellectual interest in citizenship and its gendered forms, and her increasingly sophisticated study of its workings and implementation. She argued that the Women's Budget Group (WBG), of which she had been a member (and which Diane Elson now chaired), saw women as the shock absorbers of poverty, or what she called, 'sexually transmitted poverty'.

Diane Elson, an international development expert, provided a wider perspective with her focus on work for the UN from the first international conference on women in 1975 in New York. She made the important point that not all societies are like the UK in being based on a money economy, since many have only been moving to becoming monetised in our lifetimes. This means that millions of women around the world remain with no money of their own, and thus, proxy measures, such as women's employment, need to be used to show inequalities in economic dependence. She pointed out that while countries of the Global South had become more like the Global North in being monetised, they remained fundamentally unequal with respect to women's power and resources.

Both also pointed to the early excitement and passion of creating an innovative analysis of women's relationships to men through the household and family, and especially the caring work in looking after the household and children. This had been part of political activism through the women's movement, which had gradually become incorporated into more academic, social scientific endeavour. While the research base and gendered analysis had become more central, changes in global and local political economies rendered the obstacles to broad socioeconomic changes difficult to remove. Thus the balance sheet of the successes of the WLM compared with individual women's successes with political and social change was harder to gauge.

In the concluding discussion it is clear that this is now a 'rich' discussion, as Mary Evans put it (also punning on the wealth analogies), but feminist fortunes remain in the balance. Globalisation and neoliberalism have wrought changes that increase some middle-class or elite women's economic independence and ability to work in these economies while collective change has not been equalised for women. Rather, there have been major increases in inequalities between men and women, rich and poor, and across and between classes. Women remain the majority in poverty, and collective and collaborative action to alter these balances remains fraught. In the UK, the destruction of local authorities has led to the loss of local community action and at the same time, the loss of welfare rights. Thus political parties are now more knowing with respect to the ideologies of women's rights, but do little more than pay lip service to how to transform economic inequalities and care. Misogyny continues to rule the political system, and the gains that the WLM has made on all women's lives have been relatively meagre: there are certainly no real fortunes.

In thinking about how misogyny is an everyday experience, I was also reminded of how embroiled in misogyny both Mary and I were about 10 years ago, when her excellent book, *Killing thinking: The death of the universities* (2004), was published. As I was involved with a number of HE organisations, I nominated Mary as a keynote speaker for them, on the topic of her book. Some months later, I was puzzled to discover that she had not been invited to present, and questioned why. I was told that she was too critical of university bureaucracy to be taken seriously. She had called university managers 'little Hitlers' (Evans, 2004, p 34), and had even commented on its 'unfortunate anti-German connotations' (Evans, 2004, p 35). The senior man in question objected to being called a Nazi, and thus insisted on her exclusion: surely a clear example of everyday misogyny?

Legacy of sisterhood from the WLM

On the other hand, but equally illustrative of how complex and contradictory events have become around social movements and media, the British Library celebrated International Women's Day in 2014 with a discussion panel entitled 'Sisterhood: Greenham in common'. This panel discussion was to both celebrate and take forward the British Library's online learning and educational resources that had been announced a year previously (as noted in my introductory chapter) on International Women's Day, entitled 'Sisterhood and After: The Women's Liberation oral history project', in conjunction with the Women's Library and the University of Sussex.

The chair of the panel, Jude England, director of social sciences at the British Library, pointed out that her four panellists might not, in their younger selves as social and political feminist activists, have expected to have reached their positions of eminence today. Intriguingly, and in line with a thread of my argument, one was a Baroness, one a Dame, one a Professor and one a Doctor. They are all now involved in forms of education from school to higher education!

As with the previous panel, over 35 years ago, the four women had all been involved with the women's movement through school, college or university, and especially in campaigning for peace and against nuclear deterrents, as part of the protests at Greenham Common and through CND. This is again a current issue with Jeremy Corbyn's election as Labour Party leader and the parliamentary Labour Party contestations. In 1979, just after the General Election in which Margaret Thatcher came to power as the first female but Conservative British Prime Minister, NATO announced, without any prior discussion, that the US would be placing nuclear missiles on European soil to deter the Soviet Union from nuclear strikes against the US. One major US base was to be at Greenham Common near Newbury in Berkshire, where there were to be several Cruise missiles. Women from across the UK quickly began to protest about the severity and danger of having nuclear warheads so close to their homes, children and families. Many women went as peace activists to the base and began to camp there, initially at the main gate, but eventually surrounding the whole base and decorating it with women and children's items, and with song and dance. I remember clearly going there from Bristol with my two young children as part of a relatively local feminist contingent.

Baroness Beeban Kidron was a young film-maker who had just embarked on a course and had gone to film the peace activists at Greenham as part of what she thought would be practice for her. She quickly became involved in the activities and in diverting other newscasters' and film-makers' attention from some of the women's more questionable activities, spending seven months of her life at the camp. With Amanda Richardson, she eventually made a film – 'Carry Greenham home' – that has memorialised and celebrated the women of Greenham across the world. She has since gone on to make many significant feminist films, including 'Oranges are not the only fruit' (based on the feminist novelist Jeannette Winterson's first novel) and 'Bridget Jones' diary'. She was made a Baroness in 2012 and sits as a crossbencher. She has created an educational resource, entitled 'FILMCLUB', that gives children from participating schools access to thousands of films, and organises school visits by professionals from within the film industry. She was awarded an Honorary Doctorate from

Kingston University in 2010 for her contribution to education. She became a board member of the UK Film Council in 2008 with a mandate to provide film education.

Dame Joan Ruddock was a political activist in the Socialist Campaign Group and Labour Party, and had unsuccessfully tried to obtain a parliamentary seat for Newbury in the late 1970s. She also was actively involved in CND, becoming chair during the critical years of 1981-85 when the peace camp activist women needed great support and help. Although she never lived at the camp, she had great admiration for those who lived there, and provided support and sustenance as well as distraction from the more questionable male socialist politics of the time. She resigned from being chair of CND in 1985, and stood successfully as a Labour candidate in 1988, becoming MP for Lewisham Deptford. She served as a government minister for women briefly under Blair's New Labour government, and later as Minister for Energy and Climate Change under Gordon Brown as Prime Minister. She was made a Dame in 2012, and is also an Honorary Fellow of Goldsmiths College, University of London, having graduated with a BSc from Imperial College, University of London.

Professor Sasha Roseneil, whom I have already mentioned as a fellow trustee of WTC, was still a schoolgirl in the early 1980s, and went on a women's demonstration with her mother and sister to Greenham, and became completely captivated by the peace camp. She eventually left school early and went to live at the camp for several months, seeing all the different strands and conversations as incredibly special and creatively anarchic. Later she wrote her doctoral thesis on the Greenham peace movement, and has published frequently on the topic. She is now an internationally renowned professor of gender and psychosocial studies, and director of the Birkbeck Institute for Social Research. Prior to Birkbeck, she was professor of sociology and gender studies at the University of Leeds (2000-07), where she was also the founding director of the Centre for Interdisciplinary Gender Studies (1997-2004). The WLM as the key social movement of the 20th century has been critically important to her, both personally and professionally. It has led her to conduct European and international studies on 'Gendered citizenship in multicultural Europe: the impact of contemporary women's movements'.

In a nice neat circle, Dr Rebecca Johnson had been a feminist and undergraduate student at the University of Bristol where she gained a BSc (Hons) in the 1970s and was part of our collective developments through the WLM and BWSG. She left Bristol and went to do a Master's at the University of London's School of Oriental and African Studies (SOAS) about China. Having taken her MA exams but not yet completed her thesis, she left to travel to Beijing, returning in August to visit the camp. She had intended only to spend a week there, but kept leaving and returning, eventually spending several years living as a peace activist and involved with all the creative activities, especially song and dance. She later went on to co-found the Acronym Institute for Disarmament Diplomacy in 1995, having obtained a PhD from LSE. She has had extensive experience as a grassroots activist and organiser, and is a member of the International Institute for Strategic Studies (IISS) and Women in Black. While her present research priorities are weapons of mass destruction (WMD), space weaponisation and international security, Rebecca has authored numerous articles and reports on the UN system and multilateral disarmament and negotiations, notably, the Nuclear Non-Proliferation Treaty (NPT) and the Comprehensive Test Ban Treaty (CTBT), civil society and British defence policy, and lectures on these subjects to a wide range of UN and other international meetings.

What the panellists wanted to create, and succeeded in doing so, was the atmosphere and feelings about women's creativity and activism in pursuit of peace and social justice, fighting against the un-reflexive assumption that had been made by NATO, the US and UK governments about the protection from nuclear disaster that such WMD could proffer. This was an astonishing reminder of the energy of feminist activism that has since been diverted into other critical campaigns, although not yet as successfully as the Greenham women's peace camp. Indeed, the women's peace camp and the linked women's movement activities illustrated quite how important it was to have a quiet space for conversations and reflections on the violence of war contrasted with peace in these hazardous times. What was eloquently and passionately argued was that a commitment to women's ways of knowing and thinking was vital to stem the unthinking violence implicit in the potential use of Cruise missiles.

And even more dramatically, it is clear, with the benefit of hindsight, that these women's collective, leaderless and yet anarchic actions were successful in transforming minds and political actions around the idea of mutually assured destruction (MAD). This was a point made most eloquently by Joan Ruddock. While it was both creative and extremely precarious, the women's peace camp was on the radical edge of a much wider and larger movement of women, through the WLM, trade unionists, CND, and even religious groups such as the Quakers, who all contributed to support and action.

By December 1987, just five years after the camps had begun, there was a major peace treaty and the removal of nuclear weapons and the later demolition of the base itself. Through the leadership of Mikhail Gorbachev from the Soviet Union with other European countries, including the European Nuclear Disarmament (END) campaign, a treaty was signed. So, 26 years on, there is no longer any sign of where the base actually was: it is now heathland and a nature reserve where it was once a nuclear base, covered in barbed wire. It could be said to be a victory for social movements and campaigning, although there is clearly no end to the uses of warlike rhetoric and violent actions, which continue in other avenues today. Yet we can draw knowledge and inspiration from this particular action to try to continue to transform politics and lives through alternative actions and continuing social movements.

Women, social and sexual equality and party politics

One of the key threads to my argument is how to effect sociopolitical change for better feminist fortunes and to curtail male power. One clear way, illustrated throughout the examples in this book, is by committing to a national political party, initially through membership, and subsequently through different kinds of political engagement and involvement. A particular exemplification of an extraordinary way of accomplishing this has been through, in the British case, the reform of the House of

Lords by the Labour Party, two decades ago. The resulting effect has been the creation of feminist life peers, or Baronesses! As we have already mentioned, North Americans find this quite bizarre, and yet, by some extraordinary quirk of fate, these women and feminist Baronesses, who hold positions through appointment for their professional excellence and commitment to Labour of liberal party politics, rather than parliamentary democracy, have played a major part in countering some of the worst excesses of the current neo-liberal politics of austerity.

A key instance is the role that they played in the debate about the Conservative cuts in public expenditure on social welfare planned for implementation from the autumn of 2015. Led by Baronesses Molly Meacher, a crossbench peer, who had been involved in social welfare policies for the previous 25 years or more, and Baroness Patricia Hollis, a Labour peer, and former professor of politics from the University of East Anglia, the House of Lords voted to severely delay plans to curtail tax credits to working people, to supplement their low pay. The leader of the House of Lords, Helene Hayman (mentioned in Chapter Three), also supported these moves, as did Ruth Lister and Beeban Kidron, among others. Baroness Brenda Hale, the only woman judge in the British Supreme Court, and also a former academic feminist, was also supportive.

In a recent comment, as reported by Martin Bentham (2015), Brenda Hale criticised her fellow women for allowing the Supreme Court to remain 'male-dominated' by failing to apply for promotion. She suggested that today's generation (of women lawyers) were more reticent than the 'early women' of her era. Her era, of course, was that of second-wave feminism, and she was a prominent scholar of feminism and the law, publishing *Women and the law* under her name as Brenda Hoggett with Susan Atkins in 1984. Her comments were in response to the misogynistic comments of Supreme Court Justice Lord Sumption, who had said that there could be appalling consequences if efforts to achieve equality proceeded too quickly and deterred talented men from applying. She argued for diversity, and also said 'we owe it to our sex, but also to the future of the law and the legal system for women to step up to the plate.' However, her comments, although welcome, fail to recognise the increasing everyday misogyny, as, for example, the case already mentioned of the lawyer working on sexual abuse cases, Charlotte Proudman, who was subject to misogynistic comments about her looks rather than her professionalism, and subsequently harassed because of her complaints.

The issue of tax credits illustrates especially the problems for poorer but hard-working women. Originally developed by a New Labour administration, led by the then Prime Minister Gordon Brown, they are generally paid more frequently to women, especially those in low-paid jobs. In another neat circle of revisiting social democracy, in an article based on a lecture prepared for the 50th anniversary celebration of CPAG, an organisation founded by the late Professor Peter Townsend in 1965, and led first by Frank Field MP, followed by Ruth Lister, Gordon Brown argued that 'my tax credits are a lifeline. Osborne is wrong to slash them' (Brown, 2015). He went on:

> ... it will be clear that the majority of today's poor, and the biggest losers from [his] tax credit changes, are not the unemployed or "chaotic" families but hard working parents and their children ... child poverty numbers ... will rise from 2.3 million two years ago to 3.9 million in 2020 – a level of child poverty worse than at any time in the Thatcher years.... Indeed, the biggest group of families in poverty are highly traditional families: fathers who work and mothers who stay at home, but who now cannot survive on one wage. Of course, we have to deal with a range of problems – from drugs and domestic violence to mental illness and family break-ups – but it is a fiction that the biggest army of today's poor are from "chaotic" families. And the fastest rising group of poor families are the millennials: ... 35% of women face rising household bills, with average earnings below the voluntary living wage. For them the promise of globalization lies unrealized: ... you will not necessarily get on in Tory Britain.... Over its life cycle almost every family benefits from a welfare state whose main spending is on health, education and pensions. (Brown, 2015)

While a thriving economy might be able to find alternative ways of increasing women's incomes or wages, these tax credits have been an interim life source. And it is to the feminist or liberally minded women peers that we owe a debt, for at least having made the Conservative Chancellor of the Exchequer reconsider his unkind and ultimately misogynistic budget cuts to the public purse.

On the other hand, the parliamentary Labour Party has not been unequivocally supportive of the newly elected Labour Party leader Jeremy Corbyn, contesting his values and views on a range of socialist issues. In particular, they have been unsupportive to his views about nuclear disarmament, including arguing with him publicly. Yet his views are more in keeping with many tendencies within feminism, as we have just seen in the case of the discussion about women and Greenham Common. Of course, the parliamentary Labour Party, hitherto, has not been unequivocally supportive of feminists, as instanced in how Harriet Harman, also originally a second-wave feminist, was debarred from applying for the most senior leadership position.

Again, by some curious quirk, the newly energised Scottish Labour Party, under the leadership of Kezia Dugdale, a feisty young woman leader, has voted against the renewal of Trident, the current British nuclear deterrent. This makes her policies closer to Jeremy Corbyn than the rest of the parliamentary party. It also allows for a stronger debate within Scotland, since the Scottish National Party (SNP), under the leadership of Nicola Sturgeon, since Alex Sammond's resignation when the referendum on Scottish independence from the rest of the UK was lost, has taken a strong anti-nuclear position.

Indeed, Nicola Sturgeon, together with Leanne Wood, leader of Plaid Cymru, or the Welsh independence party, and Natalie Bennett, leader of the Green Party, all appear to be of strong and feminist persuasion, despite their lack of political power and women's clout at Westminster. They are all of the generation of third-wave feminists, but may be more inclined towards older or radical feminist sensibilities. Nicola Sturgeon has increasing support in the Scottish Parliament. In May 2015, the youngest MP in Parliament was elected to represent the SNP, gaining the Paisley and Renfrewshire seat from a strong and senior member of the Labour Party and former Shadow Foreign Secretary, Douglas Alexander. This was part of the rout of the Labour

Party in Scotland, and signals seismic changes taking place in UK party politics.

In May 2015, Mhairi Black was 20 years and 237 days old, making her the youngest MP since at least the Reform Act 1832. She gained a first class honours degree in June 2015 from the University of Glasgow, in politics and public policy. At the time of her election, she was still to complete her undergraduate degree with a final exam on Scottish politics still to be undertaken. Black is an LGBT MP, and expressed her support for marriage equality prior to the referendum in Ireland. Asked about her decision to 'come out', she replied 'I've never been in.' Black describes herself as a 'traditional socialist', citing Tony Benn as her enduring political hero, as we have seen that many of my socialist feminists have also done.

Finally, enter here, the newly formed WE party, with aims to achieve party political status in time for local party elections for mayoral candidates in 2016. The WE party was launched to great fanfare in October 2015 (Hinscliff, 2015), having developed countless local branches across the country over the last six months, since it was inaugurated at the Women of the World (WOW) events for International Women's Day in March 2015. This potential party has garnered great media and online attention, given its base within the liberal and social democratic party (LibDems) and its feisty media personality, Sandi Toksvig. An avowed feminist, Toksvig has created around her a huge gathering of feisty young and mid-career women, eager to take more political power. They are, however, part of the new generation of liberal feminists in business, and pursue neoliberal methods of political organisation. For example, they are using what are now called 'crowdfunding' methods to raise funds for their political campaigns: this means appealing to rich and private donors for the means to pursue their politics. This may be the only way for the party to get off the ground, but it does not augur well for the future of public funding for their essential political purposes. I had advised them on education, and argued that achievement was not the only point, saying that they should link their aim of dealing with gender and sexual violence through a conscious education policy, but sadly, I believe that they are relatively more interested in appealing to educated and relatively elite 'lipstick' feminists, with neoliberal tendencies.

As my wise older feminist friend Dulcie Groves told me, the history of single-issue women's parties is strewn with failure! She cited examples from Norway and Canada, to mention but a few. Better to keep to being a single-issue pressure group, lobbying political parties for key issues, as in the US, with strong single-issue lobbying than to set up as a political party doomed to failure. These were also the sentiments of my U3A group – Women and Wisdom – who were all initially highly in favour of such a sterling effort by such a charming political personality. What is so fascinating to me is how my ageing friends in this feisty group have been turned on by this political act, enervated by its possibilities, and yet worried by its potential failure. And they have also reconsidered their own early WLM or feminist roots, re-reading the Canadian feminist, Margaret Atwood's *The handmaid's tale*, initially published in 1985 for its eerily prescient forebodings about the world we are now in.

Women rising, and US party politics

Given the scale and intensity of neoliberalism, there is now a question, as Nancy Fraser (2013b) argues, that we have not sufficiently challenged the turn against social democracy in the 21st century. She argues that, as second-wave feminists, we have cooperated and ourselves been co-opted into the neoliberal changes that have occurred. We have not mounted an adequate critique to allow for diverse forms of social equality. In a comment piece in *The Guardian* (2013b), she argued that feminism has now become entangled with neoliberalism. The old feminist notions of 'the personal is political' helped contribute to critiques of the welfare state under capitalism, especially on the family and economy, but as these kinds of social democratic politics gave way to neoliberalism, instead of mounting critiques of the free market society, feminist ideas contributed to developing forms of the neoliberal ethos. In other words, she developed an argument around the contradictions between gender equalities and other social equalities and feminisms. Gender equality has been captured by neoliberalism, but I don't want to argue like

Nancy Fraser does, that this is, in fact, the 'fault' of neoliberal feminists. It is much more the case that the sophistication of the arguments is lost in a media melee. And, that it is impossible to step outside of the discourse, such that only these voices can be heard in media circles. It may also be simply with the enduring power of misogyny, or is it also closely linked with developing forms of corporate capitalism: markets and globalisation? What has corporate feminism to do with the socialist-feminism of the 1970s? There are examples from the shifts and changes in politics in the US.

For instance, film stars and celebrities are now claiming to be feminists, such as the very able Jessica Laurence, nicknamed J Law, a feminist actress who contributed to Lena Dunham's celebrity *Feminist Newsletter*. There are also welcome new approaches through social media such as Facebook and Twitter. And yet we require a social movement, not just individual women. Although Sheryl Sandberg's feminist notion of 'leaning in' is nevertheless welcome, it is not enough. We must stand together for all our sakes: for men and for women. What will it take to grasp the nettle that we know that education is vitally important to make all our lives better – happier and free from constraints and from the threats of abuse, intimidation, harassment and the risks of male violence? We need to transform the way misogyny rules to ensure that women and girls are afforded dignity and respect in all aspects of their and our lives.

One Million Women Rising and WOW

The idea of moving from just one International Women's Day to a week of events was inaugurated by women film-makers about seven years ago, and has slowly gained traction among women more generally. In the UK, with the leadership of Jude Kelly at South Bank in London, the WOW festival of arts, dance and song, over about a week in early March, has been organised for the last few years. Linking WOW with One Million Women Rising (www.millionwomenrise.com), a particularly strong social media campaign around an end to violence and gender justice and equality for women, gives this enormous media attention. Events were planned around individual women's creative and poetic achievements as well as discussions across the generations of feminism, from second-wave through to fourth-wave and school-age girls.

Eve Ensler, the acclaimed US feminist playwright, began a global political movement linked with Valentine's Day rather than International Women's Day, called the V-Day movement, where the 'V' stands for *victory, valentine and vagina*. In 1998, Eve's experience performing her own play 'The vagina monologues' inspired her to create V-Day, a global activist movement to stop violence against women and girls. V-Day raises funds and awareness through annual benefit productions of 'The vagina monologues'. In 2010, more than 5,400 V-Day events took place in over 1,500 locations in the US and around the world, including in the UK. In the UK this led to an annual WOW event to coincide with International Women's Day, and eventually to a week of events.

In 2012, Eve created One Billion Rising, a global protest campaign to end violence, and to promote justice and gender equality for women, along with her V-Day movement. On 14 February 2013, V-Day's 15th anniversary, women and men in over 200 countries held dance actions to demand an end to violence against women and girls. Eve had inaugurated this novel and imaginative event in the US in 2012.[1] She chose Valentine's Day to be part of global outrage against violence against women (VAW) through rape, incest and torture and, as with many feminist social movements, it was dealt with by alternative women's activities such as song and dance. This successful dance event was repeated on Valentine's Day 2014 and 2015, and has led to a whole array of celebratory and alternative activities for International Women's Week. For instance, Bird's Eye View (BEV) has used social media to announce various such events during the first week of March. The London 70s Sisters were, indeed, strongly present at the International Women's Day One Million Women Rising demonstration and march, walking under

---

[1] 'The vagina monologues' has been translated into 48 languages and performed in over 140 countries. Eve was awarded the Obie Award in 1996 for 'Best New Play' and in 1999 was awarded a Guggenheim Fellowship Award in Playwriting.

the banner of '1971-2014/5 Still Marching: Still Fighting', and arguing that while there had been some gains for women in social and economic terms, violence against women remained endemic and barely tackled. And in 2015, this exciting spectacle of events was repeated with dance, demonstrations and marches, as well as celebratory talks etc. It was here that Sandi Toksvig launched her first bid for a Women's Equality (WE) party.

A woman for US president?

The renowned second-wave feminist from the US, Gloria Steinem, recently published a book reflecting on her own experiences over a lifetime, entitled *My life on the road* (2015a). In the book, Steinem praises Hillary Clinton's feminist sensibilities, and argues for her mature perspective as a potential first woman president of the US, and who can gainsay this wise woman? In an excerpt in *The Guardian* (2015), she argues that:

> I know Hillary Clinton mostly in the way we all do, as a public figure in good times and in bad, one who became part of our lives and dreams.... But what clinched it for me was listening to her speak after a performance of Eve Ensler's play *Necessary targets*, based upon interviews with women in one of the camps set up to treat women who had endured unspeakable suffering, humiliation, and torture in the ethnic wars within the former Yugoslavia. To speak to an audience that had just heard those heart-breaking horrors seemed impossible for anyone, and Hillary had the added burden of representing the Clinton administration, which had been criticised for the slowness in stopping this genocide.... Most crucial of all, she admitted the country's slowness in intervening. By the time she sat down, she had brought the audience together and given us a shared meeting place: the simple truth.... [But] I was blindsided by the hostility toward her from some women. They called her cold, calculating, ambitious and even "unfeminist" for using political experience gained as a wife.... [Yet] some were so opposed to her that they came to be called Hillary Haters ... often turned out to be the women most like her: white, well-educated, and married or linked with powerful men.... Also they hadn't objected to sons, brothers, and sons-in-law using family connections and political

names to further careers.... The more they talked the more it was clear that their own husbands hadn't shared power with them.... This woman that they had imagined as smart, cold, and calculating turned out to be smart, warm and responsive. Instead of someone who excused a husband's behavior, she was potentially, as one said, "a great girlfriend" who had their backs. They also saw her expertise....

The zeitgeist about feminist fortunes

Second-wave feminists, perhaps fearful of not being able to influence debates about gender and sexual relations, used the term 'patriarchy' to describe power relations between men and women. As we have seen, it is only in the 21st century that misogyny has begun to garner common usage, initially as a media term, and only relatively recently in parliamentary and/or party political debates. As far as I can discover, the term was first used by Julia Gillard, former Australian Prime Minister, in the Australian Parliament in the autumn of 2012. Indeed, it can now be argued that it was rampant misogyny that led to the vote of no confidence against Gillard as Prime Minister in June 2013, and to her decision to leave not only her office, but also politics. Since her adversary in the Australian Labor Party, Kevin Rudd, lost the election in September 2013 to the right-wing Tony Abbott, she has further reflected on how misogyny and patriarchy continue to rule. Not previously known as an explicit feminist, she has developed an international diplomatic reputation, including working with US first lady Michelle Obama, to develop girls' education in Africa. This has the explicit intention of working on forms of leadership education and against sexual harassment.

During International Women's Day 2014 across the globe, an array of events took place, which illustrates how it is now incorporated into conventional politics and is no longer only radical and critical — a sign of the times? For example, the very conservative Australian Prime Minister Tony Abbott announced to an International Women's Day breakfast that his three daughters had helped to turn him into a (neoliberal, of course, and part of the 'selfie' generation) feminist! At the breakfast he claimed that women had smashed just about every glass ceiling in Australia, referencing female premiers and former Prime Minister Julia Gillard as examples. He also compared himself to the late US President Richard Nixon, saying that his wife quipped that having three daughters had helped to turn an 'unreconstructed bloke into a feminist'. He also argued that, despite having used sexist and misogynistic methods to beat Julia Gillard, on her admission, 'so this is a nation which has smashed every glass ceiling, but we need to do more ... such as extending the Coalition's paid parental scheme.... This is one of those moments when people from all sides of politics needed to realise that a watershed had been reached.'[2]

This is a very cynical moment for him perhaps, but also one that illustrates just how significant feminism and the International Women's Day have become in a global world of social media and politics. The focus is squarely on forms of shared parenting to enable women as young mothers to work on a par with their male partners. And at least Abbott decided to mention the International Women's Day, whereas the British Prime Minister, David Cameron, in an International Women's Day speech, 'targeted forced marriage and female genital mutilation', according to a small editorial in the *London Evening Standard*, not otherwise reported! However, the editorial was headed 'Women's rights now', and it argued that 'women and girls suffer sexual violence ... we still need IWD: the fight for female equality goes on.'[3]

In an interesting and ironic turn of events, in September 2015, Abbott was involved in a similar fight to Gillard, in retaining his Prime Ministership, and lost to Malcolm Turnbull, who is perhaps a slightly less bullish and 'macho' right-winger.

Over the globe, there are indeed seismic political changes occurring, although whether women and feminists will be the beneficiaries is a moot point. For example, in Canada, against all expectations, Justin Trudeau, son of the late liberal leader Pierre Trudeau, won an outstanding victory in Canadian parliamentary

---

[2] *The Guardian,* 4 March 2014, online.
[3] *London Evening Standard*, 7 March 2014, p 14.

232

politics. Describing himself as a feminist, he vowed to create his cabinet with 50% women in October 2015.

On the other hand, in New Zealand, they have taken a significantly right-wing turn, after having been led for over a decade by a liberally minded Labour woman. Prime Minister John Key exhibited incredibly misogynistic tendencies in the New Zealand Parliament over a furore over the detention of New Zealanders by Australia in the detention centre on Christmas Island. Mr Key deflected opposition accusations that his government had been too weak in its dealings with Australia by accusing Labour of 'backing the rapists'. Labour complained, but Key refused to back down. Several women Labour and Green MPs staged a mass walk out. A day later, on 12 November 2015, there were more challenges led by the Greens' co-leader Metiria Turei, who told Parliament that, as a victim of sexual abuse, she was deeply offended, and wanted Mr Key to apologise. Several other women MPs followed suit, but Mr Key remained seated and refused to apologise, standing by his comments. The speaker then ordered other women MPs to leave the chamber for continuing to object!

Ms Jan Logie told reporters that she had taken offence at his refusal to apologise:

> Because I've experienced a sexual assault, I've worked with a huge number of people in this country who have experienced it and it's an epidemic, and for the PM to trivialise that issue just deeply offends me. And it was not an easy decision to make this personal but the fact that this is personal for so many thousands of New Zealanders and there is still shame in speaking out, I felt compelled to actually bring that to the PM's attention.[4]

A different mark on the future

We now live in a very contradictory world, where feminism is on the public agenda and is part of the current zeitgeist; while it remains nowhere truly significant and powerful, it is very

---

[4]   I am grateful to Sue Middleton for supplying this reference via Facebook on 12 November 2015.

empowering. Nevertheless, I believe, through my concluding comments, that there is now sufficient energy among an array of feisty younger generations of feminists to take the social movement forward in new and inspiring ways, whether as politicians or as writers, journalists, teachers and/or academics. As my daughter said publically to me on my 70th birthday, she was a feminist, too, but inevitably she would do things differently from me, given the different world that she finds herself in, and the new circumstances of neoliberal markets for education and schooling. She is, indeed, a feisty feminist teacher, and as with her generation of fourth-wave feminists, or women seeking new creative tendencies, inevitably she and they will put a different mark on the future, especially perhaps for their sons rather than their daughters.

Certainly, the 'selfie' generation will have its work cut out in contesting and challenging everyday misogyny, which is more in evidence than before. But this generation does have the lessons of previous waves of feminism to look back on, and use as they see fit ... protesting and signing online petitions, letters and making new demands on the ever-encroaching state, despite its claims to be reducing its spheres of influence.

As the feminist Gail Lewis (2014) argued in 'Infighting is inclusion':

> Infighting may be dangerous but in these neoliberal times – when new inequalities overlay old ones, when diversification of gender increases, and yet the visions for alternatives modes of connection multiply – to ignore the challenge of infighting is equally, if not more, dangerous. So let the work of making feminism continue but let it do so in passionate conversations.

There are new waves of feminism that ebb and flow and take the lessons of previous waves to reclaim the agenda. I take heart from the fact that even if we are not as powerful in political places as we might wish, we are at least able to stem the tide of misogyny, and not be engulfed by it.

References and
select bibliography

Acker, S. (ed) (1989) *Teachers, gender and careers*, London: The Falmer Press

Acker, S. (1999) *The realities of teachers' work: Never a dull moment*, London: Cassell & Continuum

Acker, S., Wagner, A. and Mayuzumi, K. (eds) (2008) *Whose university is it, anyway? Power and privilege on gendered terrain*, Toronto, Canada: Sumach Press

Acker, S., Smyth, E., Bourne, P. and Prentice, A. (1999) *Challenging professions: Historical and contemporary perspectives on women's professional work*, Toronto, Canada: University of Toronto Press

Aga Khan University and Institute for Educational Development East Africa (2012) *Inclusion and equity in education: Focus on gender, Current issues for research and practice*, Annual Research Institute conference, 14-16 November, Dar es Salaam, Tanzania

Ali, S. and Coate, K. (2013) 'Impeccable advice: supporting women academics through supervision and mentoring', *Gender & Education*, vol 25, no 1, January, pp 23-37

Allan, A. and Tinkler, P. (2015) 'Taking stock: a framework', Editorial, *Gender & Education*, Special issue: 'Taking stock: a framework', vol 27, no 7, pp 733-43

Alldred, P. and David, M.E. (2007) *Get real about sex: The politics and practice of sex education*, London: McGraw Hill and Open University Press

Alldred, P. and David, M.E. (2015) *Gap Work project: Training for youth practitioners on tackling gender-related violence: Final report*, London: Brunel University (http://sites.brunel.ac.uk/gap)

Altbach, P. (2010) 'Trouble with numbers', *Times Higher Education*, 23 September

Althusser, L. (1971) 'Ideology and ideological state apparatuses', in *Lenin and philosophy and other essays*, London: New Left Books

Andrews, M., Squires, C. and Tamboukou, M. (eds) (2008) *Doing narrative research*, London: Sage

Anyangwe, E. (2015) 'Misogynoir: where racism and sexism meet', *The Guardian*, 5 October (www.theguardian.com/lifeandstyle/2015/oct/05/what-is-misogynoir)

Appignanesi, L. (2013) 'How *Fifty shades of feminism* dragged the F-word out of the shade', *The Observer*, 17 March (www.theguardian.com/books/2013/mar/17/fifty-shades-feminism-lisa-appignanesi)

Appignanesi, L., Orbach, S. and Holmes, R. (eds) (2013) *Fifty shades of feminism*, London: Virago

Arendt, H. (1955) *Men in dark times*, New York and London: Harcourt Brave Jovanovich

Arnot, M. and Weiner, G. (eds) (1989) *Gender under scrutiny: New enquiries in education*, Maidenhead: Open University Press

Arnot, M., David, M.E. and Weiner, G. (1999) *Closing the gender gap: Postwar education and social change*, Cambridge: Polity Press

Assiter, A. (1987) *Althusser and feminism*, London: Pluto Press

Atkins, S. and Hoggett, B. (1984) *Women and the law*, Oxford: Blackwell

Atwood, M. (1999) *The handmaid's tale*, London: Vintage Books [first published in 1985]

Banks, O. (1985) *The biographical dictionary of British feminists, Volume One: 1800-1930*, New York: New York University Press

Banks, O. (1986) *Becoming a feminist: The social origins of first wave feminism*, Brighton: Wheatsheaf Books

Bagilhole, B. and White, K. (eds) (2011) *Gender, power and management: A cross-cultural analysis of higher education*, London: Palgrave Macmillan

Bagilhole, B. and White, K. (eds) (2013) *Battle scars: Reflections on gender and generation in academia*, Basingstoke: Palgrave Macmillan

Banyard, K. (2010) *The equality illusion: The truth about women and men today*, London: Faber & Faber

Barker, D.L. and Allen, S. (eds) (1976a) *Sexual divisions and society: Process and change*, London: Tavistock

Barker, D.L. and Allen, S. (eds) (1976b) *Sexual exploitation in work and marriage*, London: Longman

Barrett, M. and Macintosh, M. (1982) *The anti-social family*, London: New Left Books

Bates, L. (2012) '"Slut dropping" and "pimps and hoes" – the sexual politics of Freshers' week', *The Independent*, 9 October

Bates, L. (2014a) *Everyday sexism*, London: Simon & Schuster

Bates, L. (2014b) 'Facebook's "spotted" pages: everyday sexism in universities for all to see', *The Guardian*, 31 January

Bedell, G. (2015) 'Profile of Germaine Greer', *The Observer*, 1 November

Bekhradnia, B. (2009) *Male and female participation and progression in higher education*, Oxford: Higher Education Policy Institute

Belenky, M.F., McVicker Clinchy, B., Goldberger, N.R. and Tarule, J.M. (1986) *Ways of knowing: The development of self, voice and mind*, New York: Basic Books

Benjamin, J. (1988) *The bonds of love: Psychoanalysis, feminism and the problem of domination*, New York: Pantheon Books

Benn, C. and Chitty, C. (1997) *Thirty years on: The campaign for comprehensive education*, London: Heinemann

Benn, M. (2013) *What should we tell our daughters? The pleasures and pressures of growing up female*, London: John Murray

Benn, M. and Chitty, C. (2004) *A tribute to Caroline Benn: Education and democracy*, London: Continuum

Bentham, M. (2015) 'Women won't apply to be justices at Supreme Court out of fear, says judge', *Evening Standard*, 6 November

Beveridge, W. (1942) *Social and allied services* (Beveridge Report), Cmnd 6404, London: HMSO

Bidisha (2013) in L. Appignanesi, S. Orbach and R. Holmes (eds) *Fifty shades of feminism*, London: Virago

Biklen, S., Marshall, C. and Pollard, D. (2008) 'Experiencing second-wave feminism in the USA', *Discourse: Studies in the Cultural Politics of Education*, vol 29, no 4, December, pp 451–71

Blackmore, J. (1999) *Troubling women: Feminism, leadership and educational change*, Maidenhead: Open University Press

Blackmore, J. and Sachs, J. (2007) *Performing and reforming leaders: Gender, educational restructuring, and organizational change*, Albany, NY: SUNY Press

Blackstone, T., Gales, K., Hadley, R. and Lewis, W. (1970) *Students in conflict: LSE in 1967*, London: Weidenfeld and Nicolson

Boden, R., Epstein, D. and Kenway, J. (2006) *The academic's support kit*, London: Sage

Boserup, E. (1970) *Women's role in economic development*, London: Earthscan

Boston Women's Health Collective (2005 [1971]) *Our bodies, ourselves: A new edition for a new era*, New York: Simon & Schuster

Boursicot, K. and Roberts, T. (2009) 'Widening participation in medical education', *Higher Education Policy*, vol 22, no 1, March, pp 19-37

Bowers, K. (2010) 'Rethinking the possibilities of feminist scholarship in the contemporary university', Unpublished thesis, Sydney, NSW: University of Technology Sydney (UTS)

Boycott, R. (2014) 'On Germaine Greer', *The Observer*, 26 January

Brah, A. and Coombes, A. (eds) (2000) *Hybridity and its discontents: Politics, science, culture*, London: Routledge

Brah, A. and Phoenix, A. (2004) 'Ain't I a woman? Revisiting intersectionality', *Journal of International Women's Studies*, vol 5, no 3, May, pp 75-86

Brivati, B. (2014) 'Tony Benn obituary', *The Guardian*, 14 March (www.theguardian.com/politics/2014/mar/14/tony-benn-obituary)

Brooks, R. and Waters, J. (2011) *Student mobilities, migration and the internationalization of higher education*, Basingstoke: Palgrave Macmillan

Brown, G. (2015) 'My tax credits are a lifeline. Osborne is wrong to slash them', *The Guardian*, Opinion, 10 November (www.theguardian.com/commentisfree/2015/nov/10/tax-credits-osborne-poverty-working-parents-children)

Brown, L.M. and Gilligan, C. (1990) *Meeting at the crossroads: Women's psychology and girls' development*, Cambridge, MA: Harvard University Press

Brown, P., Lauder, H. and Ashton, D. (2011) *The global auction: The broken promise of education, jobs and incomes*, New York and London: Oxford University Press

Buhle, P. (2014) 'Pete Seeger obituary', *The Guardian*, 28 January (www.theguardian.com/music/2014/jan/28/pete-seeger)

Burke, P.J. (2009) 'Men accessing higher education: Theorizing continuity and change in relation to masculine subjectivities', *Higher Education Policy*, vol 22, no 1, March, pp 81–101

Burke, P.J. (2012) The right to higher education: Beyond widening participation, London: Routledge

Burke, P.J and Crozier, G. (2013) *Teaching inclusively: Changing pedagogical spaces*, Resource pack from the Formations of Gender and Higher Education Pedagogies (GaP) research project, London: University of Roehampton and the Higher Education Academy

Burman, E. (ed) (1990) *Feminists and psychological practice*, London: Sage

Burman, E. (1994) *Deconstructing developmental psychology*, London: Routledge

Butler, J. (1990) *Gender trouble: Feminism and the subversion of identity*, New York and London: Routledge

Butler J. (2004) *Undoing gender*, New York and London: Routledge

BWSG (Bristol Women's Studies Group) (1979, 1984) *Half the sky: An introduction to women's studies*, London: Virago

Callanan, R. (2012) 'North London University of the Third Age (NLU3A)', *Newsletter*, 6 June

Campbell, B. (2013) *End of equality: The only way is women's liberation*, London: Seagull Books

Cameron, D. and Scanlon, J. (2010) 'Talking about gender', *Trouble and Strife*

Carvalho, M.E. et al (2015) 'Trajectories of feminist academics in higher education in Brazilian North and Northeast', Paper presented at the biennial Gender & Education Association conference, University of Roehampton, 24 June

Chapman, L. (2014) 'The future of the Women's Library', *The Guardian*, 14 March (www.theguardian.com/lifeandstyle/2014/mar/14/future-womens-library)

Chodorow, N. (1978) *The reproduction of mothering: Psychoanalysis and the sociology of gender*, Berkeley, CA: University of California Press

Chodorow, N. (1989) *Feminism and psychoanalytic theory*, Berkeley, CA: University of California Press

Clegg, S. and David, M.E. (2006) 'Passion, pedagogies and the project of the personal in higher education', *21st Century Society: Journal of the Academy of Social Sciences*, vol 1, no 2, October, pp 149-67

Coate, K. (2011) 'Writing in the dark: reflections on becoming a feminist', in K. Davis and M. Evans (eds) *Transatlantic conversations: Feminism as travelling theory*, Farnham: Ashgate

Coate, K., Howson, C.K. and de St Croix, T. (2015) *Mid-career academic women: Strategies, choices and motivation*, London: King's College London

Cockburn, C. (1993) *Brothers: Male dominance and technological change*, London: Pluto

Cole, B. (2010) '"Good" vibrations: good girls, good wives, good mothers and ... good heavens – a PhD', in B. Cole and H. Gunter (eds) Changing lives: Women, inclusion and the PhD, Stoke-on-Trent: Trentham Books

Connell, R. (2007) *Southern theory: The global dynamics of knowledge in social science*, London: Allen & Unwin

Coote, A. and Campbell, B. (1982) *Sweet freedom and the struggle for women's liberation*, London: Picador

Corston, Baroness J. (2007) *The Corston report*, London: Home Office

Daniels, L. (2011) *Pulling the punches: Defeating domestic violence*, London: Bogle L'ouverture Press Ltd

David, M.E. (1989a) 'Prima donna inter pares? Women in academic management', in S. Acker (ed) *Teachers, gender and careers*, London: The Falmer Press

David, M.E. (1989b) *What is education for?*, Inaugural at London: South Bank Polytechnic

David, M.E. (2002) 'From Keighley to Keele: Reflections on a personal, professional and academic journey', *British Journal of Sociology of Education*, vol 23, no 2, pp 249-69

David, M.E. (2003) *Personal and political: Feminisms, sociology and family lives*, Stoke-on-Trent: Trentham Books

David, M.E. (ed) (2009a) *Improving learning by widening participation in higher education*, London Routledge

David, M.E. (2009b) 'Transforming global higher education: A feminist perspective', Inaugural professorial lecture, London: Institute of Education, University of London

David, M.E. (2011) 'Overview of researching global higher education: challenge, change or crisis?', *Contemporary Social Science*, Special issue, 'Challenge, change or crisis in global higher education', vol 6, no 2, June, pp 147–65

David, M.E. (2012) 'Feminism, gender and global higher education: women's learning lives', *Higher Education Research and Development (HERDSA)*, vol 31, no 5, pp 679–89

David, M.E. (2013) 'A "mother" of feminist sociology of education?', in M.B. Weaver-Hightower and C. Skelton (eds) *Leaders in gender and education: Intellectual self-portraits*, Rotterdam, Netherlands: Sense Books

David, M.E. (2013) 'Still personal, still political', *Times Higher Education*, 31 January, pp 40–3

David, M.E. (2014) *Feminism, gender and universities: Politics, passion and pedagogies*, Farnham: Wheatsheaf

David, M.E. (2015a) 'Gender & Education Association: a case study in feminist education?', *Gender and Education*, Special issue: 'Taking stock: a framework', vol 27, issue 7, pp 929–46

David, M.E. (2015b) *The state, the family and education*, London: Routledge [first published in 1980 in the Radical Social Policy Series]

David, M.E. (2016: in press) *A feminist manifesto for education*, Cambridge: Polity Press

David, M.E. and Clegg, S. (2008) 'Power, pedagogy and personalization in global higher education', *Discourse: Studies in the Cultural Politics of Education*, Special issue on 'Second- wave feminism and educational research', vol 29, no 4, pp 483–99

David, M.E. and Epstein, D. (eds) (2013) 'Introduction: Thinking education feminisms: engagement with the work of Diana Leonard', *Gender & Education*, vol 25, no 1, January, pp 1–6

David, M.E. and Land, H. (1983) 'Sex and social policy', in H. Glennerster (ed) *The future of the welfare state: Remaking social policy*, London: Heinemann

David, M.E. and Naidoo, R. (eds) (2013) *The sociology of higher education: Reproduction, transformation and change in a global era*, London: Routledge

David, M.E., Hey, V. and Morley, L. (eds) (2011) *Contemporary social science*, Special issue, 'Challenge, change or crisis in global higher education', vol 6, no 2, June

Davidoff, L. and Hall, C. (1987) *Family fortunes: Men and women of the English middle class, 1780-1850*, London: Taylor & Francis [new edn, 2002]

Davies, B. (1989) *Frogs and snails and feminist tales. Preschool children and gender*, London: Routledge (http://bronwyndavies.com.au)

Davis, A. (1971) *If they come in the morning: Voices of resistance*, New York: Third Press

Davis, A. (1974) *Angela Davis: An autobiography*, New York: Random House

Davis, A. (1983) *Women, race, and class*, New York: Vintage

Davis, A. (1990) *Women, culture and politics*, New York: Vintage

Davis, K. and Evans, M.S. (eds) (2011) *Transatlantic conversations: Feminism as travelling theory*, Farnham: Ashgate

Davis, K., Evans, M.S. and Lorber, J. (eds) (2006) *Handbook of gender and women's studies*, London: Sage

de Beauvoir, S. (1949, 1953 in English) *The second sex*, Paris: Editions Gallimard

de Beauvoir, S. (1958, 1966 in English) *Memoirs of a dutiful daughter*, Harmondsworth: Penguin

Deem, R. (1978) *Women and schooling*, London: Routledge

Deem, R. (2009) 'Leading and managing contemporary UK universities: Do excellence and meritocracy still prevail over diversity?', *Higher Education Policy*, vol 22, no 1, March

Deem, R. (2014) 'Kevin Brehony obituary', *The Guardian*, 7 January

Dehli, K. (2010) 'Toward a new survivalism? Neo-liberal government of graduate education in Ontario', in J. Blackmore, M. Brennan and L. Zipin (eds) *Re-positioning university governance and academic work*, Rotterdam: Sense Publishers, pp 85-100

Delamont, S. (1989) *Knowledgeable women*, London: Routledge

Delamont, S. (2003) *Feminist sociology*, London: Sage

Delphy, C. and Leonard, D. (1992) *Familiar exploitation: A new analysis of marriage in contemporary Western societies*, Cambridge: Polity Press

Dinnerstein, D. (1987) *The rocking of the cradle and the ruling of the world*, London: Women's Press

Donald, A. (2015) *Evening Standard*, 27 October

Dowd, M., quoted in Roberts, Y. (2013) 'Is Facebook's Sheryl Sandberg really the new face of feminism?', *The Observer*, 17 March (www.theguardian.com/books/2013/mar/17/facebook-sheryl-sandberg-lean-book)

Dubai International conference on 'Gender equality in HE leadership' (2013) *The Guardian*, 6 March

Dunham, L. (2015) *Feminist Newsletter*

Dyhouse, C. (1981) *Girls growing up in Victorian and Edwardian England*, London: Routledge

Dyhouse, C. (1989) *Feminism and the family in England, 1890-1939*, Oxford: Blackwell

Dyhouse, C. (1995) *No distinction of sex? Women in British universities, 1870-1939*, London: UCL Press

Dyhouse, C. (2005) *Students: A gendered history*, London: Routledge

Dyhouse, C. (2010) *Glamour: Women, history, feminism*, London: Zed Books

Edwards, R.E. (1993) *Mature women students: Separating or connecting family and education*, London: Taylor & Francis

Edwards, R.E. and Mauthner, M. (2012) 'Ethics and feminist research: theory and practice', in T. Miller, M. Birch, M. Mauthner and J. Jessop (eds) *Ethics in qualitative research* (2nd edn), London: Sage, pp 14-28

Eichenbaum, L. and Orbach, S. (1982) *Outside in... Inside out: Women's psychology – A feminist psychoanalytic approach*, Harmondsworth: Penguin

Eichenbaum, L. and Orbach, S. (1983) *Understanding women: A feminist psychoanalytic approach*, New York: Basic Books

Eichenbaum, L. and Orbach, S. (1984) *What do women want: Exploding the myth of dependency*, New York: Berkeley Books

Eichenbaum, L. and Orbach, S. (1987) *Bittersweet: Facing up to feelings of love, envy and competition in women's friendships*, London: Century Hutchinson

Eichler, M. (1991) *Nonsexist research methods: A practical guide*, New York and London: Routledge

Eisenstein, H. (2009) *Feminism seduced: How global elites use women's labor and ideas to exploit the world*, New York: Paradigm

Ellsworth, E. (1997) *Teaching positions: Difference, pedagogy and the power of address*, New York: Teachers College Press

Engels, F. (1884) *The origins of the family, private property, and the state*, London: Pluto Press [republished in 1980]

Epstein, D., Elwood, J., Hey, V. and Maw, J. (eds) (1998) *Failing boys? Issues in gender and education*, Buckingham: Open University Press

Equality Challenge Unit (2011) *Equality in higher education: Statistical report 2011, Part 1: Staff and Part 2: Students*, December

Evans, M. (2004) *Killing thinking: The death of the universities*, London: Continuum

Evans, M. (2011) 'Mary Evans' narrative', in K. Davis and M. Evans (eds) *Transatlantic conversations: Feminism as travelling theory*, Farnham: Ashgate

Farrall, S. and Hay, C. (eds) (2014) *The legacy of Thatcherism: Assessing and exploring Thatcherite social and economic policies*, Oxford: Oxford University Press for the British Academy

Figes, E. (1970) *Patriarchal attitudes: Women in society*, London: Stein & Day

Finch, J. (1983) *Married to the job*, London: Allen & Unwin

Fine, M. (1992) *Disruptive voices: The possibilities of feminist research*, Ann Arbor, MI: University of Michigan Press

Fine, M. (2004) 'The power of the Brown v Board of Education decision: Theorizing threats to sustainability', *American Psychologist*, vol 59, pp 502–10

Fine, M. and McClelland, S. (2007) 'The politics of teen women's sexuality: Public policy and the adolescent female body', *Emory Law Review*, vol 56, no 4, pp 993–1038

Fine, M. and Weis, L. (1998) *The unknown city: Lives of poor and working class young adults*, Boston, MA: Beacon Press

Fine, M., Weis, L., Powell, L. and Burns, A. (eds) (2004) *Off-white: Readings on power, privilege, and resistance* (2nd edn), New York: Routledge

Firestone, S. (1970) *The dialectic of sex: The case for feminist revolution*, New York: Morrow

Fraser, N. (1989) *Unruly practices: Power, discourse, and gender in contemporary social theory*, Minneapolis, MS: University of Minnesota Press

Fraser, N. (1997) *Justice interruptus: Critical reflections on the 'postsocialist' condition*, New York and London: Routledge

Fraser, N. (2013a) *Fortunes of feminism: From state-managed capitalism to neoliberal crisis*, London: Verso

Fraser, N. (2013b) 'How feminism became capitalism's handmaiden – and how to reclaim it', *The Guardian*, 14 October (www.theguardian.com/commentisfree/2013/oct/14/feminism-capitalist-handmaiden-neoliberal)

Freeman, H. (2014) 'Her: the movie every internet addict should be forced to watch', *The Guardian*, Opinion, 28 January (www.theguardian.com/commentisfree/2014/jan/28/spike-jonze-her-movie-internet-addict-sex-phone)

Freeman, J. (1972) 'Tyranny of structurelessness', *The Second Wave*, vol 2, no 1, p 20

French, M. (1977) *The women's room*, New York: Jove Books

Friedan, B. (1963) *The feminine mystique*, Harmondsworth: Penguin

Gaskell, J. (2008) 'Learning from the Women's Movement about educational change', *Discourse: Studies in the Cultural Politics of Education*, vol 29, no 4, December

Gavron, H. (1966) *The captive wife: Conflicts of housebound mothers*, London: Routledge

Gilbert, S. and Gubar, S. (1980) *The mad woman in the attic*, New Haven, CT: Yale University Press

Gill, R. (2011) 'Sexism reloaded, or, it's time to get angry again', *Feminist Media Studies*, vol 11, no 1, pp 61-71

Gilligan, C. (1982) *In a different voice*, Cambridge, MA: Harvard University Press

Gilman, C.P. (1892) 'The yellow wallpaper', *New England Magazine*, vol 5, pp 647-56, [Boston, MA: Small, Maynard & Co, 1899; New York: Feminist Press, 1973]

Gilman, C.P. (1915) *Herland*, New York: Forerunner

Glasgow Women's Studies Group (1983) *Uncharted lives: Extracts from Scottish women's experiences, 1850-1982* (Ruth Madigan's essay), Glasgow: Pressgang

Glazer-Raymo, J. (ed) (2008) *Unfinished agendas: New and continuing gender challenges in higher education*, Baltimore, MD: Johns Hopkins University Press

Glazer-Raymo, J. (1999) *Shattering the myths: Women in academe*, Baltimore, MD: Johns Hopkins University Press

Glazer-Raymo, J., Townsend, B.K. and Ropers-Huilman, R. (eds) (2000) *Women in higher education: A feminist perspective*, Needham Heights, MA: Pearson Publishing

Glendinning, C. and Millar J. (eds) (1992) *Women and poverty in Britain*, Brighton: Harvester-Wheatsheaf

Glennerster, H. (ed) (1983) *The future of the welfare state: Remaking social policy*, London: Heinemann

Grant, J.W. (2016) *In the steps of exceptional women: The story of the Fawcett Society 1866–2016*, London: Francis Boutle Publishers

Greer, G. (1970) *The female eunuch*, London: Picador

Griffin, G. (2011) 'On not engaging with what's right in front of us: Or race, ethnicity and gender in reading women's writing', in K. Davis and M. Evans (eds) *Transatlantic conversations: Feminism as travelling theory*, Farnham: Ashgate, pp 157-67

Griffith, A. and Smith, D.E. (1987) 'Constructing cultural knowledge: Mothering as discourse', in J. Gaskell and A. McLaren (eds) *Women and education: A Canadian perspective*, Calgary, Canada: Detselig Press, pp 87-104 [reprinted in 1990]

Griffith, A. and Smith, D.E. (2005) *Mothering for schooling*, New York: Routledge

Grove, J. (2015) '"Striking" inequalities in higher education fuel gender pay gap', *Times Higher Education*, 5 November

Hall, C. (1992) *White, male and middle class: Feminism and history*, London: Wiley

Hall, P., Land, H., Parker, R. and Webb, A. (1975) *Change, choice and conflict in social policy*, London: Heinemann

Harding, S. (1987) *Feminism and methodology*, Bloomington, IN: Indiana University Press

Haraway, D. (1988) 'Situated knowledges: The science question in feminism and the privilege of partial perspective', *Feminist Studies*, vol 14, no 3, Autumn, pp 575-9

Hartman, H. (1981) 'The unhappy marriage of Marxism and feminism', in L. Sergent (ed) *The unhappy marriage of Marxism and feminism: A debate on class and patriarchy*, London: Pluto Press

Havergal, C. (2015) 'IoE centre's agenda aims to make case for higher education research', *Times Higher Education*, 30 October (www.timeshighereducation.com/news/ioe-centres-agenda-aims-make-case-higher-education-research)

Hemmings, C. (2006) 'The life and times of academic feminism', in K. Davis, M. Evans and J. Lorber (eds) (2006) *Handbook of gender and women's studies*, London: Sage

Henderson, E. (2015) *Gender pedagogy: Teaching, learning and tracing gender in higher education*, London: Macmillan

Heron, L. (ed) (1985) *Truth, dare or promise: Girls growing up in the 1950s*, London: Virago

Hewitt, M. (1958) *Wives and mothers in Victorian industry*, London: Barrie and Rockcliffe

Hewitt, N. (ed) (2010) *No permanent waves: Recasting histories of US feminism*, New Brunswick, NJ: Rutgers University Press

Hey, V. (2011) 'Affective asymmetries: academics, austerity and the mis/recognition of emotion', *Contemporary Social Science*, Special issue, 'Challenge, change or crisis in global higher education', vol 6, no 2, June, pp 207-23

Hey, V. and Leathwood, C. (2009) 'Passionate attachments: Higher education, policy, knowledge, emotion and social justice', *Higher Education Policy*, vol 22, no 1, March

Hey, V. and Morley, L. (2011) 'Imagining the university of the future: eyes wide open? Expanding the imaginary through critical and feminist ruminations in and on the university', *Contemporary Social Science*, Special issue, 'Challenge, change or crisis in global higher education', vol 6, no 2, June, pp 165-75

Hills, J., Brewer, M., Jenkins, S.P., Lister, R., Lupton, R., Machin, S., et al (2010) *An anatomy of economic inequality in the UK: Report of the National Equality Panel*, CASEreports 60, London: Centre for Analysis of Social Exclusion, London School of Economics and Political Science

Hinscliff, G. (2015) 'The Women's Equality Party has a problem – no one hates it', *The Guardian*, Opinion, 22 October (www.theguardian.com/commentisfree/2015/oct/22/womens-equality-party-problem-wep-ukip-eu-feminism)

Hollingsworth, S. (1994) *Teacher research and urban literacy education*, New York: Teachers College Press

Hollingsworth, S. (2002) *Personal, community and school literacies: Challenging a single standard*, New York: Teachers College Press

hooks, b. (1981) *Ain't I a woman? Black women and feminism*, Boston, MA: South End Press

Horowitz, H.L. (1993) *Alma mater: Design and experience in the women's colleges from their nineteenthcentury beginnings to the 1930s*, Amherst, US: University of Massachusetts Press

Hoskins, K. (2012) *Women and success: Professors in the academy*, Stoke-on-Trent: Trentham Books

Hughes, C. (2002) *Key concepts in feminist theory and research*, London: Sage

Jackson, C. and Sundaram, V. (2015) '"Lad culture" and higher education: exploring the perspectives of staff working in higher education institutions', Paper presented to Gender & Education Association conference, University of Roehampton, 25 June

Jackson, C., Dempster, S. and Pollard, L. (2015) '"They just don't seem to really care, they just think it's cool to sit there and talk": laddism in university teaching-learning contexts', *Educational Review*, vol 67, no 3, pp 300-14

James, E.L. (2012) *Fifty shades of grey*, London: Arrow Books

Jencks, C. et al (1973) *Inequality: The effects of family and schooling in the USA*, New York: Basic Books

Joffe, C. (1971) 'Sex role socialization and the nursery school: as the twig is bent', *Journal of Marriage and the Family*, vol 33, no 3, August, pp 467-75

Judt, A. with Snyder, T. (2013) *Thinking the twentieth century*, London: Vintage Books

Keller, E.F. (1985) *Reflections on gender and science*, New Haven, CT: Yale University Press

Kennedy, H., Update, E. Welch, E. and Tillyard, S. (2015) 'Lisa Jardine obituary', *The Guardian*, 26 October (www.theguardian.com/books/2015/oct/26/lisa-jardine)

Kenway, J. and Bullen, E. (2001) *Consuming children: Education – entertainment – advertising*, Maidenhead: McGraw Hill/Open University Press

Kenway, J. and Fahey, J. (eds) (2008) *Globalizing the research imagination*, London: Routledge

Kenway, J. and Willis, S. with Blackmore, J. and Rennie, L. (1998) *Answering back: Girls, boys and feminism in schools*, London: Routledge

Kerry, J. (2013) 'Malala's vital lesson for US foreign policy', *Evening Standard*, 8 March

Kim, T. and Brooks, R. (2013) *Internationalisation, mobile academics and knowledge creation in universities: A comparative analysis*, SRHE Research Award, London: Society for Research into Higher Education (SRHE) (www.srhe.ac.uk/downloads/TerriKimReport.pdf)

King, R., Marginson, S. and Naidoo, R. (eds) (2011) *Handbook on globalization and higher education*, Cheltenham: Edward Elgar

Klein, N. (1999) *No logo*, New York and London: Picador

Kozol, J. (1960s) *Free schools*, Harmondsworth: Penguin

Land, H. (1975) 'The myth of the male breadwinner', *New Society*, 9 October

Land, H. (1976) 'Women: Supporters or supported?', in D.L. Barker and S. Allen (eds) *Sexual divisions and society: Process and change*, London: Tavistock

Langa Rosado, D. and David, M.E. (2006) '"A massive university or a university for the masses?" Continuity and change in higher education in Spain and England', *Journal of Education Policy*, vol 21, no 3, pp 343-65

Lather, P. (1991) *Getting smart: Feminist research and pedagogy with/in the postmodern*, New York and London: Routledge

Lawson, A. (1966) *The recognition of mental illness in London: A study of the social processes determining compulsory admission to an observation unit in a London hospital*, Oxford: Oxford University Press

Lawson, A. (1990) *Adultery: An analysis of love and betrayal*, New York: Basic Books

Le Guin, U. (1974) *The dispossessed: An ambiguous utopia*, New York: Harper Row

Leathwood, C. and Read, B. (2008) *Gender and the changing place of higher education*, London: Society for Research in Higher Education and Open University Press

Lees, S. (1986) *Losing out: Sexuality and adolescent girls*, London: HarperCollins

Lees, S. (1999) *Ruling passions: Sexual violence, reputation and the law*, Milton Keynes: Open University Press

Leonard, D. (2002) *A woman's guide to doctoral studies*, Milton Keynes: Open University Press

Levitt, R. (ed) (2015) *Prelude to the Holocaust: Pogrom, November 1938, Testimonies from Krystallnacht*, London: The Wiener Library and Souvenir Press

Lewis, G. (2014) 'Infighting is inclusion', *The Guardian*, 7 March (www.theguardian.com/commentisfree/2014/mar/07/international-womens-day-defence-feminist-dissent-argued-priorities)

Lister, R. (2010) *Understanding theories and concepts in social policy*, Bristol: Policy Press

Luttrell, W. (1997) *School-smart and mother-wise: Working-class women's identity and schooling*, New York and London: Routledge

McLean, M. (2006) *Pedagogy and the university: Critical theory and practice*, New York and London: Continuum

McLeod, J. and Yates, L. (2006) *Making modern lives: Subjectivity, schooling and social change*, New York: State University of New York Press (SUNY)

Maher, F. and Tetreault, M.K. (2001) *The feminist classroom: Dynamics of gender, race and privilege*, New York: Rowman & Littlefield

Maher, F. and Tetreault, M.K. (2007) *Privilege and diversity in the American academy*, New York and London: Routledge

Mahony, P. (1985) *Schools for the boys? Co-education reassessed*, New York and London: Routledge

Malamud, B. (1961) *A new life*, Harmondsworth: Penguin

Malos, E. (ed) (1995) *The politics of housework*, Cheltenham: New Clarion Press

Marshall, C. (ed) (1997a) *Feminist critical policy analysis I: A perspective from primary and secondary schooling*, London: Falmer Press

Marshall, C. (ed) (1997b) *Feminist critical policy analysis II: A perspective from post-secondary education*, London: Falmer Press

Marsden, L. (2008) 'Second wave breaks on the shores of U of T', in W. Robbins, M. Luxton, M. Eichler and F. Descarries (eds) *Minds of our own: Inventing feminist scholarship and women's studies in Canada and Quebec 1966-76*, Ontario, Canada: Wilfrid Laurier University Press, pp 210-17

Marsden, S. (2013) 'New Year Honours: women outnumber men for the first time', *The Telegraph*, 30 December

Martin, J. (2006) 'On Olive Banks', *British Journal of Sociology of Education*, Special issue, 'Olive Banks (1923-2006)', vol 29, no 4

Martin, J. (2013) 'Gender, education and social change: a study of feminist politics and practice in London 1870-1990', *Gender & Education*, vol 25, no 1, January, pp 56-75

Massey, D. (1994) *Space, place and gender*, Cambridge: Polity Press

Matthews, D. (2013) '"Miss" no hit with revered alumna', *Times Higher Education*, 28 November

Matthews, D. (2014) 'The numbers don't look good guys', *Times Higher Education*, 6 March, pp 24-5

Mauthner, N. and Edwards, R. (2010) 'Feminist research management in higher education in Britain: possibilities and practices', *Gender, Work and Organization*, vol 17, no 5, pp 481-502

Mead, M. (1928) *Coming of age in Samoa*, New York: Blue Ribbon Books, Harmondsworth: Penguin [republished]

Mead, M. (1930) *Growing up in New Guinea*, New York: W. Morrow & Company, Harmondsworth: Penguin [republished]

Middleton, S. (1993) *Educating feminists: Life histories and pedagogies*, New York: Teachers College Press

Middleton, S. (1998) *Disciplining sexuality: Foucault, life histories and education*, New York: Teachers College Press

Milburn, A. (2014) *Social Mobility and Child Poverty Commission: call for evidence annual report*, May (www.gov.uk/government/uploads/system/uploads/attachment data/file/3149)

Millett, K. (1970) *Sexual politics*, New York: Doubleday

Mills, C.W. (1959) *The sociological imagination*, Oxford: Oxford University Press

Mirza, H.S. (ed) (1990) *Black British feminism*, London: Routledge

Mirza, H.S. (1992) *Young, female and Black*, London: Routledge

Mirza, H.S. (2009) *Race, gender and educational desire: Why black women succeed and fail*, London: Routledge

Mitchell, J. (1966) 'Women: The longest revolution', *New Left Review*, I/40 Nov–Dec

Mitchell, J. (1973) *Women's estate*, Harmondsworth: Penguin

Mitchell, J. (1984) *Women: The longest revolution: Essays on feminism, literature and psychoanalysis*, London: Virago Press

Mitchell, J. and Oakley, A. (eds) (1975) *The rights and wrongs of women*, Harmondsworth: Penguin

Monroe, J. (2015) 'We're all a bit non-binary inside. So why do we segregate by gender?', *The Guardian*, 29 October (www.theguardian.com/commentisfree/2015/oct/29/binary-gender-feminism-transgender-womens-award)

Mooney, C. (senior ed, special sections, B3) (2012) 'Diversity in academe: The gender issue', *The Chronicle of Higher Education* (http://ucd-advance.ucdavis.edu/post/diversity-academe-gender-issue)

Moran, C. (2011) *How to be a woman*, London: Ebury Press

Morley, L. (1999) *Organising feminisms: The micropolitics of the academy*, London: Palgrave Macmillan

Morley, L. (2011) 'Misogyny posing as measurement: disrupting the feminisation crisis discourse', *Contemporary Social Science*, Special issue, 'Challenge, change or crisis in global higher education', vol 6, no 2, June, pp 223–37

Morley, L. (2012) 'Cycles of domination of top roles by men must be broken', *Times Higher Education*, 6 December

Morley, L. (2013) 'The rules of the game: women and the leaderist turn in higher education', *Gender & Education*, vol 25, no 1, January, pp 116–31

Morley, L. and David, M.E. (eds) (2009) 'Celebrations and challenges: Gender in higher education', *Higher Education Policy*, vol 22, no 1, March, pp 1–2

Morley, L. and Lugg, R. (2009) 'Mapping meritocracy: Intersecting gender, poverty and higher education opportunity structures', *Higher Education Policy*, vol 22, no 1, March

Moss, G. (1989) *Un/popular fictions*, London: Virago

Mullender, A., Hague, G., Imam, I., Kelly, L., Malos, E. and Regan, L. (2002) *Children's perspectives on domestic violence*, London: Sage Publications

Myrdal, A. and Klein, V. (1956) *Women's two roles: Home and work*, London: Routledge & Kegan Paul

Naidoo, R. (2011) 'Higher education and the new imperialism: Implications for development', in S. Marginson, R. King and R. Naidoo (eds) *Higher education and globalisation reader*, London: Edward Elgar

Nava, M. (1992) *Changing cultures: Feminism, youth and consumerism*, London: Sage

Nava, M. (2007) *Visceral cosmopolitanism: Gender, culture and the normalisation of difference*, Oxford: Berg Publishers

New, C. and David, M.E. (1985) *For the children's sake: Making child care more than women's business*, Harmondsworth: Penguin

Newman, J. (2012) *Working the spaces of power: Activism, neoliberalism and gendered labour*, London: Bloomsbury

Nnaemeka, O. (ed) (1998) *Sisters, feminism and power*, Trenton, NJ: Africa World Press

Oakley, A. (1972) *Sex and gender*, London: Martin Robertson

Oakley, A. (1974) *The sociology of housework*, London: Martin Robertson

Oakley, A. (1976) *Housewife*, Harmondsworth: Penguin

Oakley, A. (1979) *Becoming a mother*, London: Martin Robertson

Oakley, A. (2000) *Experiments in knowing: Gender and method in the social sciences*, Cambridge: Polity Press

Oakley, A. (2002) *Gender on planet earth*, London: New Press

Oakley, A. (ed) (2005) *The Ann Oakley reader: Gender, women, and social science*, Bristol: Policy Press

Okin, S.M. (1979) *Women in Western political thought*, Princeton, NJ: Princeton University Press

Okin, S.M. (1989) *Justice, gender, and the family*, Princeton, NJ: Princeton University Press

Orbach, S. (1978) *Fat is a feminist issue*, London: Century Hutchinson

Pence, E. and Paymar, M. (1993) *Education groups for men who batter: The Duluth Model*, Amsterdam: Springer

Pengelly, M. (2014) 'Obama highlights military and colleges in an effort to tackle sexual violence', *The Guardian*, 25 January

Penny, L. (2014) *Unspeakable things: Sex, lies and revolution*, London: Bloomsbury

Petersen, E.B. and Davies, B. (2010) 'In/difference in the neoliberalised university', *Learning and Teaching in the Social Sciences*, vol 3, no 2, pp 93-109

Piercy, M. (1976) *Woman on the edge of time*, New York: Alfred A. Knopf

Phillips, A. (1991) *Engendering democracy*, Cambridge: Polity Press

Phipps, A. (2010) *Hidden marks: A study of women students' experiences of harassment, stalking, violence and sexual assault*, London: National Union of Students

Phipps, A. (2013) *That's what she said: Women students' experiences of 'lad culture' in HE*, London: National Union of Students

Phipps, A. and Young, I. (2014) 'Lad culture in higher education: agency in the sexualisation debates', *Sexualities*, vol 18, no 4, pp 459-79

Phoenix, A. (1991) *Young mothers?*, Cambridge: Polity Press

Phoenix, A. (2011) 'Re-narrating feminist stories: Black British women and transatlantic feminisms', in K. Davis and M. Evans (eds) *Transatlantic conversations: Feminism as travelling theory*, Farnham: Ashgate, pp 55-69

Plesch, D. (2011) *America, Hitler and the UN*, London: I.B. Taurus

Plummer, K. (2013) 'Mary McIntosh obituary', *The Guardian*, 24 January (www.theguardian.com/education/2013/jan/24/mary-mcintosh)

Purvis, J. (2014) 'Support for the Women's Library', *The Guardian*, 18 March

Quinn, J. (2003) *Powerful subjects: Are women really taking over the university?*, Stoke on Trent: Trentham

Rapp, R. (2000) *Testing women, testing the fetus: The social impact of amniocentesis in America*, New York: Routledge

Rathbone, E. (1924, 1986) *The disinherited family*, Bristol: Falling Wall Press [2nd edition with an introduction by Suzie Fleming]

Raven, C. (2013) 'Feminist times', *Observer Magazine*, 13 October, pp 10-11

RCUK (Research Council UK) (2009) *Sustainability of the UK research workforce: Annual report to the UK Research Base Funders Forum 2009*, London: RCUK

Rees, T. (1992) *Women and the labour market*, London: Routledge

Rich, A. (1977) *Of woman born: Motherhood as experience and institution*, New York and London: W.W. Norton

Riley, D. (1983) *War in the nursery: Theories of the child and mother*, London: Virago

Riley, D. (1988) *Am I that name? Feminism and the category of 'women' in history*, London: Macmillan

Ringrose, J. (2012) *Post-feminist education? Girls and the sexual politics of schooling*, London: Routledge

Ringrose, J. and Renold, E. (2011) 'Teen girls, working class femininity and resistance: Re-theorizing fantasy and desire in educational contexts of heterosexualized violence', *International Journal of Inclusive Education*, pp 1–17

Ringrose, J. and Renold, E. (2012) 'Slut shaming, girl power and "sexualisation": Thinking through the politics of the international SlutWalks with teen girls', *Gender & Education*, vol 24, no 3, pp 333–43

Robbins, Sir Lionel (1963) *Higher education* (Robbins Report), Cmnd 2154, London: HMSO

Robbins, W., Luxton, M., Eichler, M. and Descarries, F. (2008) *Minds of our own: Inventing feminist scholarship and women's studies in Canada and Quebec 1966-76*, Ontario, Canada: Wilfrid Laurier University Press

Roberts H. (ed) (1981) *Doing feminist research*, London: Routledge

Robinson, J. (2009) *Bluestockings: The remarkable story of the first women to fight for an education*, London: Viking

Roby, P. (1973) *Child care – Who cares? Infant and early childhood development policies*, New York: Basic Books

Roby, P. (1981) *Women in the workplace*, Cambridge, MA: Schenkman Publishing Company

Rose, J. (2014) *Women in dark times*, London: Bloomsbury

Rowbotham, S. (1972) *Women, resistance and revolution*, Harmondsworth: Penguin

Rowbotham, S. (1973a) *Hidden from history*, London: Pluto Press

Rowbotham, S. (1973) *Women's consciousness: Man's world*, Harmondsworth: Penguin

Rowbotham, S. (2012) 'Discovering the other America', Public lecture as writer in residence at the British Library, 22 October

Rubin, G. (2012) *Deviations: A Gayle Rubin reader*, Durham, NC: Duke University Press

Ruebain, D. (2012) 'Diversity, and equality', The Equality Challenge Unit talk in the CHEER lecture series, University of Sussex, 16 April

Rushe, D. (2014) 'Senate confirms Janet Yellen as next chair of the Federal Reserve', *The Guardian*, 6 January (www.theguardian.com/business/2014/jan/06/senate-confirms-janet-yellen-chair-federal-reserve)

Saada Saar, M. (2014) 'President Obama's Task Force on College Sexual Assault', *Huffington Post*, 24 January

Sandberg, S. (2013) *Lean in: Women, work, and the will to lead*, New York and London: W.H. Allen

Sayers, J. (1991) *Mothering psychoanalysis*, Harmondsworth: Penguin

Scott, J. and Butler, J. (eds) (1992) *Feminists theorize the political*, New York: Routledge

Scott, J. and Tilly, L. (1978) *Women, work and family*, New York: Holt, Rinehart & Winston

Seth, V. (1993) *A suitable boy*, London: Phoenix House

Sen, A. (2005) *The argumentative Indian. Writings on Indian culture, history and identity*, London: Penguin Books [especially chapter 11, Women and men, pp 220-385]

European Commission (2009) *She figures 2009: Statistics and indicators on gender equality in science*, Brussels: European Commission Directorate-General for Research (https://ec.europa.eu/research/science-society/document_library/pdf_06/she_figures_2009_en.pdf)

Shuller, T. and Watson, D. (2010) *Learning through life: Inquiry into the future for lifelong learning (IFLL)*, London: National Institute for Adult and Continuing Education (NIACE)

Skeggs, B. (1997) *Formations of class and gender: Becoming respectable*, London: Sage

Skelton, C. and Francis, B. (2009) *Feminism and 'The schooling scandal'*, London: Routledge

Skevington, S. (1995/2009) *Psychology of pain*, New York and London: Wiley

Slaughter, S. and Leslie, L. (1997) *Academic capitalism: Politics, policies and the entrepreneurial university*, Baltimore, MD and London: Johns Hopkins University Press

Slaughter, S. and Rhoades, G. (2004) *Academic capitalism and the new economy markets, state and higher education*, Baltimore, MD and London: Johns Hopkins University Press

Smart, C. (1976) *Women, crime, and criminology*, London: Routledge and Kegan Paul

Smart, C. (1990) 'Feminist approaches to criminology or postmodern woman meets atavistic man', in A. Morris and L. Gelsthorpe (eds) *Feminist perspectives in criminology*, Milton Keynes: Open University Press

Smith, D.E. (1987) *The everyday world as problematic: A feminist sociology*, London: Routledge

Spender, D. (1980) *Manmade language*, London: Routledge

Spender, D. (1982) *Women of ideas and what men have done to them: From Aphra Behn to Adrienne Rich*, London: Routledge

Spender, D. (1983) *There's always been a women's movement this century*, London: Pandora Press

Squire, C. (ed) (1993) *Women and AIDS: Psychological perspectives*, London: Sage

Stacey, M. and Price, M. (1981) *Women, power and politics*, London: Tavistock

Stambach, A. and David, M.E. (2005) 'Feminist theory and educational policy: How gender has been "involved" in family school choice debates', *Signs: Journal of Women in Culture and Society*, vol 30, no 2, winter, pp 1633–58

Stanley, L. and Wise, S. (1983) *Breaking out: Feminist Consciousness and Feminist Research*, London: Routledge and Kegan Paul

Stansgate, M. (1992) *My exit visa*, London: Hutchinson

Stasinopoulos, A. (1973) *The female woman*, London: Random House

Steedman, C. (1986) *Landscape for a good woman*, London: Virago Press

Steedman, C., Urwin, C. and Walkerdine V. (eds) (1985) *Language, gender and childhood*, London: Routledge & Kegan Paul

Steinem, G. (2015a) *My life on the road*, London and New York: Oneworld

Steinem, G. (2015b) 'Gloria Steinem: Why the White House needs Hillary Clinton', *The Guardian*, 19 October (www.theguardian.com/us-news/2015/oct/19/gloria-steinem-hillary-clinton-white-house)

Stone, L. (ed) *The education feminism reader*, New York and London: Routledge

Strathern, M. (ed) (2000) *Audit cultures. Anthropological studies in accountability, ethics and the academy*, London: Routledge

Summers, A. (2015) 'There is a museum of female emancipation: The Women's Library', *The Guardian*, Letter, 10 November (www.theguardian.com/culture/2015/nov/10/there-is-a-museum-of-female-emancipation-the-womens-library)

Szreter, S. (2006) 'Olive Banks obituary', *The Guardian*, 12 December

The Chronicle of Higher Education (2012) 'Diversity in academe: The gender issue' (http://ucd-advance.ucdavis.edu/post/diversity-academe-gender-issue)

Taylor, H. (2014) *Scarlett's women: Gone with the wind and its female fans* [republished by Virago, London, from the 1989 edition published originally by Rutgers University Press, New York]

Teekah, A., Scholz, E.J., Friedman, M. and O'Reilly, A. (eds) (2015) *This is what a feminist slut looks like: Perspectives on the SlutWalk Movement*, Bradford, ON, Canada: Demeter Press

Thomson, E.P. (1963, 1968) *The making of the English working class*, London: Victor Gollancz (2nd edn), Harmondsworth: Penguin

Tomlinson, S. (2013) 'My university life as a woman professor', *The Guardian*, in the Higher Education Network series, 31 January (www.theguardian.com/higher-education-network/blog/2013/jan/31/female-professor-university-life-equality)

Townsend, L.F. and Weiner, G. (2011) *Deconstructing and reconstructing lives: Auto/biography in educational settings*, London, Canada: The Althouse Press

Ungerson, C. (ed) (1985) *Women and social policy: A reader*, London: Macmillan

Ungerson, C. (1990) *Policy is personal: Sex, gender and informal care*, London: Tavistock

Ungerson, C. (2014) *Four thousand lives: The rescue of German Jewish men to Britain, 1939*, Stroud: The History Press

Unterhalter, E. (2013) 'Connecting the private and the public: pregnancy, exclusion, and the expansion of schooling in Africa', *Gender and Education*, Special issue, 'Thinking education feminisms: Engagements with the work of Diana Leonard', vol 25, no 1, pp 75-91

Unterhalter, E. and Carpentier, V. (eds) (2010) *Global inequalities and higher education. Whose interests are we serving?*, Basingstoke: Palgrave

UNESCO (United Nations Educational, Scientific and Cultural Organization) (2012) *World atlas of gender equality in education*, Paris: UNESCO Publishing (www.uis.unesco.org/Education/Documents/unesco-world-atlas-gender-education-2012.pdf)

Vallance, E. (1979) *Women in the House: A study of women Members of Parliament*, London: Continuum

Vallance, E. and Davies, E. (1985) *Women in Europe: Women MEPs and equality policy*, Cambridge: Cambridge University Press

Viorst, J. (1999) *It's hard to be hip over thirty ...And other tragedies of married life*, London: Persephone Books [first published 1968 in the USA]

Walby, S. (2011) *The future of feminism?*, Cambridge: Polity Press

Walker, A. (1982) *The color purple*, New York: Harcourt Brace Jovanovich

Walker, A. (1982) *You can't keep a good woman down: Stories*, New York: Harcourt Brace Jovanovich

Walker, A. (1983) *In search of our mothers' gardens: Womanist prose*, New York: Harcourt Brace Jovanovich

Walkerdine, V. (1997) *Daddy's girl: Young girls and popular culture*, London: Macmillan

Walkerdine, V. (2011) 'Neoliberalism, working-class subjects and higher education', *Contemporary Social Science*, Special issue, 'Challenge, change or crisis in global higher education', vol 6, no 2, June, pp 255-73

Walkerdine, V., Lucey, H. and Melody, J. (2002) *Growing up girl: Psychosocial explorations of gender and class*, London: Palgrave

Walter, N. (2009) *Living dolls: The return of sexism*, London: Vintage

Weaver-Hightower, M.B. and Skelton, C. (eds) (2013) *Leaders in gender and education: Intellectual self-portraits*, Rotterdam: Sense Publishers

Weedon, C. (1987, 1996) *Feminist practice and poststructuralist theory* (2nd edn), Oxford: Blackwell

Weiler, K. (1988) *Women teaching for a change: Gender, class and power*, Greenwood, CT: Bergin and Garvey

Weiler, K. (ed) (2001) *Feminist engagements: Reading, resisting, and revisioning male theorists in education and cultural studies*, New York and London: Routledge

Weiler, K. (2008) 'The feminist imagination and educational research', *Discourse: Studies in the Cultural Politics of Education*, vol 29, no 4, December, pp 499–509

Weiler, K. (2011) *Democracy and schooling in California: Historical studies in education*, Palgrave Macmillan

Weiler, K. and David, M. (eds) (2008) 'Introduction', *Discourse: Studies in the Cultural Politics of Education*, Special issue on 'Second wave feminism and educational research'

Weiner, G. (2008) 'Olive Banks and the collective biography of British feminism', *British Journal of Sociology of Education*, Special issue, 'Olive Banks (1923-2006)', vol 29, no 4

Weis, L. (2004) *Class reunion: The remaking of the American white working class*, New York: Routledge

Weis, L. and Fine, M. (2004) *Working method: Research and social justice*, New York: Routledge

West, J. (ed) (1980) *Women, work and the labour market*, London: Routledge

West, J. and Austrin, T. (2002) 'From work as sex to sex as work: networks, "others" and occupations in the analysis of work', *Gender, Work and Organization*, vol 9, no 5

White House Council on Women and Girls, The (2014) *Rape and sexual assault: A renewed call to action*, Washington, DC: The White House Council on Women and Girls and the Office of the Vice President

White House Office of the Press Secretary, The (2014) Memorandum for the Heads of Executive Departments and Agencies, 'Establishing a White House Task Force to protect students from sexual assault', 22 January

Williams, R. (2013) 'The university professor is always white', *The Guardian*, 28 January (www.theguardian.com/education/2013/jan/28/women-bme-professors-academia) [featuring a photograph of Heidi Mirza]

Willetts, D. (2011) *The pinch: How the baby boomers took their children's future – and why they should give it back*, London Atlantic Books [2011 paperback edn]

Willetts, D. (2013) *Robbins revisited: Bigger and better higher education*, London: Social Market Foundation

Williams, F. (1989) *Social policy: A critical introduction, Issues of race, gender and class*, Cambridge: Polity Press

Wilson, E. (1977) *Women and the welfare state*, London: Tavistock

Wilson, E. (1977) 'Women in the community', in M. Mayo (ed) *Women in the community*, London: Routledge

Wilson, E. (1980) *Only halfway to paradise: Women in postwar Britain, 1945-1968*, London: Tavistock

Wilson, E. (1982) *What is to be done about violence towards women?*, Harmondsworth: Penguin

Wilson, E. (1983) *Mirror writing*, London: Virago

Wiseman, E. (2013) 'Lad culture: just say no', *The Guardian*, 28 April (www.theguardian.com/lifeandstyle/2013/apr/28/lad-culture-just-say-no)

Winterson, J. (1985) *Oranges are not the only fruit*, London: Vintage

Wolf, A. (2013) *The XX factor: How working women are creating a new society*, London: Profile Books

Wolf, N. (1991) *The beauty myth*, London: Vintage

Wollstonecraft, M. (1792) *A vindication of the rights of woman, with strictures on moral and political subjects*, London: Joseph Johnson

Woolf, V. (1989) *A room of one's own*, London and New York: Harcourt Brace Jovanovich [originally published in 1929]

WSWW (Women's Studies Without Walls) (2013) Conference at the Feminist Library, 20-21 January

Yates, L. (2004) *What does good education research look like? Situating a field and its practices*, Milton Keynes: Open University Press

Yates, L. (2008) 'Revisiting feminism and Australian education: Who speaks? What questions? What contexts? What impact?', *Discourse: Studies in the Cultural Politics of Education*, vol 29, no 4, December, pp 471-83

Young, I.M. (1990) *Justice and the politics of difference*, Princeton NJ: Princeton University Press

Yousafzai, M. with C. Lamb (2013) *I am Malala: The girl who stood up for education and was shot by the Taliban*, London: Weidenfeld & Nicholson

Yuval-Davis, N. (2011) *The politics of belonging: Intersectional contestations*, London: Sage

Zweig, F. (1963, republished in 1977) *The student in the age of anxiety*, London: Heinemann

Index